Othello

NEW ESSAYS BY BLACK WRITERS

Othello

NEW ESSAYS BY BLACK WRITERS

Edited with a Background Essay by

Mythili Kaul

HOWARD UNIVERSITY PRESS
Washington, D.C.
1997

Howard University Press, Washington, D.C., 20017

Copyright © 1996 by Mythili Kaul
All rights reserved

Manufactured in the United States of America

This book is printed on acid-free paper.

10 9 8 7 6 5 4 3 2 1

Library of Congress Cataloging-in-Publication Data

Othello : new essays by Black writers / edited with a background essay
   by Mythili Kaul.
      p.   cm.
   Includes bibliographical references (p.   ) and index.
   ISBN 0-88258-191-0 (pbk.)
   1. Shakespeare, William, 1564-1616. Othello.   2. Muslims in
literature.   3. Blacks in literature.   4. Tragedy.   I. Kaul,
Mythili, 1938-
PR2829.086   1997   96-47192
822.3'3—dc21   CIP

Contents

III ACADEMIC CRITICS

Preface

I n his introduction to the Cambridge *Othello*, John Dover Wilson, a foremost Shakespearean critic of the century, recorded that when he first saw Paul Robeson play the role, he felt that he "was seeing the tragedy for the first time," and "not merely because of Robeson's acting" but because Robeson's being "a true Negro seemed to floodlight the whole drama. Eveything was slightly different. . . . [N]ew points, fresh nuances, were constantly emerging; and all had, I felt, been clearly intended by the author."

This anthology has been inspired by a similar conviction. As a Third World scholar of Western literature, I have always been alive to the importance of historical, cultural, and ethnic factors involved in literary response and interpretation. In some cases, these factors are obviously more important than in others. *Othello* not only has a black protagonist but is deeply involved with questions of racial attitudes and interracial relationships that, if anything, are more live and crucial today than ever before. If Robeson's Othello could prove so illuminating over sixty yeas ago, further important points, nuances, and insights were bound to emerge when contempary black theater personalities, creative writers, and scholars addressed themselves to the play. This view, I may add, was endorsed by all those with whom I discussed the project and even by those potential contributors who were finally unable to write.

Those who did, and whose essays are here assembled, include two eminent theater persons (Earle Hyman, Shelia Rose Bland); six distinguished creative writers (James A. McPherson, Ishmael Reed, Maryse Condé, Playthell Benjamin, Al Young, John Williams); and five scholarly critics (Jacquelyn McLendon, Elliott Butler-Evans, S. E. Ogude, Edward Washington, Lucille Fultz).

The major theme of this anthology is, of course, race and racism in *Othello*. This fact should not, however, obscure the diversity of the essays included in it. For instance, on the critical question whether *Othello* is a racist play or a play *about* racism, opinion is almost equally divided between those contributors who see it as a racist play, written by a racist playwright, for a racist audience, and those who see it as a play *about* racism, with Iago (and not the playwright or the play itself) as the embodiment of racist attitudes.

Further, there is at least one essay that is minimally concerned with the question of race. Earle Hyman, an outstanding stage Othello, treating the characters as real men and women (because "that is the way of the actor"), focuses on ego as the play's central theme. James McPherson pointedly draws attention to the contemporary relevance of *Othello* by framing his essay with a discussion of the recent O. J. Simpson trial. For McPherson, Shakespeare's "core theme" is not race so much as the conflict between Othello's "natural nobility of soul" and Iago's "natural depravity." This theme, he argues, is worked out in terms of a conflict between Venetian ethics on the one hand and, on the other, the backdrop of the Levantine ethical system, which, though not fully articulated in the play, functions as Othello's "private ethic" and helps us to understand the complexity of his character. While all the other essays are concerned with race, they focus either on different aspects of the theme or on same or similar themes from different perspectives leading to different, often startlingly opposed conclusions. In a background essay, Mythili Kaul surveys the stage history of the play concluding with the widely acclaimed emergence of black actors in the title role—a point highlighted also by Playthell Benjamin's detailed account of the sensational successes of Ira Aldridge and Paul Robeson. Shelia Bland, on the other hand, would restore the all-white, all-male cast of Shakespeare's time. Writing as a director, she presents the outline of a radically innovative production: part comedy, part minstrel show—with Othello in blackface and Iago as interlocutor—which would bring to life again "the bawdy, lewd, white male ritual of in-group bonding" and emphasize what she sees as the play's twin themes of racism and homoeroticism. S. E. Ogude, too, maintains that *Othello* makes sense as comedy or farce but not as tragedy. He argues against black actors playing the role because Othello is not a black man but a white man's "grotesque caricature" of an African, and since no black actor can obviate this grotesqueness, a black Othello becomes an "obscenity."

Ishmael Reed treats the question of racism in *Othello* (in conjunction with the relation between academic power and the acceptability of radical literary interpretations) in a fictional scene, a tense comic exchange between a worried conservative white professor, who has lost his clout, and a lowly black lecturer suddenly elevated to the higher echelons of college administration. Both Maryse Condé and Al Young, writing in terms of personal experience, compare Othello's situation in a racist society with their own. For Condé, a native of Guadeloupe, exposure to Europe, European theater, and especially *Othello* marked the beginning of a process of recognition of racism as well as the "ambiguous construction" of her own identity under white colonial rule. Young's experience as a black in America leads to a more emphatic recognition that nothing much has changed since Othello's time four centuries ago. Jacquelyn McLendon explores the continued problem of racism in Western civilization through a comparative study of *Othello* and some recent African American texts. She sees Shakespeare's play as a paradigmatic narrative of miscegenation, which figures as a subtext in, and against which we can read, Chester Himes's *The Primitive* and Amiri Baraka's *Dutchman* and *The Slave*.

John Williams suggests that racism in the play is best approached by focusing not on Othello but on Desdemona's enigmatic behavior. Edward Washington argues that Othello's dependence on image at the expense of truth and reality prevents him from understanding that "the black image he strives to protect has already found acceptance in Venice." Elliott Butler-Evans, using social semiotics to deconstruct the ideology of the text, suggest that Othello appropriates and valorizes the culture of the Other in an attempt to identify with the dominant group. Lucille Fultz focuses on the way in which characters are empowered or destroyed through control of language, particularly Iago whose discourse "devours" other discourses.

Taken together, the essays constitute not a chorus but a wide-

ranging debate involving diverse perspectives, approaches, and conclusions. The one thing that all the contributors do share in common, however, is the recognition that the issues raised by the play are, indeed, of
utmost relevance today in terms of politics, colonial exploitation, cultural
relativism, and, above all, race. From the other side, the essays collectively
also make clear the extent to which an engagement with *Othello* can
enable black writers to discuss these pressing contemporary issues in
ways that are both pointed and complex.

On a personal note, I should make it clear that I have not intervened
directly in this critical debate. Given the concept behind the project, to
do so would have been inappropriate. My essay is concerned with a
historical survey of audience and reviewer responses and their relation
to the changing stage representations of Othello—which will, I hope,
provide a useful background to the essays that follow.

I am indebted to the United States Educational Foundation in India
for the grant of a fellowship that enabled me to collect materials in the
United States as well as discuss the project with my contributors. I also
acknowledge with pleasure the courtesy extended to me by the library
staff at the University of Rochester, Oberlin College, and the University
of Delhi. The Frederick Douglass Institute was the host institution during
my stay at Rochester, and I wish to thank its staff and faculty, particularly
Professor Karen Fields and Professor Joseph Inikori, for their generous
assistance. I also wish to thank Profssors Kim Hall and Peter Nazareth
for their many valuable and detailed suggestions that have helped in the
revision of the manuscript. I am grateful to Edwin J. Gordon, Director,
Howard University Press, for providing the right help and guidance at
the right time, and to Prem Kumar Katarmal for the care with which he ﹢
prepared the typescript.

Finally, this project has been supported in more ways than I can
record by my children, Aditya, Chipu, and Padma, and, above all, by my
husband, A. N. Kaul.

Rochester   Mythili Kaul
August 1995

Othello

NEW ESSAYS BY
BLACK WRITERS

Background: Black or Tawny? Stage Representations of Othello from 1604 to the Present

MYTHILI KAUL

Othello's color and race became a matter of controversy in the late eighteenth and early nineteenth centuries. Earlier, he was assumed to be black, and his character was played as such on the stage.

The word *Moor* had a wider, more ambiguous reference at first. Originally derived from either an ancient North African language or from the Greek *mauros,* which means black, the term was first used to identify the natives of Mauretania—a region of North Africa corresponding to parts of present-day Morocco and Algeria—and later applied to people of mixed Berber and Arab race, Mohammedan in religion, who conquered Spain in the eighth century. But, as the Oxford English Dictionary (OED) points out,

> In the Middle Ages, and as late as the 17th c., the Moors were commonly supposed to be mostly black or very swarthy (though the existence of "white Moors" was recognized), and hence the word was often used for "negro," cf. Blackamoor.

Thus the ambiguity was narrowed, if not erased, and *Moor*

came to mean almost exclusively a blackamoor, or a person of black or very swarthy color—which is how it was used by John Gower in 1390, Trevisa in 1398, and Caxton in 1485.

As to the "white Moors," or light-skinned Africans, their existence is acknowledged in only one sixteenth-century account of that continent, John Leo Africanus's *The History and Description of Africa,* a work well known to Shakespeare and his contemporaries. A Moor himself whose life presents parallels with Othello's, Africanus belonged to a family of status; was captured, probably by Venetian corsairs; and was brought to Rome as a gift for Pope Leo X, who freed him and converted him to Christianity. Being a native, he not surprisingly reintroduces the old distinction between "white or tawnie Moores, and Negros or blacke Moores" (I.20). No such distinction is made by contemporary white writers for whom *Moor* by now generally means a black African. As a passage in Richard Eden's translation of three early travel accounts (again a work well known to writers and dramatists of the period), states, "The people which now inhabite the regions of the coast of Guinea and the mydde partes of Affrica . . . were in oulde tyme cauled Ethiopes and Nigrite which we now caule Moores, Moorens, or Negros" (384). Ethiopians earlier are described as "all blacke, havinge theyr heare curld more lyke wulle then heare" (88).

This general view is reflected in English stage history from the early Middle Ages onward. For instance the faces of participants in the "Morisce" or "Morisco" dance—a term probably derived from a combination of the words *Moor* and *Morocco*—were traditionally blackened. During the sixteenth century, "Moors" or "Morians," black in color, were used as "Bogey-man figures" in civic pageants. They later appeared in masques, to which their presence lent exotic appeal, and later still in drama proper.

In sixteenth- and seventeenth-century drama, several if not all Moorish characters are black. Muly Hamet in Peele's *The Battle of Alcazar* is referred to as the "Negro Moore," and Eleazer in *Lust's Dominion* is a black Moor. Aaron the Moor in Shakespeare's *Titus Andronicus,* always spoken of in terms of racial traits, is "raven-colored" (II.iii.83) with a "fleece of woolly hair" (II.iii.34), and his child is "dismal, black" (IV.ii.66), a "thick-lipp'd slave" (IV.ii.176).

Coming to Othello, we notice that Shakespeare again attributes the same unambiguous racial traits to the Moor: blackness, "thick lips" (I.i.67), "sooty bosom" (I.ii.70). As to the stage in Shakespeare's own time, there is no record of how Burbage, whose funeral elegy describes "the grieved Moor" as his "chiefest part"[1] (Collier, 53), represented Othello. However, "The Tragedie of Othello the Moore," an anonymous ballad written around 1625, mentions "Dicke Burbidge" in the part and refers to Othello as "blacke" and "swarthie" (*Variorum*, 398–402); thus, it is reasonable to assume that Burbage's Othello was black. Every succeeding Othello on the British stage up to the nineteenth century—Thomas Betterton, James Quin, David Garrick, John Philip Kemble, and others—also was black.

Garrick not only played the Moor as black but, connecting blackness with jealousy, expressed the view that Shakespeare had made Othello black in the interests of a larger theme: the jealousy of "white men" that he had shown in other plays "had limits. . . . [I]n Othello he . . . wished to paint that passion in all its violence, and that is why he chose an African in whose veins circulated fire instead of blood" (Hedgecock, 341). Garrick's black Othello was, however, a disaster, and he played the part on the London stage only three times during his entire career. He was a small man, and to gain a few inches he added an Oriental turban to his costume. But still he reminded his predecessor Quin, who was in the audience, of the little Negro page in Hogarth's *The Harlot's Progress,* and when Quin called out, "Here's Pompey, but where's the tea-kettle and lamp," the comment brought the house down (Fitzgerald, I.154). Quin himself, in the words of a contemporary reviewer, played the Moor "in a large powdered major wig, which, with the black face, made such a magpye appearance of his head, as tended greatly to laughter" (Salgado, 259). The point about the audience reaction to Garrick and Quin, however, is that they excited laughter not because they played Othello as black but because their appearance was at variance with the general expectation of a noble and dignified Moor. A black Othello was both expected and, by and large, accepted by the audience.

The audience's acceptance of the black character cannot, however, be interpreted as sympathy or friendliness. Racial consciousness or racial prejudice existed in the sixteenth and seventeenth centuries in Europe. In England, the color black was associated with sin, malignity, wickedness, and baseness, whereas white connoted purity, beneficence, goodness, and

---

1. Laurence Olivier's "theory" about the inception of the play is that Shakespeare and Burbage got drunk one night and Burbage boasted that he could act any role Shakespeare could invent. Shakespeare accepted the challenge—and wrote *Othello* ("The Great Sir Laurence," *Life,* LVI, May 1, 1964).

blessedness. Queen Elizabeth's edict of 1601 ordered the wholesale trans-
portation of "negars and blackmoores" out of England (E. Jones, 87).
Othello itself, as Winthrop Jordan warns us, "loses most of its power
and several of its central points if it is read with the assumption that
because the black man was the hero English audiences were friendly or
indifferent to his blackness. . . . Shakespeare was writing both about and
to his countrymen's feelings concerning physical distinctions between
kinds of people" (37). The sixteenth century thus, far from being innocent
of what we would call racist ideology, was in historical terms its point
of origin in Europe.

Because this ideology spread and developed over the centuries, it is
important to note the changes of kind, degree, and extent. As Philip
Mason has suggested, the reasons for race prejudice in the seventeenth
century, unlike in the centuries following, were "psychological and cultural" and not "political and economic," that is, not "due to any struggle
for power or wealth" (122). Clearly, racist ideology involves factors that
range from the economic to the psychological, and the question is which
of its aspects is dominant at what time. Race by itself, as Louis Snyder
puts it, denotes a biological category and "implies the existence of groups
which have certain similarities . . . perpetuated according to laws of biological inheritance," whereas

> *Racism* assumes inherent racial superiority or the purity or superi-
> ority of certain races; also it denotes any doctrine or program of
> racial domination based on such an assumption. Less specifically,
> it refers to race hatred and discrimination. *Racialism* assumes sim-
> ilar ideas, but describes especially race hatred and racial prejudice.
> (9–10)

"Racialism" in these terms—or a full-blown racist ideology encom-
passing programs of domination and theories of racial superiority and
especially emphasizing race hatred and racial prejudice—began to manifest itself in the late eighteenth century. In the seventeenth century, there
was not yet the widespread racialism that would make it impossible to
view a black as possessing any sympathetic human qualities or to sympathize in any way with the presentation of an interracial marriage on
stage. On the contrary, when Shakespeare's company, the King's Men,
presented *Othello* at Oxford in 1610, men wept. Emotional involvement
was the rule, not the exception, and exceptions were noted and condemned. Remarking on the "flat insensibility" of female members of the

audience during a performance in 1709, Sir John Perceval, Earl of Egmont, wrote that "those who cannot be moved at Othello's story so
artfully written by Shakespeare, and justly played by Betterton, are capable of marrying again before their husbands are cold, of trampling on
a lover when dying at their feet, and are fit to converse with tygers only"
(240). Most Englishwomen, however, would seem to have been guilty of
excessive rather than deficient sensibility, for a year later we find the Earl
of Shaftesbury noting with alarm that "a thousand Desdemonas" were
so obsessed with stories of African men that they were ready to abandon
husbands, families, and country to "follow the fortunes of a hero of the
black tribe" (Cowhig, 13)!

A radical shift in attitudes to race and stage presentations of Othello
occurs with the rise of colonialism and imperialism—the operation of
the new political and economic forces and the new "struggle for power
and wealth" discussed by Philip Mason and others—and leads to strik-
ingly altered perceptions and reactions. For instance, questions about
Othello's color, whether the Moor was meant by Shakespeare to be
black—indeed, whether a person who was noble could possibly be black
at all—were repeatedly raised in the nineteenth century, the era of ex-
panding colonization and imperialist consolidation when arguments for
and against slavery were at their height. In the seventeenth century,
Othello's descent from "men of royal siege" (I.ii.22) would tend to make
this outsider much more acceptable. In Britain, prejudice, as Mason observes, is much reduced for anyone who can establish that he or she
belongs "to the upper half of the class structure. . . . And here is Shakespeare knowing his audience, using this native English snobbery . . . three
and a half centuries ago" (162). But in the nineteenth century, aristocratic
origins could no longer compensate for racial difference.

As would be expected, such an attitude led to a questioning if not
outright rejection of the idea of treating a black–white marriage sym-
pathetically. Emotionally charged comments to this effect were occasionally made in the earlier years too. As far back as 1692, Thomas Rymer
expressed disgust at Shakespeare's coupling a "Blackamoor" with the
daughter of a "great Lord" instead of "some little drab, or Small-coal
Wench" (134). Seventeen years later, Charles Gildon stated that Desdemona's love for a man "so opposite a Colour . . . takes away our Pity
from her, and only raises our indignation against him" (410). But, in
keeping with the intensification of racialism, such strong and adverse
reactions to Shakespeare's interracial marriage became insistent and com-

mon—almost common—on both sides of the Atlantic. Indeed, the most significant aspect of the stage history of *Othello* during the nineteenth and twentieth centuries is the linkage between the ideological climate and audience and reviewer responses on the one hand and, on the other, the question of the degree of the hero's color—black, tawny, or almost white.

The question was first raised, somewhat guardedly, as early as October 29, 1787, in a review of Kemble's performance in the *Public Advertiser*: "We must approve his [Kemble's] dressing Othello in Moorish habit . . . but is it necessary the Moor should be as *black* as a native of Guiney?" Clearly, a black Othello alienated the audience. Abigail Adams, the wife of John Adams, then ambassador and later the second president of the United States, who saw Kemble's Othello in London, "lost much of the pleasure of the play from the sooty appearance of the Moor," and was filled with "disgust and horror" every time she saw him touch Desdemona (2, 125).[2] Charles Lamb was repelled by Desdemona's "laying aside every consideration of kindred, and country, and colour, and wedding with a *coal-black Moor*," and appealed to everyone who had seen the play whether "he did not . . . find something extremely revolting in the courtship and wedded caresses of Othello and Desdemona" (299).

John Quincy Adams, the eldest son of Abigail and John Adams and a president of the United States himself, found Desdemona's "fondling of Othello" on stage "disgusting." John Quincy Adams was against slavery, opposed the so-called "Gag Rules" that prevented abolitionist petitions from being presented in the House, and successfully defended in court the black mutineers in the famous *Amistad* case. But his views on interracial marriage were, if anything, more virulent than those of his mother. According to him, had Othello been white, Desdemona "could have made no better match." But because of Othello's color, because "he *had been* a slave," her feeling for him is not love but "unnatural passion." Nobody, Adams asserted, could sympathize with a woman who "born and educated to a splendid and lofty station in the community . . . makes

---

2. John Adams did not share his wife's distaste for racial intermarriage. Influenced by Puritan doctrine, he rather emphasized human frailty and saw the play as a moral demonstration of how love, when betrayed, turns to hatred and revenge (I.114). When *Othello* was first performed in 1761 at Newport in the liberal Puritan colony of Rhode Island, the play was advertised as a "Moral Dialogue in five parts Depicting the evil effects of Jealousy and other Bad Passions." The playbill carried epigrams on each character, and the one on Brabantio read: "Fathers beware what sense and love ye lack, / Tis crime not color, makes the being black" (Shattuck, I.12).

a runaway match with a blackamoor" and "violates her duties to her father, her family, her sex, and her country." Hence "when Othello smothers her in bed she has her just deserts" (224–26, 235).

If such hostile reactions were to be avoided and if a more sympathetic audience reception was to be ensured, clearly a black Othello would not do. Not only should the stage Othello not be "as black as a native of Guiney," he should not be black at all. In fact, the view gained ground that the error in making Othello black in the strict sense was not Shakespeare's but that of stage producers and actors. For instance, replying to John Quincy Adams's outburst, Richard Grant White in *Shakespeare's Scholar* argued that Shakespeare "could not fail to know the difference between the position and character of the nation which built the Alhambra, and that which . . . [was supplying] the plantations with slaves," and Othello was not a Negro but a Moor (432–33). Samuel Coleridge had made the point much earlier and with greater force and vehemence, arguing that it is Roderigo who, because of "rivalry," willfully confuses *Moor* and *Negro*. Shakespeare surely knew better.

> Can we imagine Shakespeare so utterly ignorant as to make a barbarous *negro* plead royal birth? Were negroes then known but as slaves? . . . No doubt Desdemona saw Othello's visage in his mind; yet it would be something monstrous to conceive this beautiful Venetian girl falling in love with a veritable negro. It would argue a disproportionateness, a want of balance in Desdemona, which Shakespeare does not appear to have in the least contemplated. (I.46–47)

On stage, the man responsible for introducing the first nonblack Othello was Edmund Kean, who became the model for stage representations of Shakespeare's protagonist for almost a century. At the time, several reasons were put forward to account for the change: black makeup obscured facial expression, and because of the disappearance of the apron stage and the greater distance between actors and audience, lighter makeup was necessary; also, actors were no longer prepared to accept the discomfort of blacking.[3] But although these technical factors

---

3. Cowhig cites the story of a German actor who turned up at a formal lunch with a black face, explaining that he had "gone through so much fatigue and trouble in blacking his face" for the previous performance of *Othello* that rather than undergo the same painful process again he had sat up the whole night without washing his face (15).

justified the change, they did not cause it. The determining factor was racial. Kean himself asserted that he "regarded it as a gross error to make Othello either a negro or a black, and accordingly altered the conventional black to a light brown which distinguishes the Moors by virtue of their descent from the Caucasian race" (Hawkins, I.221). Using a combination of burnt cork and brown pigment, Kean represented the Moor as an Arab.

Neither at this time nor at any subsequent time did scholars and critics display the same degree of consensus as actors and producers in banishing the black Othello in favor of the light-skinned Moor. For example, William Hazlitt did not approve of Kean's innovation and maintained in the *Examiner* of January 7, 1816, that Othello was "black" (v.271). Coleridge, of course, welcomed and endorsed it: "Othello must not be conceived as a negro, but a high and chivalrous Moorish chief" (II.350). The rising tide of racism favored, not Hazlitt, but Coleridge and particularly Kean, who thus may be said to have ushered in the so-called "bronze age" of Othello.

Incidentally, models for bronze Othellos were provided not only by Arabia but in one or two instances by India. For Thomas Campbell, the "Indian Prince Ramohun Roy" (Raja Rammohan Roy, a nineteenth-century social and religious reformer who visited and died in England) was "the only living being . . . who came up to Othello's appearance" (*Variorum*, 420). For Daniel[4] Bandman, a German American actor who had previously toured India, it was a follower of Roy, the tall, broad-shouldered, deep-chested, light–olive-complexioned, black-haired Keshub Chander Sen, who "incarnated" Othello, so much so that Bandman made himself up to resemble Sen as closely as possible whenever he performed the part (Grebanier, 359). Exceptions aside, however, British and American actors for the next hundred years followed Kean's lead in representing Othello as Semitic and tawny rather than black.

A light-skinned Othello was particularly welcome to American audiences. In fact, the play was so frequently performed in the United States that it has been called "Shakespeare's American Play." It was acted before audiences as diverse as Cherokee Indians in Virginia in 1752—who intervened during the performance to prevent actors from, as they thought, killing each other with the naked swords they were brandishing—and miners in mining camps in California during the Gold Rush in the nine-

---

4. See Carlisle (193). Given erroneously as David in Grebanier.

teenth century—who probably saw nothing unusual in a black-faced Othello!

Given its racial and sexual content, it is curious that *Othello* should be "Shakespeare's American Play." To explain the play's popularity in England in the seventeenth and eighteenth centuries, I suggested that there was, generally speaking, acceptance, perhaps at times even a sentimentalization, of the black hero. But how does one explain its even greater popularity in America where racism entered together with the first settlers in the seventeenth century, and where, unlike Europe, there was, through the nineteenth century, a steady intensification of racism and racialist attitudes culminating, beyond the Civil War, in the Jim Crow legislation enacted by the southern states?

In view of this, it may seem surprising that *Othello* should have been so repeatedly performed even in the South. As the Richmond *Dispatch,* January 17, 1888, put it: a "miscegenation" play is not "calculated to enthuse the southern heart." Or, as the Montgomery *Daily Advertiser,* February 4, 1888, concluded, after arguing that if Iago is to be hanged, "the black-a-moor murderer of the fair haired, blue eyed Desdemona . . . should be hanged, and drawn and quartered too." *Othello* "cannot, in the nature of things, be appreciated by a Southern audience."

The play would thus seem to be a prime candidate for failure rather than popularity. Charles Lower's essay, "*Othello* as Black on Southern Stages, Then and Now," however, provides statistics that point in the opposite direction. Up to the Civil War, there were sixty-three performances of the play in Charleston, twenty in Memphis, forty-one in Mobile, twenty-two in Louisville, and so on.

Lower himself provides an explanation. "*Othello* and the slavery controversy could coexist" because, according to him, "antebellum southern audiences regarded theatrical performances as Art quite distinct from life" so that the resultant "emotional experiences were aesthetic not sociological" (201–02, 216, 223). James Dorman, on the other hand, suggests an explanation based on opposite reasoning. Far from seeing art as distinct from life, southern audiences saw it as a reflection of life, and "commonly viewed [*Othello*] as an anti-miscegenation play" (276), a cautionary tale confirming their deepest prejudices. John Quincy Adams, too, saw it in this light:

> The great moral lesson of the tragedy of *Othello* is that black and white blood cannot be intermingled in marriage without a gross

outrage upon the law of Nature; and that, in such violations, Nature will vindicate her laws. (224)

Combining the two reasons, Tilden Edelstein, in his brilliant essay "*Othello* in America," gives a more complex account of America's fascination with *Othello*. The play, Edelstein argues, dramatized America's "racial reality" and "racial fantasies" (179) and helped American audiences "define their own racial morality." Although it engaged their racial attitudes at the deepest level, the engagement took place at "the physical and psychological distance that the theater allowed." *Othello* on stage was thus popular with directors, actors, and audiences alike because it provided an ideal site for the enactment and observation of "the real tragedy of America's racial history" (194).

The preceding arguments should not, however, be taken to imply that American audiences, unlike those in Britain, actually wanted to see a black-faced Othello. If nineteenth-century Britain could tolerate none but tawny Othellos, much less could America with its history of greater intensification of racist attitudes with each passing decade of the century. No matter how much they saw *Othello* as an anti-miscegenation play vindicating natural law, and no matter how fascinated they were by the theatrically distant enactment of their real racial tragedy, the "wedded caresses" and the "fondling" of a white woman and a black man would be for them just too disgusting and repugnant to watch or endure. Although the spectacle was no doubt theatrically distanced, they could still take it only at a further remove or displacement with regard to Othello's race and color. As Edelstein himself points out, from the early nineteenth century onward for about one hundred and twenty five years, American audiences would simply not accept such a hero on stage if his skin color was black.

Thus the bronze age of *Othello* was more tenacious in America than on the other side of the Atlantic. There were fewer exceptions to the rule that the character be played as brown rather than black. There was also a greater variety of tawny shades, tending at times to white. For instance, when Edwin Forrest, deleting lines referring to race and color, played the part as an octoroon, a critic remarked that he looked more like an American Indian, a Shawnee or Mohican, than a Moor. Edwin Booth was even lighter. His Othello, following Kean's, was Arabian, and he appeared in a Moorish burnoose, resplendent with jewels and gold-embroidered robe and shoes. He, too, expunged lines that emphasized race.

His Othello was genteel, so genteel that the *New York Herald* of April 25, 1869, saw him not as a "fiery Arab" but "a young Jesuit student, calm, cultivated, even subdued." The *New York Evening Mail* of April 24, 1869, caustically remarked that Booth seemed to confuse Othello with his own Hamlet. Earlier, Harry Watkins, a strolling player, performing in Macon, Georgia, in 1852, played the role as almost white in order to avoid trouble. The attitude of Mary Preston, author of an 1869 book entitled *Studies in Shakespeare,* points further in the same direction: "In studying the play . . . I have always *imagined* its hero a *white* man. It is true that the dramatist paints him black, but this shade does not suit the man. It is a stage decoration which *my taste* discards. . . . I have, therefore, dispensed with it" (*Variorum,* 395). In view of this demand for white or "whitewashed" Othellos, it is hardly surprising that the British actor Henry Irving, who played Othello in black makeup in England, never played the part on any of his eight American tours.

The darkest Othello seen on the American stage during this period was that of the Italian actor Tomasso Salvini, a blend of copper and coffee. In his portrayal, however, the Moor was no longer noble but, in words taken from several reviews, a "barbarian," a "bestial savage," "a sweating beast," an "animal" who looked at Desdemona as no "Christian gentleman" ever looked at a woman. Salvini took New York by storm (Henry James greatly admired him), and it is obvious that even a dark-brown Othello became acceptable to critics and viewers only if he conformed to a familiar nineteenth-century racial stereotype. Other players, however, continued to play Othello as light-skinned. When Salvini's son played the part in the 1890s, he stated that his father had been wrong in making Othello so dark, for Desdemona could never have loved a man with a dark skin unless she were a pervert. He decided to make Othello attractive—which, of course, meant lightening his color.

From 1890 to 1920, the Jim Crow era, when fear of miscegenation reached the proportions of a national phobia, the play was seldom staged. But when it was revived, so to speak, in 1925, with a record fifty-seven performances, Othello was still light-skinned, except in minstrel-show versions and occasional all-black productions of the play.[5]

The end of the bronze age and the return of a black Othello to the

---

5. One such production in 1916 seems to have made the audience apprehensive that, since all the actors were black, they might not be able to recognize Othello when he first appeared. "As it turned out," observed the reviewer in the *Boston Herald* of May 8, 1916, without any trace of humor, "there was no difficulty."

stage has often been attributed to the emergence of great black actors on the scene. Although this is true, changes in the political situation on both sides of the Atlantic played a still more crucial role. In an overall sense, the bronze age, as I have maintained, lasted well into the twentieth century in Europe as well as America. But in Europe, events like the early abolition of slavery and the revolutions of the mid-nineteenth century led to some mitigation of the racial situation. America, in fact, was behind Europe by a hundred years in introducing the novelty of a black actor playing Othello. As Errol Hill points out in his history of black Shakespearean actors, it took the United States a depression, World War II, and a period of "reluctant integration" (xiv)—to which may be added the challenge in terms of racial equality and justice posed by the now defunct Soviet Union—to recognize and accept black actors on the professional stage.

The first great black actor to play Othello was Ira Aldridge in the 1830s, and it is illustrative that although he was a native American and performed to great acclaim in Britain and throughout Europe, especially Russia where he was paid four hundred rubles for a single performance, he could never appear as Othello or in any other role in his own country. In Europe on the other hand, he actually played *white* roles as well—Richard III, Hamlet, Macbeth, Lear.

A colorful character, Aldridge liked to draw attention to himself. Among other things, he claimed that there were analogies between Othello's situation and his own. That his forefathers were princes of a Senegalese tribe seems to have been largely a fabrication. But it is true that he married not one but two "Desdemonas." His first wife was an Englishwoman who looked after the illegitimate children he fathered, and his second the Swedish mistress who had borne his illegitimate children and whom he married after the first wife died. He modeled his interpretation on Edmund Kean's—he first appeared on the London stage as "Mr. Keene" and only later as Ira Aldridge, the "African Roscius."

Aldridge achieved his first great success in Dublin at the Theatre Royal in 1831–32. A black actor "naturally" playing Othello—and, indeed, emphasizing his blackness at several points during the performance—seems to have struck everyone immediately as a significant stage event. As a Dublin advertisement put it, Aldridge represented "the most singular novelty in the Theatrical World, viz., an actor of colour" (Marshall and Stock, 99).

But how much the subsequent sustained acclaim and general acceptance of this "African Roscius" had to do with the race question and how much with his great abilities as an individual actor remains debatable. That both were contributory factors in some measure is, however, clear. For instance, when Kean saw Aldridge perform in Dublin, he not only sent for him and complimented him but wrote a letter recommending him to the manager of the Theatre Royal in Bath. What impressed Kean was Aldridge's acting ability and versatility—and, indeed, it can hardly be supposed that the man who thought it a "gross error" to make Othello black would welcome a black actor in the role. In truth, Kean seems to have praised Aldridge not because but in spite of his color.[6] One can, likewise, cite the following exchange between the manager of the Dublin Theatre Royal and an American whose wife, Madame Celeste, a well-known figure in popular melodrama, was also to appear at the theater during the 1833–34 season. When this man, "a Yankee of the genuine type," confronted the manager and told him that his wife would not perform under the same roof as a "nigger. . . . In America we don't associate with blacks," the manager replied: "Neither do we, as a national habit. But he is a good actor and the public like him. His color is nothing to me, though it were green, blue or red" (Marshall and Stock, 105). On the other hand, such an attitude also argues a degree of racial tolerance that, among the Irish, may have had something to do with the sense of being themselves a subject if not a colonized people, but that, in any case, was simply unthinkable across the Atlantic at this time. Neither Aldridge's greatness as an actor nor his value as a novelty could ever put him on the stage anywhere in America.

In Britain, and especially London—where acceptance did not come as easily as in Dublin—Aldridge on his debut was openly involved in the controversy about race and slavery that was then at its height. The proslavery lobby, of which London was the center, saw his appearance on the London stage as a threat to racist theories of black inferiority and attacked "the unseemly nigger" who relied "solely on colour for his inspiration." The antislavery lobby put forward its views equally strongly and hailed the achievement of "*a black man,*" a member of an "ill-used and degraded race" (Marshall and Stock, 138).

By the time Queen Victoria came to the throne, Aldridge's reputation was well established, although more in the provinces than in the

---

6. "But Kean, when sober praised everybody. When drunk or approaching thereto he called all his professional brethren humbugs" (Marshall and Stock, 103).

metropolis, and audiences everywhere responded enthusiastically to what they considered a historic moment in the stage history of *Othello* and of Shakespeare generally. William Wells Brown, the black abolitionist, records that the Haymarket Theatre was "jammed" at one of Aldridge's performances—he recognized Bulwer Lytton in the audience—and "thunders of applause" greeted the appearance of Othello. When Othello seized Iago by the throat in Act III, the audience "with one impulse, rose to their feet amid the wildest enthusiasm" and was not satisfied until Aldridge took repeated curtain calls at the end of the act (487).

In Europe, Aldridge, a black playing Shakespeare's black hero, was greeted as a revelation. Kemble's biographer and admirer, James Boaden, had said even of that great actor's Othello that although he "was grand and awful and pathetic," he "was a European" and therefore it was "at most, only a part very finely played" (I.256–57). Aldridge now seemed the true embodiment of Othello at last. To Theophile Gautier, French author, poet, and critic, watching a performance in Russia, Aldridge had the "natural skin" for the part and was, indeed, "Othello himself, as created by Shakespeare . . . with that Negroid grace of movement which no European can imitate" (Marshall and Stock, 229). A reviewer in the *Preussische Zeitung* said, "After this Othello it would be an anti-climax to have to see an ordinary Othello again," and the Russian critic K. Zvantsev likewise stated that after Aldridge it was "impossible to see Othello performed by a white actor" (Marshall and Stock, 181, 232). Following his success on the Continent, when Aldridge appeared in the Lyceum Theatre, London, *The Illustrated London News* of July 31, 1858, spoke of the "triumph achieved over the usual prejudice against colour. . . . The veritable Moor, so to speak, stood before the spectator and appealed in his living and natural lineaments to human sympathy."

Aldridge's undoubted success notwithstanding, it should not be imagined that black actors appeared in droves in Europe from this time onward or that the "African Roscius" had signaled the end of the bronze age. Despite the above encomiums, white actors continued to play tawny Othellos, barring exceptions such as Henry Irving who performed in blackface. Irving, however, performed late in the century and then, too, only in Britain and never in America. As to black actors, far from ushering in a new age for them on the professional stage, Aldridge himself by the end of the century came to be viewed as a rare exception. In America, he was regarded as a curiosity, according to the testimony of Laurence Hutton's *Curiosities of the American Stage* (1891) in which

Aldridge is mentioned as "the negro tragedian" who played Othello "in his natural skin" (94). The day of the black actor had not yet come—racism was still much too potent a force. Indeed, it was not until 1930 that another "negro tragedian," Wayland Rudd, was to make theater history by being the first black actor to play Othello in a white professional company's production in America.

But the man who made the breakthrough, also in 1930, was Paul Robeson in London. It took, as Errol Hill points out, his charismatic personality and international reputation and "the social security of a nation that, for all its chronic chauvinistic and horrible historical record, had no domestic color problem of its own at the time," to establish "the undisputed right of the black man to perform a great Shakespearean role in the commercial theater purely on the basis of quality" (xiv). And, indeed, a survey of the reviews in leading London newspapers makes clear how the overwhelming praise of Robeson's Othello focused on the quality of his performance and, in so doing, side-stepped the question of race. Eight out of twelve London critics, according to *The World's Bureau,* May 30, 1930, hailed Robeson's Othello mainly as a "magnificent and outstanding achievement." The *Daily Telegraph* did touch on the question by admitting that Robeson's race had given him an advantage over English actors in the role but went on to conclude that whether Othello was "a Negro or an Arab can be left to the professors." The *Morning Post,* May 30, 1930, asserted that the interest aroused by Robeson was due not to the fact that he was "a man of colour" or that "Shakespeare gave to Othello many characteristics that belong rather to the Negro than to the Moor" but to the fact that Robeson was a "great artist." Herbert Farjeon was one of the few critics to focus on race but to Robeson's disadvantage. According to him, Robeson being "a member of a subject race, still dragging the chains of his ancestors . . . was not noble enough. . . . The fact that he is a negro did not assist him. . . . Shakespeare wrote this part for a white man to play" (166).

Although at this time Britain did not have a "domestic color problem," America did, and the question of race figured prominently in reviewer and audience response from the outset. In fact, Robeson did not perform in his country until 1942–43 when the racial climate was more moderate. It was only then, as the *New York Times* of August 16, 1942, observed, "that a Negro actor [was] acceptable, both academically and practically, as Othello." The *New York Daily News* of October 20, 1943, praised the production for presenting a black man of dignity and intelligence in the role of a black man of dignity and intelligence. Howard Barnes, in the New York *Herald Tribune* of October 31, 1943, considered it a great success because

> Robeson's color as much as his fine acting skill . . . brings a rather tricky melodrama into sharp and memorable focus. Lines which meant nothing when a white man played the part . . . loom impressively.

On the other hand, when *Life* magazine of September 21, 1942, published a picturespread of Robeson and Uta Hagen, there were denunciatory letters to the editor. A reader from South Carolina observed that such pictures would only create a feeling of frustration in Negroes, while another from Kentucky saw the printing of pictures of a Negro with his arm around a white woman as evidence of the fact that white men had lost all respect for themselves and their race.

Altogether, then, no matter how divided the positions taken on the race question, there was a general recognition that Robeson in playing this Shakespearean role had brought into vital focus a deep and continuing problem of Western societies. As Robeson's biographer, Edwin Hoyt, puts it, when the play opened in New York

> hundreds knew they were witnessing a historic performance. Never before in America had a Negro played the role of Othello in a cast of whites. . . . As they saw Paul Robeson in the role for the first time many of them realized how deep and ingenious had been William Shakespeare's writing, for the Moor, like Robeson, was different from the others—the whites—and the play, with all its overtones of racial conflict in sixteenth-century Venice, took on a new life four centuries later. . . . [Audiences] sensed that in this four-hundred-year-old melodrama lay the wellsprings of the emotional and racial conflict which was even in 1943 and 1944 burgeoning in America. (2–3)

Robeson himself, as a black and an American, was only too conscious of the racial issue in its historical as well as contemporary manifestations. In an interview with the *New York Times*, June 6, 1943, he revealed that at the time of his first London performance, he was so "bothered" by the proximity of Desdemona that "that girl couldn't get near to [him]," since he was "backin' away from her all the time . . . like a plantation hand in the parlor, that clumsy." He was convinced that "Shakespeare meant Othello to be a 'black moor' from Africa, an African of the highest nobility of heritage. From Kean on, he was made a light-skinned Moor because Western Europe had made Africa a slave center, and the African was seen as a slave." But he also realized that English critics even in the twentieth century would see him as slavish and ignoble—as, indeed, Herbert Farjeon did—and was determined to correct and alter this view (Rosenberg, 195). In her biography, *Paul Robeson, Negro,* his wife, Eslanda Goode Robeson, reports Robeson as saying early in his career that if some day he could play Othello as Shakespeare meant him to be played, he would "bring to the stage the nobility, sympathy, and understanding Shakespeare put into the play" (96).

Robeson, like Aldridge before him, saw *Othello* as "the tragedy and pathos of a black man in a white world" (Hoyt, 51). It was said of Aldridge that he stood on the Covent Garden stage "as the lone protagonist of his oppressed and villified people." The Russian critic Zvantsev, seeing Aldridge, "the tamed Othello . . . in the power of the educated European (the Iago of contemporary history)," involuntarily thought of the many generations of blacks who had suffered at the hands of American slave-traders. The Russian historian M. P. Pogodin likewise saw Aldridge as the embodiment of what had happened to a whole people (Marshall and Stock, 119, 232, 233). In *The Rising Sun; or the Antecedents and Advancement of the Colored Race,* William Wells Brown puts Ira Aldridge alongside Frederick Douglass and Phyllis Wheatley as one among those "representative" men and women who contributed to the "Freedom" of the "Race."

Robeson saw himself as inheritor of Aldridge's legacy and derived strength from it as a black actor on a stage controlled and dominated by whites. He studied voice and diction with Aldridge's youngest daughter, Amanda, and wrote the following inscription on the photograph he gave her: "With many thanks for the fresh inspiration received from all reports of her father's greatness. I realize I can only carry on in the tradition of Aldridge" (Marshall and Stock, 1).

Even more than Aldridge, Robeson in his time came to understand that the black actor had a special and urgent responsibility toward his people. What is distinctive about Robeson and Aldridge, then, is not that they played Othello as noble. Several white actors had done the same. What is distinctive is that they presented him as a representative figure, and that they saw the role and their enactment of it as a challenge to complacent and entrenched assumptions about the black race to which he and they belonged.

It may finally be said that if Kean banished the black Othello from the stage, Robeson, unlike Aldridge, succeeded in bringing him right back. Robeson was followed by several outstanding black actors including Earle Hyman (a contributor to this volume), William Marshall, Paul Winfield, James Earl Jones, and others right up to the present. Once again, what contributed most was the political changes already indicated and, particularly, the resurgence of Africa and the emergence of radical black movements in the United States. Of course, there were a few dissident voices. Bernard Grebanier stated that a very "dangerous tradition" was started by Robeson's Othello, the tradition that "a black man was indispensable in the role if the play was to be understood"—adding that this was just a way for people to salve their social conscience (463). Clive Barnes of the *New York Times* also disapproved of black actors playing Othello because they were too "obvious," and he reminded directors and audiences that Shakespeare wrote the part for a white actor in blackface.

Dissidence, however, was marginal, and black actors were widely hailed in the role. Hyman was described by the *New York Times* of October 30, 1953, as a "magnificent Moor." William Marshall was called the "best Othello of our time" by the London *Times* of September 30, 1962. Moses Gunn was similarly described by the *New York Post* for his performance at the American Shakespeare Festival Theater in Connecticut in 1970.

Even in the South, when the Alliance Theatre Company of Atlanta, Georgia, chose to stage *Othello* in 1979, it was decided that only a black actor should play the title role. Paul Winfield was selected, the play ran for four weeks, there were only six unsold seats during the entire run, and whites constituted 95 percent of the audience. What is more, Winfield "Africanized" Othello. Whereas nineteenth-century performers expunged references to race and color, he not only emphasized them but introduced innovative features to underline Othello's African heritage. For the trance in Act III, he substituted a tribal chant. Clad in African robes he squatted, intoning over a pile of bones, beating the floor rhythmically with his hand. In the final scene, barefoot and in a caftan, he performed a silent ritual before approaching the sleeping Desdemona. The production prompted some hostile letters but, as in the case of

Robeson, audiences got so involved in the performance that any racial antipathy they may have started with was by and large overcome.

Of course, Othello has not been played only by black actors in recent years. But with one or two exceptions, white actors too have reverted to presenting him as black. Donald Wolfit rejected the light brown color of his predecessors and represented Othello as a curly-haired, savage but noble North African. Laurence Olivier blacked himself—overblacked himself in the opinion of some critics and viewers—wore a crinkly wig, and "remade" his whole personality from speech to gesture to gait. He tried to look, sound, and walk like a "Negro." (A reviewer sardonically remarked that Olivier portrayed Othello as sensuous, savage, narcissistic, and even stupid, an interpretation one might be tempted to see as racist but that cannot be so simply dismissed in the light of arguments advanced by Hyman and one or two other contributors to this volume in support of a similar interpretation of Othello's character.)

The change from tawny to black, or at least its beginnings, may be seen as still more significant when it happens on a medium of mass entertainment like television. In 1981, Jonathan Miller, director of the BBC productions of Shakespeare, invited James Earl Jones to play Othello, but Jones was barred by the British actors association. Miller then cast Anthony Hopkins and, in a curious turnabout, had him play Othello as an Arab, justifying the decision by reinvoking arguments first put forth in the nineteenth century. Discounting Othello's blackness as "the myth of performance over the text," he argued that it has "assumed an importance out of all proportion to its role in the play." To the Elizabethans, *Moor* meant no more than "dark stranger," and if the lines referring to Othello's racial features were eliminated, the play would "work perfectly well"—in fact, better, since the hero's blackness was a distraction (*Shakespeare on Television*, 278, 58). On the other hand, in the Bard Production *Othello*, televised three years later, the black actor William Marshall played the role very successfully, modeling his performance on Robeson's. More recently, a major breakthrough has been achieved on film with the release of *Othello* starring Laurence Fishburne in the title role.

Thus, while making inroads into television and cinema, the black Othello, after the lapse of over a century, stands firmly reestablished on the stage.

I

Theater Persons

Othello:
Or Ego in Love, Sex, and War

EARLE HYMAN

I have seen five productions of *Othello* in my lifetime, two of them quite successful, but in my opinion, the greatest Othello of them all was Paul Robeson. I do not expect to see a greater in my lifetime. Some of the actors acted Othello better than Paul Robeson, and almost all of them spoke Othello's verse better, but he simply *was* Othello. He did not have to act. He chopped up the verse at times, but the resonance of his uniquely bass-baritone voice will sound in my memory always. The majesty—there is no other word for it—of his sheer presence on stage was electric. When Paul Robeson kissed his Desdemona (Uta Hagen) full on the mouth, an audible gasp went through the entire audience at the sold-out Schubert Theater on Broadway. This was in 1943, and I feel certain that all of us in the audience knew we were seeing *Shakespeare's Othello* for the first time.

For off and on twenty-five years, I have played Othello in ten productions in three languages—English, Norwegian, and New Norwegian—stacking up roughly 758 performances. I feel that I am too old to play the role now, but I still study it from time to time, and during the past thirty years I have come to certain conclusions about the role and the play that I think are valid. I wish I could be less clumsy in expressing them.

Othello is not about jealousy or racism, although both these elements make the play more sensational and powerfully affecting. The play is about ego. Ego, used well, is a great blessing. Ego, used badly, is a great evil. An example of the former is Mother Teresa, who used her ego to forget self and to serve the poor in Calcutta. An example of the latter is Hitler, who used his ego in an attempt to magnify self as king of the world. Were I the only human being in the world, my ego would not matter. Ego has to do with a sense of self as far as identity is concerned, a sense of self-respect and dignity, and an ability to function within the human condition. Ego problems occur as a result of one's relations and dealings with other human beings. I believe that one can have too much ego or not enough, especially in the realms of love, sex, and war. When one loves the loved one at least as much as one loves oneself, that is good ego and love. When in the sex act, one tries to give as much sexual fulfillment to one's lover as one receives, that is good ego and good sex. When I was a little boy, I once wandered into a room where a man and a woman were having sex. I stood frozen, fascinated, and yet terrified. I thought the couple were fighting and the man was hurting the woman. Sexual intercourse can at times feel like a battle or war. I am not saying that war is good, but let us face it, if we cannot stop a Hitler with treaties and diplomacy, then it is necessary to gird our healthy egos and beat him as soon as possible.

Othello is a man, a black African prince, between thirty-five and forty-five years old, an age that in Shakespeare's time was closer to old age than to middle age. His tribe or nation was attacked and beaten by a foreign nation and tribe. His king father and queen mother were killed. Seven-year-old Othello and his somewhat older brother managed to escape. Later, Othello was captured and sold into slavery, but he managed to gain his freedom.

Iago does speak objective truth sometimes: "And, like the devil, from his very arm / Puffed his own brother; and is he angry?" Iago was present during the battle in which Othello's brother was killed, and he saw that Othello did not lose control. Othello is a survivor and therefore very aware that he must keep his emotions under control if he is to survive. In a sense, he has fought all his life. He is a soldier, and eventually he becomes a great general and commander. His work as a warrior is also his love and, therefore, his art. He is a poet. No warrior in all of Shakespeare speaks of war in such beautifully romantic terms. "Othello's occupation is gone" becomes, therefore, an unbearably tragic statement.

Even today, in a white-oriented society, a black man, in order to achieve success and any appreciable sense of security, has to make his services well-nigh indispensable. And the general and commander Othello *is* indispensable to Venice, one of the great city-states of all time. There is racism—a black man has to be *better* than a white man at the same job.

And now for sex—and love. Othello has had sex with several women, some of them white, aristocratic, and married. But love for a woman never entered the picture until he met Desdemona. Before Desdemona, his love was his art. He must have known a kind of orgasmic fulfillment with every brilliant military victory; however, no military victory could begin to compare with the wonder of the consummation of his betrothal to Desdemona. He must have been trembling like a schoolboy when he entered their bridal chamber, and to his amazement found a girl uninhibited and free, giving and taking with open physical passion. In short, the consummation of their marriage must have been passionately sexual. On the day after, I imagine them finding it difficult to keep their hands off each other—although Othello is a man who has built up an almost rigid control that allows him to be in command and true to his art. It is little wonder that Othello cocks an eyebrow or two in wonder when Iago begins to make insinuations about Desdemona's infidelity and sensuality. It is tragic that something as natural and beautiful as the physical consummation of Desdemona's and Othello's love should be thought of as unnatural and ugly. As a black man, he has a little more ego than he needs. Othello has to survive in a white society and therefore has to think more of himself, and about himself, than is really good for him. Othello simply had to say to Desdemona, openly and freely, "I know this may sound crazy, but is there now, or has there ever been, anything between you and Cassio?" But that little bit of unnecessary ego will not allow him to say this until it is too late. Then, out of control, and that unnecessary bit of ego rampant, not freely or openly *asking,* he *accuses* her of infidelity to him with Cassio and kills her.

What about the *divine* Desdemona? Could she, too, suffer from a little too much ego? The answer is "Yes." I see Desdemona as a beautiful, intelligent young woman between nineteen and twenty-one years of age, well brought up as an upper-class Venetian lady of her time. Her mother died when Desdemona was quite young, nine or eleven or so. She has had no one to whom she could tell her innermost thoughts. She loves her father, but he is part of the "super-subtle" Venetian society into which she is expected to marry, to become a "super-subtle" Venetian matron married to a "super-subtle" Venetian husband. This does not appeal to Desdemona. On the outside a beautiful, well-bred, obedient young Venetian woman, she craves on the inside to know something about the "wonder of life." When she meets Othello, she knows what that "something" is. She falls totally in love with him, even though she does not "totally" know Othello, any more than Othello "totally" knows her. Although Desdemona is not a tomboy, I still see her as wanting to ride a horse bareback. I think she would love to stand outside Othello's tent at his side while he gives commands to his troops for battle. She is intelligent enough to know that she will never get her father's consent or sympathy, so she elopes, and the physical act of their love is as natural to her as breathing. This black prince, with his muscled and battle-scarred body, is the "wonder of life" to her. But when she first sensed that all was not *perfectly* well between them—"Where should I lose that handkerchief, Emilia?"—she should have asked, "Othello, I don't like to say this, but I have a feeling you are jealous. Are you?" But that little extra dash of ego does not allow her to ask until it is too late and she is fighting for her life. "What, *my* Othello, *my* man, jealous? *No way.*"

Shakespeare gives us a key to the interpretation of his characters in the first and last words they speak. For instance, Othello says " 'Tis better as it is," and Desdemona, "I do perceive here a divided duty." In other words, both of them believe that they are in total command of the situation. Now let us look at their last words. Othello's are, "Killing *myself*, to die upon a kiss," and Desdemona's are, "Nobody; *I myself.* Farewell: / Commend me to my kind lord: O farewell!" They kill themselves, that unnecessary bit of extra ego in themselves, and by doing so Desdemona and Othello die in pure and selfless love.

The only two characters in the play who are truly jealous are Bianca and Iago. Bianca—whose name in Italian means *white*—is healthily jealous. She tells Cassio to his face and in the street for everyone to hear that she is jealous. Iago is unhealthily jealous because he does not consciously know that he is jealous. I believe that Iago does not have enough ego. He sees himself as the supreme egoist, yet he has continually to feed and build up his ego. Shakespeare, in perhaps a private joke, gives him a double dose of ego in his very name. The Latin verb *ego*, which means "I do" or "I make," gets an extra dose of "I" or ego from Shakespeare by the placing of the English personal pronoun *I* before the Latin verb *ego*, which means "a double I do or make." Shakespeare certainly had enough Latin to know what he was doing when he named Iago.

Everyone believes Iago is honest—honest in the sense that as a brusque, open-hearted, soldier type, he can get away with saying exactly what he means and wants, from making wisecracks about the Establishment to rolling off dirty jokes that anyone else would be condemned for, but coming from him rate only shocked laughter. You can almost hear people around him saying, "Isn't that Iago a card? He ought to be ashamed of himself, but he *is* funny." The real reason why Iago gets laughs and indulgent shakes of the head is because he is a good actor in life. People believe him and that is dangerous; what is even more dangerous is that Iago believes himself.

Iago is a good actor in life because he *has* to be. In his subconscious lies a truth that would cause him searing agony if he ever had to face up to it. Tyrone Guthrie and Laurence Olivier, I have read in several accounts, consulted the psychologist Ernest Jones about Othello before they went into rehearsals of the play with Ralph Richardson playing Othello. The production was a failure, probably because they never let Richardson/Othello in on the results of their consultation with Dr. Jones, who told them that Iago was a latent homosexual. Director Guthrie and Olivier/Iago believed Jones's theory and tried to put it into action.

I also believe Jones was right. As a latent homosexual, Iago must act all the time, even when he is alone. He is the greatest misogynist of all time; he has absolutely nothing good to say about women. He will cast filth on them all at any given moment. He *is* married, but at the age of twenty-eight he had to be or tongues might begin to wag. I am sure Emilia is at least two years older than he is and not too beautiful at that. She probably is not *too* unhappy that "I nothing [I know nothing], but to please his fantasy." I am also sure that Iago's fantasies in bed with Emilia must have been, to use a current word, a little on the "kinky" side. Iago is attracted to Cassio because Cassio is handsome ("a daily beauty in his life"), but Othello is whom he most desires. The black majesty of Othello is strange, but all the more potently attractive to Iago's subconscious self. Even today, many whites "hate" blacks because they believe blacks are possessors of a more potent sexuality than they, the whites, are. It is all right for a white man to have a physical relationship with a black woman, but the idea or fact of a black man as more virile and better endowed sexually than a white man is an utterly repellent and yet fascinating horror. A black man's physical relationship with a white woman is, therefore, in the minds of many white people, a crime punishable by death. Iago cannot and must not allow his subconscious desire for Othello to surface. It manifests itself in another way. He states that he, Iago, supreme ego that he thinks he is and good actor that he *really* is, will set his plans in motion as though Cassio and Othello had actually gone to bed with Emilia. It seems to me that he is fantasizing a physical relationship between Cassio and Othello. *He* has not had any such, but *Emilia* has.

During all the years I played Othello, I often thought that I could have played a better Othello if I had had the opportunity to play Iago just once. I do not believe with Coleridge that Iago is a creature of "motiveless malignity." Let us give him also the first and last line test. He tells Roderigo (who is accusing him of concealing the true state of relations between Othello and Desdemona from him): "'Sblood but you'll not hear me. / If ever I did dream of such a matter, *abhor* me" (emphasis mine). Yes, no one *hears* the real Iago, not even Iago himself, until it is too late. Yes, *abhor* Iago, with emphasis on the "hor" or "whore," if he ever did *dream* that Othello would or could woo, win, and marry a beautiful young white woman without telling him, Iago, about it. His last words are, "Demand me nothing. What you know *you* know. / Henceforth, I shall never speak word" (emphasis mine). I believe that when Iago sees Othello's dead body on the bed, Iago's subconscious heaves the repressed, unthinkable truth into his consciousness. That truth causes him a searing agony that is worse than any slow torture, so that, indeed, Iago does not speak another word.

It is possible that many people will disregard what I have written because I have treated characters in the play as though they were real men and women, flesh and blood creatures. But that is the way of the actor. He or she has to use all of himself or herself to become what *seems* to be a living person on stage or before a camera.

How I Would Direct Othello

SHELIA ROSE BLAND

I would direct *Othello* as a comedy, almost as a minstrel show. The entire show would be played for laughs—even the murders and suicides. I would make Othello the butt of the jokes, and Iago the hero—saving the values of white purity. I would make Desdemona a woman who deserves what she gets. Both Desdemona and Othello would be effigies—there for the "hanging." Cassio I would make a drunkard, Roderigo, a fool—both worthy of being laughed at.

I would cast the show entirely with white males, having Othello played by a white male in blackface. White males dressed in female clothing would play Desdemona, Emilia, and Bianca. I would allow the white male homoerotica to be played for both humor and titillation.

In fact, I would treat the entire production as a white male fraternity initiation skit—including the audience as initiates—where the insiders ridicule the outsiders and those who betray the insiders. Othello represents the outsiders; Desdemona betrays the insiders. I would use Iago as the president of the fraternity. He would be the host, the charmer who sings, tells jokes, narrates the story, and creates the dramatic action. The initiates/audience would be his accomplices.

I would create blocking and stage business that would encourage the audience to laugh *at* Othello, and *with* Iago.

The word *coward* would be repeated when Othello draws on Emilia. However, when Iago draws on Emilia and kills her, I would use recorded laughter. Then I would play the homoerotica of "Ay, Ay, O lay me by my mistress' side" (V.ii), and also of:

> *Emilia:* What did thy song bode, lady?
> Hark, canst thou hear me? I play the swan
> And die in music (Sings) "Willow, willow, willow"
> Moor, she was chaste. She loved thee, cruel Moor,
> So come my soul to bliss as I speak true.
> So speaking as I think, alas, I die. (V.ii)

I would create a lewd, loud evening of rude sexual jokes:

> *Iago:* I am one, sir, that comes to tell you your daughter and the Moor are making the beast with two backs. (I.i)

> *Iago:* Would you, the supervisor, grossly gape on? Behold her topped? (III.iii)

Iago would give some kind of joyous victory sign when Othello kills himself in the end, perhaps having "plants" (actors who pretend to be audience), in the audience, who join him, adding verbal approval.

The demonic, damned, devil motif that recurs throughout the play would be emphasized.

I would play up the notion that men are violent, but women find violence erotic, as illustrated by Othello's explanation of why Desdemona was attracted to him.

Overall, I would create an evening where hatred, vengeance, and murder were fun and entertaining.

Twenty white men come out on stage, bow, and make three semi-circles, with one of the males to play a woman in the center of each. The actor playing Othello stands center stage facing the audience. The males who are to play women don their wigs. As the three circles enclose the three female impersonators, they dress on stage. The actor playing Othello ritualistically begins to don his blackface makeup in full view of the audience. As he finishes, the three circles open to reveal Desdemona, Emilia, and Bianca. The actor playing Iago is now revealed in some spectacular fashion. The lights black out. The play begins. . . .

Why such a radical concept for a production of *Othello?*

At one time, I thought I would love to direct *Othello* with an all-black cast, except for Othello who would be played by a white actor. That is, all-black actors would be on a stage calling a white actor "beast" and so on. My guess as a director was that white as well as black audiences would be shocked; for in such a production, the negative black "name calling" found in the play's dialogue would be aimed at a person of white complexion. I thought this concept would be interesting and novel. It would put to rest once and for all the debate concerning issues of racism in Shakespeare's *Othello.*

Then, I sat down to really study the play. . . .

Many things occurred to me as I studied the script. The first major discovery was that the play, although called *Othello,* is actually about Iago. The next major discovery was that Iago was a remake of the character Richard III—that is, the villain made charming. Iago tells jokes, speaks to the audience directly more than any other character, sings songs, moralizes, and acts as general "host" to the audience throughout the play—in fact, to the very last scene in Act V. Another thing that struck me was that the play is very, very funny. Although predating American minstrels, *Othello* struck me as a minstrel show, with Iago as Mr. Interlocutor. *Othello* has a minstrel "feel" to it up until the last scene in Act V, when Iago no longer speaks directly to the audience.

Hence I had the idea to do the play as a minstrel show. I would cast the entire production with men, all of them white. Women would be played by men. Othello would be played by a white man in blackface. I am aware that this is how the original production was cast. It struck me that this would amplify the racist nature of the play in a far more authentic manner than my original concept with an all-black cast. The blackfaced Othello would be seen by the audience, both black and white, as "other"—an outsider—a caricature. This would alienate and cause discomfort to the audience. By casting "real" blacks to play Othello, and real women to play Desdemona, Emilia, and Bianca, Shakespeare's original intent in writing *Othello* may well have been cloaked. Because black actors are real people, with real human feeling, they have been striving for centuries to humanize Othello, a character who perhaps was never meant to be more than a caricature. Because women are real people, with real human feeling, they have been striving for centuries to humanize Desdemona, Emilia, and Bianca, characters who were never meant to be real women. Doing Othello as it was originally staged would illuminate the racial and gender connotations of the language immensely.

I said earlier that the play *Othello* is not about the character Othello, but about Iago. Character motivations at the opening of the play support this notion.

When the play begins, Emilia, Cassio, Desdemona, and Othello have everything they want. Emilia has Iago; Cassio has both his position as lieutenant and Bianca; Desdemona has Othello; and Othello has Desdemona, a military command, and a war. In terms of dramatic structure, characters who have everything they want have no motivation to propel a plot into action. In other words, the play can go nowhere.

There are two characters who have wants when *Othello* opens—Roderigo and Iago. Roderigo wants to have Desdemona, by any means necessary. Iago wants vengeance against Othello for copulating with his wife and for overlooking him for the position of lieutenant. He wants Cassio's position, which is lieutenant to Othello. He also wants vengeance against Cassio for copulating with his wife and for being more physically attractive than he is. Finally, Iago wants Roderigo's money—as much of it as he can wrench from him. Iago has the most to gain by propelling a plot into action. Character motivation clearly suggests that the play is about Iago.

The plot also supports this notion. The play moves to Cyprus and the war against the Turks, but the war is resolved before Othello sets foot on land. The tempest resolves the war—not Othello. Once this happens, Othello loses his reason for existing for the Venetians who have sent him to fight. Although this move makes Othello the ruling force in Cyprus, the governor, he has no war to fight. He throws a party and goes off to sensual pleasures with Desdamona. He goes to "bed" and leaves the stage to the doings of Iago. It is here that Iago gains total control of the play—control of all of the characters on stage—and control of the audience that has come to see the play. Iago charms. He chats. He sings. He pours wine. He also plots.

The play is about Iago's vengeance—it only appears to be about Othello's vengeance. Othello is acted upon by Iago. Iago acts; Othello merely reacts. The play *Othello* could well be called *Iago*. Trying to trace a directing concept around the character Othello becomes a trip down a blind alley.

What of my conclusion that *Othello* is not a tragedy? I need to validate that conclusion for my directing concept.

There are at least seventy-eight instances of humor in *Othello*—some are merely passing comments, and some are whole scenes. When you make the women male actors in women's clothing, the humor in *Othello* multiplies immensely. When you make Othello a white male actor in blackface makeup, the humor both increases and intensifies. The quality of the humor even changes. Instead of laughing with the character Othello, the audience will tend to laugh at him. In fact, much of the seemingly "tragic" dissipates.

But what of the murders? Do they automatically make *Othello* a "tragedy"?

Because Desdemona is a mere effigy, a man in a dress, her murder is a mere tableau that serves as a moral warning to wayward women in the audience. (She gets her "comeuppance.") There is pleasure in this for the men in the audience. The murder of Emilia is the same, a warning to wives to obey and submit to their husbands even when their husbands perform unjust acts. There is a pleasure in this also for the men in the audience.

Roderigo is murdered. There is no real tragedy in this, for he is trying to murder the man who wounds him. Iago strikes Roderigo the fatal blow—there is no tragedy here because Roderigo is in league with Iago. Cassio loses his leg, but he is a drunk and a whoremonger. Besides, he is rewarded at the end of the play. He is given Othello's command, though he is now a drunk and a whoremonger and has only one leg.

Finally, Othello dies. Is his death tragic? His death is self-inflicted. The question becomes, does he deserve to die? He is ungrateful to the Venetian state and Brabantio's hospitality. He uses his position to sway a white woman to marry him against all that whites consider "natural" and against the will of Brabantio, who is the white woman's father:

> *Brabantio:* A maiden never bold,
> Of spirit so still and quiet that her motion
> Blushed at herself; and she, in spite of nature,
> Of years, of country, credit, everything,
> To fall in love with what she feared to look on!
> It is a judgment maimed and most imperfect
> That will confess perfection so could err
> Against all rules of nature, and must be driven
> To find out practices of cunning hell
> Why this should be. (I.iii)

Othello himself is made to say:

And yet, how nature erring from itself—

Iago replies:

Ay, there's the point, as (to be bold with you)
Not to affect many proposed matches
Of her own clime, complexion, and degree,
Whereto we see in all things nature tends—
Foh! One may smell in such a will most rank,
Foul disproportions, thoughts unnatural. (III.iii)

Othello also abuses the white woman he has married, striking her
in public; verbally abusing her in front of others; putting the label *whore*
on her; and finally, murdering her—the very white woman who has
betrayed her father and her race for the love of his black being. Is the
death of such a black man tragic? Because the white woman Othello kills
was meant to be played by a white man in a dress, and Othello himself
was meant to be played by a white man in blackface, Othello, too,
becomes an effigy. He gets his comeuppance in the eyes of the white
audience viewing the play, and the white actors *doing* the play, and the
white man who *wrote* the play. Othello's *only* redeeming quality under
these circumstances is that he has the good sense to kill himself. Othello
himself recognizes what an abomination he is—even to himself. He says:

Then must you speak
Of one that loved not wisely, but too well;
Of one not easily jealous, but, being wrought,
Perplexed in the extreme; of one whose hand,
Like the base Judean, threw a pearl away
Richer than all his tribe. (V.ii)

No human being of *any* race, in his *right mind*, would say such a thing
about his own race! One white woman is worth more than all the black
men, women, and children in the world? This is preposterous. This is
laughable. It was not, however, laughable to the white writer, actors, and
audience who created and sustained such a character—an effigy that
stands as a warning to all *non*white men, mercenary or not, who might
consider wooing a white woman. Othello's actions toward Desdemona
also stand as a warning to all white women who might find black or
other nonwhite men attractive.

The play is good fun—humorous, frightening, cathartic—rather than tragic. This notion is strengthened by the fact that the playwright makes all the characters demons. They are "not like us."

The name *Othello* itself contains the root word *hell*. *Desdemona* contains the root word *demon*. Perhaps the playwright intended to condemn these two characters from the beginning. Iago says all women are "devils being offended." That would take care of Emilia (to whom he speaks), Desdemona, and Bianca. Iago calls Cassio "a devilish knave." Cassio is also a "devil" in his drink.

> *Cassio:* O thou invisible spirit of wine, if thou has no name to be known by, let us call thee devil. (II.iii)

Speaking of his own condition, Cassio goes on to say:

> It hath pleased the devil drunkenness to give place to the devil wrath. (II.iii)

Iago calls himself a devil.

> Divinity of hell!
> When devils will the blackest sins put on,
> They do suggest at first with heavenly shows,
> As I do now. (II.iii)

Speaking to Roderigo, Iago says:

> If thou wilt needs damn thyself,
> do it a more delicate way than drowning. (I.iii)

Also, serving as the devil Iago's assistant, Roderigo is assured a place in hell.

All these "hellish" characters are to be avoided. Watching them serves as a warning of the chaos that can ensue if one hires black mercenaries; trusts black men; marries against one's father's will; marries a black man; or bestows power and authority on black men.

A further argument against viewing *Othello* as tragic is the manner of Iago's undoing. If the play is seen as a tragedy, it would seem at this point as if the playwright had lost control of the dramatic structure.

Othello tells Iago *exactly* when he plans to kill Desdemona:

> Ay, let her rot, and perish, and be damned tonight; for she shall not live. (IV.i)

and again,

> Get me some poison, Iago, this night. I'll not expostulate with
> her, lest her body and beauty unprovide my mind again. This
> night Iago. (IV.i)

Therefore, Iago should have known better than to send Emilia, that very
night, to the scene of the crime. Yet he does so.

> *Iago:* Kind gentlemen, let's go see poor Cassio dressed.
> (To Bianca). Come, mistress, you must tell's another tale.
> Emilia, run you to the citadel
> And tell my lord and lady what hath happed.
>
> (Exit Emilia)
>
> Will you go on afore? (Exeunt all but Iago)
> This is the night
> That either makes me or fordoes me quite. (Exit) (V.i)

Iago, in essence, sends Emilia to discover Othello murdering his wife in
bed—because he knows this is what is happening. He then conveniently
turns up at the scene of the crime, creating the situation of his own
undoing. No one is "on" to Iago. There is no threat of discovery. He
himself manufactures his *own* undoing. This action by Iago is illogical
and out of keeping with a character who up to this point has behaved so
cunningly. Iago "hangs" himself, in essence—then turns to the audience
and says, tonight, either I shall be successful, or I shall be "hung." As
tragedy, this is awkward and illogical. This is, however, the very "stuff"
of which comedy is made.

Though he is under arrest, Iago is even given the pleasure and
privilege of watching Othello kill himself—the final and ultimate fruit of
his plotting. This is a gift given to the white Iago by the white playwright.
It is yet another indication that much of the sympathy of the playwright,
and therefore the audience, is with Iago—the white man. And although
Othello is dead, Iago, though wounded, is still alive as the play ends.
When wounded by Othello, he exults:

> *Iago:* I bleed sir, but not killed. (V.ii)

When asked by Othello for an explanation for his actions, Iago is given
the victoriously defiant words:

> Demand me nothing. What you know, you know. From this time
> forth I never will speak word. (V.ii)

Triumphantly, Iago never says another word in the play. Villain though he might appear, all sympathies lie with Iago. He need give no explanations to the audience, for through his narrations he has succeeded in making that audience an accomplice to his schemes, his plotting, and even to his murders. If Iago is guilty, so is the audience. The playwright, Iago, and the white audience, however, all feel that Iago is in the *right* somehow; that Othello and Desdemona had violated nature and God in the very act of choosing each other; that Iago merely was the instrument of God in bringing down divine wrath on the heads of these two; that no white man should have to serve a black one—it is unnatural, and Iago has a right, therefore, to seek vengeance. The playwright, Iago, and the audience all feel that no white man should lose his position and be at the mercy of a black man, as Cassio is; that no white man should have to compete for the affections of a white woman with a black man, as Roderigo does; that no white woman should have to serve as a maid to a black man's wife, as Emilia does. All three feel that no white nation should be at the mercy of a black man for military defense. All these situations seem unnatural to the white audience—and somehow subtly lure them into sympathy and league with Iago.

The playwright goes so far as to have Desdemona and Othello condemn themselves. Even they do not believe they deserve better than they get in the play.

> *Othello:* Haply for I am black
> And have not those soft parts of conversation
> That chamberers have, or for I am declined
> Into the vale of years—yet that's not much—
> She's gone. I am abused, and my relief
> Must be to loathe her. (III.iii)
> *Desdemona:* 'Tis meet I should be used so, very meet. (IV.ii)
> *Desdemona:* It is my wretched fortune. (IV.ii)

These characters are effigies. They deserve what they get. *Othello* does not seem to be a tragedy. Perhaps it was never intended to be a tragedy.

The idea of a tragic Othello becomes even less supportable if, as I said earlier, the script is examined in respect to traditional casting in Elizabethan times. The fact that the original cast of *Othello* would have been entirely male suggests humor in the script, which eludes modern productions because of the "realistic" casting of actual women and an actual black man.

The images of men in women's clothing and white men in blackface make the murders resemble melodrama more than tragedy. The imagery is more potent with all male actors. To see an actual black man kissing an actual white woman on stage is a powerful image—but one that misrepresents an even more powerful image on stage intended by Shakespeare: to see a white man in blackface kiss a white man in woman's clothing.

I would accentuate the homoerotica found in the play. An example would be the speech where Iago tells Othello of sleeping with Cassio, and Cassio's mistaking him for Desdemona:

> *Iago:* I do not like the office.
> But sith I am entered in this cause so far,
> Pricked to't by foolish honesty and love,
> I will go on. I lay with Cassio lately,
> And being troubled with a raging tooth,
> I could not sleep.
> There are a kind of men so loose of soul
> That in their sleeps will mutter their affairs.
> One of this kind is Cassio.
> In sleep I heard him say, "Sweet Desdemona,
> Let us be wary, let us hide our loves."
> And then, sir, would he gripe and wring my hand,
> Cry "O sweet creature!" Then kiss me hard,
> As if he plucked up kisses by the roots
> That grew upon my lips; laid his leg o'er my thigh,
> And sigh'd and kiss'd, and then cried, "Cursed fate
> That gave thee to the Moor!" (III.iii)

The complex humor of the situation involving Iago, Cassio, and Desdemona becomes obvious with an all-male cast.

Another scene that is customarily seen as tragic, but opens up to tremendous humor and homoeroticism, is the scene where two men in women's clothing, pretend to "undress" in a woman's bedroom, while talking of infidelity between men and women.

> *Emilia:* Shall I go fetch your nightgown?
> *Desdemona:* No, unpin me here.
> This Lodovico is a proper man.
> *Emilia:* A very handsome man.

Desdemona: He speaks well.
Emilia: I know a lady in Venice would have walked barefoot to
    Palestine for a touch of his nether lip. (IV.iii)

This is both humorous and erotic when the cast is entirely male. Desdemona "delicately" sings in falsetto, perhaps a cause for more humor.
Then:

Desdemona: I have heard it said so. O, these men, these men.
Dost thou in conscience think, tell me, Emilia,
That there be women do abuse their husbands
In such gross kind?
Emilia: There be some such, no question.
Desdemona: Wouldst thou do such a deed for all the world?
Emilia: Why, would not you?
Desdemona: No, by this heavenly light!
Emilia: Nor I neither by this heavenly light. I might do't as well i'
    th' dark. (IV.iii)

This is humorous in and of itself. However, the knowledge that it is two
men, pretending to be women, speculating on women's fidelity, multiplies
this humor significantly. This same knowledge makes Emilia's final
speech in this scene a virtual tour de force:

Emilia: Yes, a dozen; and as many to th' vantage as would store
    the world they played for.
But I do think it is their husbands' faults
If wives do fall. Say that they slack their duties
And pour our treasures into foreign laps;
Or else break out in peevish jealousies,
Throwing restraint upon us; or say they strike us,
Or scant our former having in despite—
Why, we have galls; and though we have some grace,
Yet, have we some revenge. Let husbands know
Their wives have sense like them. They see, and smell,
And have their palates both for sweet and sour,
As husbands have. What is it that they do
When they change us for others? Is it sport?
I think it is. And doth affection breed it?
I think it doth. Is't frailty that thus errs?
It is so too. And have not we affections?

Desires for sport? and frailty? as men have?
Then let them use us well; else let them know,
The ills we do, their ills instruct us so. (IV.iii)

This passage could easily be mistaken for some kind of feminist statement because of the modern method of staging Shakespeare with women in the parts traditionally played by men. By doing the play as it was originally done, the "man-to-man" message becomes apparent. Rather than this passage reflecting the "tragic" state of women, it shows men acting out an amusing awareness of their power over women. This was an "in joke." The whole play was an "in" thing.

My casting choices and my production of *Othello* would once again give life to the bawdy, lewd, white male ritual of in-group bonding, of group definition, by exclusion of others. The humor would continue throughout my production of *Othello*—to the very end.

When my blackfaced white male Othello steals his last kiss from my white male Desdemona and falls on the bed alongside my white male Emilia, who has denounced her husband because of her love for the white male Desdemona, saying "Ay, ay. O, lay me by my mistress' side" (V.ii), the full impact of the homoeroticism will be felt. The audience will never be allowed to forget that these are white men, acting out a white male ritual. There will be joy. There will be humor. There will be titillation.

When finally, the audience hears,

Lodovico: (To Iago) O Spartan dog,
More fell than anguish, hunger, or the sea!
Look on the tragic loading of this bed.
This is thy work. The object poisons sight;
Let it be hid. (V.ii)

they will feel satisfaction, a sense of accomplishment, a sense of things made right somehow. They will feel as Iago does. When Lodovico says,

Gratiano, keep the house,
And seize upon the fortunes of the Moor,
For they succeed on you. (V.ii)

the audience will be made to cheer, perhaps with plants in the audience who would initiate such cheering. The fortunes of the black Moor have rightfully returned to white male hands. This is cause for in-group celebration. Lodovico says to Cassio:

To you, lord governor,
Remains the censure of this hellish villain,
The time, the place, the torture. O, enforce it! (V.ii)

The audience will be made aware that it is also in Cassio's power to pardon Iago. The fact that the playwright does not give Cassio a response here, either positively or negatively, is significant. Iago may well go free. This is not tragic. The audience will be led to believe that there is some hope for Iago. Finally, the play concludes:

Lodovico: Myself will straight aboard, and to the state
This heavy act with heavy heart relate. (V.ii)

Perhaps Lodovico will have the only heavy heart in the theater house. It is over; the unnatural is made natural. The impression will be given that the state will be elated to hear that all that was ill has been made well with their world. . . .

The audience of initiates may now be sworn in. The twenty white males must once again gather on the stage. They form their semicircles again. The "dead" rise ritualistically from their deathbeds, returning to their respective places at the opening ritual. The three men who played Desdemona, Emilia, and Bianca ritualistically remove their wigs. The circles enclose them. The white male who played Othello begins ritualistically to remove his makeup. Iago mounts a podium above them all and opens his arms in welcome. He begins a joyous laugh, which is picked up by the plants in the audience. The laughter gets bigger and bigger. Perhaps the circles open, with the twenty men on stage and the audience initiates joining in the laughter. The lights black out. It is done.

II

Creative Writers

Three Great Ones of the City and One Perfect Soul: Well Met at Cyprus

JAMES A. McPHERSON

I

During the past eighteen months, the complex factual events surrounding the murders of Nicole Brown Simpson and Ronald Goldman in Los Angeles, and the trial of O. J. Simpson for the crime, have been twisted and mutated into what has been called a "media circus," if not a monumental mess. Still, despite the thousands of assertions and counterassertions that make up the record of this historic trial, it is possible that, years from now, someone will locate within the factual mess a narrative thread that, when drawn into closer focus, will attempt to make sense of what began as a simple tragedy. As a matter of fact, the CBS newsman Dan Rather, on June 17, 1994, when the media first focused their full attention on O. J. Simpson cruising along the Los Angeles freeway in his now-famous white Bronco, introduced the narrative premise that made the most sense to his viewers. Rather spoke with passion about William Shakespeare's tragedy *Othello* and compared O. J. Simpson to that tragic character and Nicole Brown Simpson to the wronged and saintly

Desdemona. After tabloids printed revelations about Nicole Brown Simpson's personal life, however, part of this narrative line was edited from the story.

With the tapes of Officer Mark Fuhrman's racial feelings introduced as evidence by Simpson's defense team, a second narrative thread from the same play was introduced: Officer Fuhrman as Iago, enraged that he, and other Anglo-Saxons like himself, have been displaced by black men, and by women, through affirmative action policies. If these two narrative threads are eventually knit into the deep emotional structures essential to English-speaking people to provide understanding of the tragedy, it might be fair to speculate, in a comic vein, whether Kato Kaelin will be viewed as a stand-in for Michael Cassio; prosecutor Marcia Clark as a stand-in for Emilia, Iago's wife; Faye Resnick as a stand-in for Bianca; Judge Ito as a stand-in for the Duke; and the mysterious bloody glove, as a substitute for Othello's handkerchief.

Such comic speculations, however, tend to diffuse emotional understanding of the human tragedy cheapened in all the media, day after tedious day, for eighteen months. The tragic facts are that Nicole Simpson and Ronald Goldman are dead, O. J. Simpson's children are permanently wounded, the families of Nicole Brown and Ronald Goldman are embittered, and the entire media-watching world has relearned that deep, killing racial hatreds are still rampant in this country. But much more tragic, in my view, is that the search for the causal elements at the basis of the tragedy has been relentless in its focus on what is considered the most potentially explosive combination of elements in the emotional imagination of Western physics: the cojoining of a black male and a white female. On its surface, Shakespeare's play *Othello* has instructed us in this causality, and we are still slaves to its hidden language. This emotional predisposition is so ingrained in the Western imagination that it is most often employed as a convenient convention, as a substitute for thought.

I relearned the potent power of this hidden language in the early summer of 1994, when a very eager black reporter for *U.S.A. Today* called me at home and asked for my perceptions into the events leading up to what has been called "the trial of the century." At the time, I was trying my best to achieve some ironic, if not comic, distance on the tragedy. I noted that the murder, on June 11, and all events following it represented a narrative commentary on the ritual movements of American society over the past three or four decades. During this time, the technological bias of the culture outpaced, and then began to overpower, the *human* capacity to compete with its power to define reality, most especially in the area of communications. I noted that the real underlying issue, apart from the tragedy itself, was the manufacturing of images and O. J. Simpson's participation in the mechanics of this industry, if not his mastery of the process. To make a joke, I said that he had used his physical grace and attractiveness to turn himself into a marketable image. He might have slowly accepted that image as reality and lost all the values with which he grew up; he might have fallen in love with another image (the nubile, blond, nineteen-year-old Nicole Brown); and he might have settled into a lifestyle based on false fronts and "thinness" of personality, of shining surfaces and tinsel, of improvised emotions ungrounded in the deeper stratas of selfhood, that is Los Angeles in this postmodern and material age. I went on to say that, if indeed O. J. Simpson had committed the murders with which he was charged, I could understand his motivation, no matter how bloody his action. He might simply have grown jealous of other, younger, much more stylish images competing with him for Nicole's attention, and acted out a narrative line from some movie plot inside his head. I added that, given the unreal and unnatural context of Los Angeles, the upcoming trial itself would be steeped in thin images over meaningful substance, because the entire affair was already being drained of human reality and existed only in the thin and bloodless provinces of the mass media. Continuing with this crazy logic, I told the young reporter that there was still hope for an outcome appropriate to the surreal context of the trial. At around the same time as the murder of Nicole Brown, it should be recalled, the media baron Lawrence Tisch was negotiating to merge his own Home Shopping Network with the CBS Network. If he succeeded, I noted (as the Disney Company succeeded in its acquisition of ABC News), Tisch would then be King of Medialand, as well as of all its images. As such, no matter what decision the O. J. jury reached, Tisch, as King of Medialand, and especially of the domain that was the focus of the trial, could say, with media-vested authority, to O. J. Simpson, a simple, wayward image, "*I pardon you.*"

The young reporter made a tape-recording of all my mad speculations. Several days later, his story appeared in *U.S.A. Today* with only one quotation attributed to me: "James McPherson said that O. J. should not have married that white woman in the first place." I then began receiving calls and letters. Producers of a CBS talk show, as well as the producers of "Larry King Live," invited me to appear as an advocate of racial purity. My daughter, who like all teenagers is captivated by the celestial unreality of the mass media, was very excited to talk with a producer from CBS. She pleaded with me to appear. But by this time it became clearer to me that I had begun to enlist in the spread of a cancer, one with no possibility of complexity or even of isolation, and so I refused both offers to have my own day under the camera lights. Instead, I took my daughter to The Mall of America, in Minneapolis.

During this time, I returned to Shakespeare's *Othello* for a sense of the human complexity that would never surface during the eighteen months of the trial's integration into the mass media. I returned to the play for something deeper than celluloid understanding. I reread it, much more carefully this time, looking for new insights into the issues, racial or others, being raised in Los Angeles.

Shakespeare's *Othello* confirms for all English-speaking people, perhaps in keeping with the European mode of causality, a certain narrative line: "Once upon a time, a certain combination of elements came together and the results were tragic for all involved. Looking back at that tragic event, one can trace a line of movement from then into this present moment; and then, secure within this present moment, one can project the same causality into the future." These are the emotional physics that are imposed on the complex and ever-changing growing edge of human life. These physics may provide some troubled people, who adapt their thinking to this settled emotional order, with a greater sense of security. But, at times, it becomes necessary to stand apart from the assumptions in which we have been so thoroughly educated and search for alternative ways of seeing. The European view of causality may well be only *one* of many points of view about the nature of reality, even a reality as thoroughly accepted as the motivations of Orenthal J. Simpson or Shakespeare's great character Othello, the Moor of Venice.

II

Shakespeare's *Othello,* after centuries of varied interpretations, has become almost a text in sociology. It has been called a warning to all good wives to look well to their linen. It has been viewed as an object lesson in the negative consequences likely to follow from contacts across racial lines. It has been interpreted as a meditation on the nature of evil. What is not often studied is the context of the play, the backdrop against which the tragedy is played out (the full title of the play is *Othello, the Moor of Venice*). We have been educated to search for insights into the tragic events in the foreground of the drama rather than in the implied drama or unstated assumptions that exist in the background and that influence the actions of the characters. That is, there are, in addition to the two different "races" at the center of the drama, the cultural assumptions of each that influence the actions of the participants in the drama.

Othello's Venice, one assumes, is the same Venice inhabited by Shylock, another alien, in Shakespeare's *The Merchant of Venice*. In the latter play, the Christian traditions of Venice are at the very center of the actions of the major characters. Antonio, the merchant, and Portia, the heiress, embody values that are employed by Shakespeare to put into contrast the alien values of Shylock. It might even be said that the two different value systems, or traditions, are "actors" in the play, with the Christian values demonstrating themselves to be superior to the Jewish ones. The ruling ethic of the play is derived mainly from the biblical codes drawn from the Book of Matthew, Chapters 5, 6, and 7—the core of the ethical teachings of Jesus of Nazareth. Shylock's code, evoked in contrast, is derived exclusively from the Jewish traditions of the Old Testament. The Venice of *The Merchant* is steeped in the ethics of Matthew 5–7, so much so that the *interface* between it and the written law of Venice provides the chief dramatic action of the play. This is much the same Venice that Othello inhabits, except that the Christian tradition in this tragedy seems to play no significant role. As a matter of fact, Christian tradition is mentioned only three times in the entire play: once by Iago during his initial complaint against Othello, once by Othello himself as a casual reference, and once by Desdemona in protestation of her loyalty to Othello. There are no references to Jesus of Nazareth and the ethics he taught. One might assume that the Christian ethic is simply "there," implicit in the motivations and the actions of the characters. Or one might assume that it is held in check, in a calculated way, in order for Shakespeare to bring into fuller focus, a focus uncluttered by ethical dogma, his core theme—the contrast between Othello's natural nobility of soul and Iago's natural depravity of soul. It is also of interest to note that although Othello is a Moor, assumedly derived from Levantine traditions, there are no overt references to his being in possession of a different ethical system. Like the Venice he inhabits, he has been stripped by Shakespeare of any connection with an ethical system beyond that of immediate concern to the drama. Othello's Venice, then, becomes only a backdrop, a stage, against which, in contrast to the Venice of *The Merchant*, a very different kind of drama is played out.

That Othello's racial background makes him an outsider in Venice goes without saying. He is black, a Moor, an experienced warrior, and an exclusive servant of the State. His only claims to personal distinction are his nobility of birth, but in another cultural context, and his nobility of soul. There is another very important sociological point of distinction: because of his extensive services to the State, the Duke, who is most powerful, is in his debt. But the Venice over which the Duke presides is a Venice seemingly stripped of the veneer of Christianity that was essential to the action of *The Merchant*. The Duke's Venice seems to be closer to the mode of an ancient European territorial state and its values than it is to the Venice of Christian tradition.

The territorial state over which the Duke presides is characterized by common language, blood, and borders. It is dynastic in that it is rooted in family ties that emphasize loyalty and liens of obligation. This web of obligations imposes a series of vertical duties: obligations of obedience upward, obligations of care and responsibility downward. In such a tightly knit living arrangement, issues of right and wrong are reduced to concrete matters of loyalty and disloyalty. To be loyal is right. To be disloyal is wrong. The core ethic in this arrangement is the survival of the dynastic family, or the State, far beyond the lives of its individual members. In this very special and non-Christian sense, purposeful endurance becomes the paramount value of each active member of the community or institution.

Othello, the Moor, did not originate within this community and therefore has only an outward coating of its innermost values. Shakespeare does not give us many clues of Othello's place of origin, but the emotional connections he has with Egypt (the place where his mother's handkerchief was made) and the Middle East suggest that he derives, in terms of ethical influences, from the Levantine tradition. This tradition subscribes to its own ethical system. Whereas in the Duke's Venice the paramount ethic is willed, purposeful endurance, whether of the individual, the family, or the State, in the ancient Levantine tradition, the paramount ethic, what is to survive, is the consensus of the faithful, those who have received the same spirit, in the Kingdom of Heaven. Because, according to this ethic, the world itself is sinful but one is obliged to live in it, salvation can be assured only by predestination, by evidence of one's membership in the body of the faithful. The conflict between these two ethical systems, although both are understated and only alluded to, provides, I believe, the basis for the true dramatic conflict in *Othello*.

Iago is the first to tell us, directly, in Act I, scene i, that two sets of values are in conflict and that the traditional ethic, and liens of loyalty and vertical obligation, are being threatened by Othello's presence. Three great ones of the city, he tells Roderigo, petitioned Othello to make Iago his lieutenant. But Othello rejects their suits and makes Michael Cassio, a Florentine and a foreigner, his second in command. From this experience Iago concludes:

> Preferment goes by letter and affection
> And not by old gradation, where each second
> Stood heir to the first.

As a demonstration that the basic ethic is being eroded, even in the homes of the Venetians, Iago informs Brabantio, who is a senator of Venice, that his own daughter, Desdemona, has proved disloyal and has demonstrated this disloyalty by marrying Othello. Both Brabantio and Iago then acknowledge recognition of their paramount obligations: loyalty to the existing vertical arrangement. Though Brabantio is a senator, as well as Desdemona's father, he can take no private action without doing violence to this ethic. He must appeal fatherly concerns upward, to the judgment of the Duke. And although Iago has plots of his own, he too recognizes that the authority of the State has a special role to play in whatever fate is assigned to Othello:

> [F]or I do know, the state
> However this may gall him with some check,
> Cannot with safety cast him, for he's embark'd
> With such loud reason to the Cyprus wars,
> Which even now stand in act, that, for their souls,
> Another of his fathom they have none
> To lead their business; in which regard,
> Though I do hate him as I do hell-pains,
> Yet, for necessity of present life,
> I must show out a flag and sign of love,
> Which is indeed but a sign.

The first scene of Act I sets up the basic dramatic conflict in the play. Venice, a small territorial state, is in a state of war with the Turkish Empire. In such an emergency, foreign mercenaries have been recruited to help the Venetians in their battles. Among these mercenaries are Othello, a Moorish officer and a veteran of many battles, and Michael Cassio, from the rival territorial state of Florence. The necessities of war have compelled the State (in the person of the Duke) to integrate Othello, and then Cassio, into the command levels of the military structure. The existing ethic is applied to them.

The Duke is thus loyal to Othello, and like any other Venetian general, Othello is allowed to exercise his own lien of obligation downward—to choose as his lieutenant the foreigner Michael Cassio, passing over even Iago, a native Venetian who has been proposed for the office in the customary way by men of high status in the dynastic state. Acting on this same sense of status, Othello has courted, and won for his wife, Desdemona, the daughter of Brabantio, a Venetian senator. But these actions by a foreigner, and a Moor at that, have undermined the existing hierarchical order. The liens of loyalty that traditionally flowed downward, from the Duke and his nobles and senators to fellow Venetians like Iago, and upward from Desdemona to her father, Brabantio, are threatened with erosion. This is the concern voiced by both Iago and Brabantio—that the "old gradation" has been threatened.

Othello himself appears as a somewhat innocent example of the outsider who has been integrated into a preexisting hierarchical order, one with its own exclusive ethic. Like the court Jew, the foreigner or outsider who has been elevated to a position of power within such a structure leaves behind, out of practical necessity, his former loyalties and associates. He becomes "captive" to the power structure that sustains his status. He lacks an infrastructure for the support of his own values. Although the preexisting liens of loyalty may extend downward to him from the ultimate source of power, they do not always extend upward, from below him, with the same degree of obligation. Like the court Jew, such a person must always depend exclusively on the powers above him for protection and must be wary of those who are ostensibly under his immediate authority, since they are native and he is not. Unlike Shylock, in this very same Venice, Othello has no coreligionists representing alternate sources of values through which he can sustain himself. Such a figure is totally alone. If the structure into which he has been integrated subscribes to values that are so closely held or assumed that they go all but unspoken, and if the outsider has nothing but a surface understanding of those values, conflict becomes inevitable. If the person has been assigned great authority, and if he assumes a deep personal involvement without a complete understanding of the unspoken values of the world in which he operates, destruction of the self becomes almost an inevitability. Such is Othello's situation.

It is unfortunate that very little is known about the relation of the Western territorial states to the more ancient traditions of the Levantine cultures out of which Othello comes. It is speculated that the culture of ancient Greece was greatly influenced by the culture of ancient Egypt (Immanuel Velikovsky in *Oedipus and Akhnaton* and much more recently Martin Bernal in *Black Athena*). It is known that the Levantine peoples, some of whom are now called Arabs, preserved in their languages the records of the best of Greek philosophy. It also is known that the culture of the ancient Greeks was reintroduced into western Europe by these peoples. It is known that the essence of Levantine religious thought was distilled in the teachings of Jesus of Nazareth and was adapted, with some significant modifications, by Europeans many centuries later. And it is known that what became the Western tradition of romantic love resulted from the infiltration of Levantine religious rituals and myths into southern France, where it found expression in the religion of the Cathari in the ninth and tenth centuries, and from whom it spread to the troubadours who carried it into all parts of Europe as an expression of a secular art. For the most part, however, the deeper influences of Levantine culture on the territorial states of western Europe have remained obscure. Apart from the scholarship of a few specialists, there is little general understanding of the ethical system that predated that of the West and that once had great influence on Western culture. This deficiency in understanding limits our insights into Levantine peoples when they appear against the backdrop provided by the ruling assumptions of Western tradition. We do not see that they, too, are operating out of an unstated value system, and that this value system, though alien to Western understanding, may play some large part in the choices they make.

Although it is presumptuous of any writer to second-guess Shakespeare, I am tempted to speculate, nonetheless, that a character as complex as Othello would be better understood if he were viewed against the backdrop provided by his own ethical system instead of against the backdrop provided, almost exclusively, by the values of the Venice he inhabits. Viewed from such an intimate perspective, Othello's fate, although still tragic, becomes more clearly the result of his own attempt to participate in some private ethic while at the same time serving out his obligation to the State. I believe that this conflict between his loyalty to the State and his attempt to be loyal to his own private ethic is the source of his tragic flaw and his fall from grace.

One sees in Othello the very same merger of noble birth and noble nature that Prince Mishkyn, in Dostoevsky's *The Idiot,* possesses. In the Western literary tradition, there is a convention of noble natures appearing in the most unlikely of places. In modern American democracy, we have been conditioned to expect the appearance of such people. From Melville's Billy Budd to Twain's Huck Finn, such natures have appeared, confirming our belief that nature is a wonderful moral factory, capable of throwing up models of moral balance that, in more traditional cultures, would be expected to find expression only in an established aristocracy. In fact, as a practical matter, virtue in pre-Christian Europe was assumed to be invested in dynastic lines and their observances of vertical obligations. Nobility of intention and of action were not so much matters of personal choice as practical matters of necessity. Othello, although an outsider to Venice, claims for himself a form of nobility that would be very familiar to the Venetian aristocracy. He says in Act I, scene ii, to Iago, in defense of his marriage to Desdemona:

> I fetch my life and being
> From men of royal siege, and my demerits
> May speak unbonneted to as proud a fortune
> As this that I have reach'd.

But Othello also lists for Iago two additional merits, both of which will become active agents in his eventual undoing. He claims a right to fairness of treatment with respect to Desdemona based on his past and present services to the State:

> Let him [Brabantio] do his spite;
> My services which I have done the signiory
> Shall out-tongue his complaints.

His third source of personal merit seems almost arrogant:

> My parts, my title, and my perfect soul
> Shall manifest me rightly.

This seeming arrogance in Othello, threaded throughout the play, proves to be his undoing. In a traditional view of tragedy, it may be construed as his "tragic flaw." Like some royal character in Greek drama, Othello seems to dare to appropriate to himself what should be the exclusive judgment of the gods. He seems to believe in his own mythology, thus running the risk of offending the gods and attracting their jealousy and wrath. It might be questioned, however, whether what Othello expresses is true arrogance or a fundamental belief in a value system, an ethic, that has sustained his life thus far and about which he is merely speaking honestly. The problem raised by this speculation is made even more difficult by the fact that, if indeed there is an independent ethic to which Othello subscribes, its sources are not apparent in the play. Othello's statements provide evidence of its existence, but no full statement of its content, no assertion of its causative principles, is made. Othello merely testifies, throughout the play, to his belief that what he calls his "perfect soul" will not lead him into error. When speaking before the Duke about his courtship of Desdemona, he says:

> She loved me for the dangers I had passed
> And I loved her that she did pity them.

And when he does fall into error, after having been manipulated by Iago, he does not admit to any error on his own part and is still captive to his old sense of his personal nobility:

> Yet, 'tis the plague of great ones;
> Prerogativ'd are they less than the base.
> 'Tis destiny unshunnable, like death.
> Even then this forked plague is fated to us
> When we do quicken.

Even after killing Desdemona, when Othello sees his fatal mistake, he still maintains that the error is not entirely his fault:

> Who can control his fate? . . .
> When we shall meet at compt [accounting],
> This look of thine will hurl my soul from heaven,
> And fiends will snatch at it.

And when asked by Lodovico how a man as good as he seemed to be could have fallen to such a slavish deed, Othello replies with a peculiar absence of self-blame:

> An honorable murderer, if you will;
> For nought I did in hate, but all in honor.

I speculate that, beneath this seeming obtuseness on Othello's part, there is an unarticulated ethic at work, one on which he has based a view of the world, the place of loyalty in that world, and his own sense of his soul's worth. I further speculate that Othello is operating in accordance with a Levantine ethical system that selects as its core value a passive stance toward matters of personal fate. Whether a person is elected to enter heaven or doomed to hell is not, in this view of things, a matter that can be influenced by individual action. According to this ethic, an individual is predestined either to join the community of the faithful in heaven or to remain forever outside of it.

Such an ethic based on predestination directly contradicts an ethic based on personal will. It assumes that God predetermines the fates of men and that the will of the individual is meaningless. It assumes that the will of the individual is not under his own control but is only God's instrument in effecting what he has already determined. I believe that a subscription to this same ethic, to a belief in his own predetermined election, motivates Othello. I also believe that the chief dramatic conflict in the drama is the conflict between Othello's private ethic and Iago's personal will.

III

The nature of this conflict between Iago and Othello might be brought into much clearer focus by being viewed through the dramatic action in the play symbolized by the Signoria of Venice and the Island of Cyprus. In the minds of Shakespeare and his contemporaries, the rational world inherited from Greco-Roman tradition tended to make a division between the material world and the irrational forces of nature. As Edward Said has suggested, the use of the word *Orientalism* is, in reality, an intellectual device employed to block out, or else to reduce in importance, almost anything that is intellectually or emotionally uncomfortable for Western people. Beneath this intellectual device reside the psychological habits that give rise to the accepted divisions between "West and East," "us and them," "white and black." In *Othello,* Venice and its Senate embody order, reason, justice, and concord—binding forces that hold the city together. Cyprus, on the other hand, is associated with chaos and violent storms, the Turk, the Ottoman, and unharnessed forces of nature—the "Other." If one were to reject the conventional interpretation of Iago as a malignant or evil soul in action, and view him instead as an expression of a settled point of view, his interaction with Othello, as I have argued earlier, might then be read as a conflict between two different ethical systems. They are put into contrast by Shakespeare in much the same way as, but on a larger scale than, the Signoria of Venice and the Island of Cyprus are put into contrast and also into conflict.

Shakespeare's Venice is drawn from Giraldi Cinthio's *Hecatommithi*, a collection of 100 tales printed in Italy in the sixteenth century (1565). One of the tales involves a Moor who kills his Christian wife. All the key elements of Shakespeare's *Othello* can be found in this morality tale: the wicked ensign, a handkerchief ("finely embroidered in the Moorish fashion"), a cruel and vengeful Moor, and a Disdemona, whose dying sentiments are much *unlike* the dying sentiments of Shakespeare's Desdemona:

> [A]nd much I fear that I shall prove a warning to young girls not to marry against the wishes of their parents, and that the Italian ladies may learn from me not to wed a man whom nature and habitudes of life estrange from us.

There are mentions of Cyprus in Cinthio's story, but Cyprus is not an active "participant" in his account.

It took the peculiar genius of Shakespeare to transform Cinthio's character sketches, as well as his morality tale, into a great drama. Shakespeare added Cyprus to Cinthio's story and made Othello an intermediary between these two worlds. This movement on Othello's part, between reason and emotional chaos, is, in my view, at the basis of the tragic events in the play. If it is indeed true, as Jesus of Nazareth taught, that "no man can serve two masters," then Othello's heroism consists, for English-speaking readers of the play, in his resolution of his deep emotional conflict by killing that part of himself that had dishonored Desdemona, as well as her father, and through them the Signoria of Venice. In this conventional view, Othello dies a Christian subject of Venice. It is open to speculation what other part of Othello, an equal partner in his internal conflict, also dies with him.

But Othello is much more than a convert to Christianity. Even before he appears in Act I, scene ii, we are told, through allusions, that the Venetians view him as an alien. This prejudice is expressed in the exchange between Brabantio, Desdemona's father, and Roderigo, in Act I, scene i:

Brabantio: What tell'st thou me of robbery? This is Venice; my
house is not a grange.
Roderigo: You'll have your daughter covered with a Barbary
[Arabian] horse, you'll have your nephews neigh to you, you'll
have coursers for cousins, and gennets for germans.

Roderigo also calls Othello "a lascivious Moor." And Brabantio, when
he confronts Othello, states the Venetian case:

Damned as thou art, thou hast enchanted her!
For I'll refer to all things of sense,
If she in chains of magic were not bound,
With a maid so tender, fair and happy,
So opposed to marriage that she shunned
The wealthy, curled darlings of our nation,
Would 'ever have, t'incur a general mock,
Run from her guardage to the sooty bosom
Of such a thing as thou . . . to fear, not to delight.

But Othello, in his own self-concept, is certain of his equality of *rank*
with Desdemona's family. When Iago orders him to run, Othello says:

Not I. I must be found.
My parts, my title, and my perfect soul
Shall manifest me rightly.

Later, before the Duke, the Venetian Senate and the officials, and Desdemona's father, Othello meets anger with reasoned discourse. He gently
recounts his courtship of Desdemona. In his famous speech in Act I, scene
iii, Othello speaks in the "high" style of the court, recollecting the incidents of a hero's life, incidents that might have also come from the
mouths of Tristan, Lancelot, Percival, or any other knight in the tradition
of courtly love so familiar to Shakespeare and his audiences. The speech
is beautiful in its childlike simplicity and honesty, but it betrays no sense
of psychological depths or insights on Othello's part. He refutes the
charges against him, of witchcraft and betrayal of loyalty, by placing his
story within a literary convention, or form, familiar to the Duke and his
senators:

She loved me for the dangers I had passed.
And I loved her that she did pity them.
This only is the witchcraft I have used.

But the "rational" nature of his speech before the Duke and his senators causes Othello to omit any reference to the handkerchief he has given Desdemona. This handkerchief, of *great* symbolic significance to the play, is not mentioned, for some reason, until Act III, scene iii, *after* Othello and the Venetians have arrived on Cyprus. Only then do we learn of its emotional importance to Othello. It is, we learn in Act III, scene iv, a symbol of both the continuity of Othello's own moral identity and his bond with Desdemona:

> *Othello:* That handkerchief
> Did an Egyptian to my mother give.
> She was a charmer, and could almost read
> The thoughts of people. *She told her, while she kept it*
> *'Twould make her amiable and subdue my father*
> *Entirely to her love; but if she lost it*
> *Or made a gift of it, my father's eye*
> *Should hold her loathed, and his spirits should hunt*
> *After new fancies. She, dying, gave it me,*
> *And bid me, when my fate would have me wived*
> *To give it to her. I did so;* and take heed on't;
> Make it a darling like your precious eye.
> To lose't or give't away were such perdition
> As nothing else could match. (emphases mine)

In Venice, before the Duke, before the senators, even before Desdemona and Brabantio, her father, there is no mention of the handkerchief. Perhaps Shakespeare's use of the conventions of courtly love, essential to his viewers for recognition of the emotional understanding expressed by the Duke, negated the introduction of any real evidence of witchcraft. Even though Cinthio, in his story, mentions a handkerchief "finely embroidered in the Moorish fashion," Shakespeare delays in raising it to a level of dramatic importance until *after* the action of the play moves to Cyprus. Perhaps Othello's loyalty to the rationality of the Signoria causes him to forget the handkerchief as a symbol of his bond with Desdemona. Or perhaps, in Shakespeare's view, the handkerchief achieves dramatic significance *only* when it and Othello are reintegrated into the "landscape" from which they both derived. Once removed from the rationalizing structure of Venice, in Shakespeare's view, Othello "reverts" to the irrationality represented by "Egypt," Moorish, Turk, Ottoman, *Cyprus*. This convention of "place" defining types of responses runs through many of Shakespeare's plays: *Antony and Cleopatra, Troilus and Cressida, King Lear, Henry IV, Parts One and Two, The Tempest, Richard II, A Midsummer Night's Dream.* But it is in *Othello,* as in *Antony and Cleopatra,* that a far distant landscape—that of an imagined Cyprus—is employed to suggest the hold of a foreign and alien ethic on a character. The symbolic background, represented by Cyprus, in addition to its emotional correlation with the handkerchief, thus becomes of great importance to the developing tragedy.

Moreover, while he is still in Venice, Othello makes before Brabantio and the Signoria a formal gesture as important as the handkerchief to the tragic developments in the play. Still conforming to the "high" style of the courtly love tradition, Othello has this exchange with Brabantio, Desdemona's father:

> *Brabantio:* Look to her, Moor, if thou hast eyes to see:
> She has deceived her father, and may thee.
> *Othello:* My life upon her faith.

To Shakespeare's audiences, such an exchange would probably recall to mind the psychological, or emotional, subtext of traditional narratives about the courtly love tradition: The lovers are doomed *not* to live happily ever after. They may separate (as Othello and Desdemona do just after this exchange), and reunite, and maintain their passion for each other, but ultimately their fate is death. Passionate pursuit of the unobtainable "Other" leads to death. This was the familiar passion of Tristan and Isolde, of Lancelot and Guinevere, and so on. Such is the conventional implication of Othello's foreshadowing "My life upon her faith." But, on a much deeper level, this line, spoken by Othello to Brabantio, the heartbroken father, might refer back to Othello's initial statement of his personal ethic, in Act I, scene ii:

> I must be found.
> My parts, my title, and my perfect soul
> Shall manifest me rightly.

Othello's statement to Brabantio may well be an oath that his personal honor and that of Desdemona have now merged. He vows to restore the faith that Brabantio has lost in Desdemona. In a deep emotional sense, Othello is making a "contract" with Brabantio, saying that he will give his life if what Brabantio perceives as deceit is a true assessment of his daughter, Othello's wife. Moreover, Othello is making his vow *through Brabantio* to the entire ordered, rational world of the Signoria. Within the context of this reading of the vow, the significance of the handkerchief, though not mentioned, once again becomes of great symbolic importance. It becomes a symbol of Othello's own lifeline, though steeped in "Orientalism"; and because it is then in Desdemona's hands, it becomes the symbolic proof of Othello's own faith in their bond. Othello thus carries to the Island of Cyprus, from Venice, a "rational" contract with Brabantio based on an "irrational" sense of his own parts, titles, and perfect soul. In this reading of the play, Othello's struggle to honor both the rationality of the Venetian State and the emotional chaos set off once he is settled into the Cyprus landscape (and what it represented to the Elizabethan mind) is at the basis of the tragic action of the play. It is being suggested that, the plots and malicious machinations of Iago aside, the tragedy of the play is centered in Othello's own struggle to contain these conflicting obligations inside himself, as these conflicting obligations increase on the Island of Cyprus.

Shakespeare's creative genius led him to add the Island of Cyprus, its "Oriental" landscape, to Cinthio's story. The conflict between it and the Signoria of Venice parallels and also contrasts the conflicting emotional states of Othello. It should be noted that, although the Signoria of Venice provides the backdrop of the play for only one act, the backdrop of Cyprus overshadows *four* full acts of the play, as well as its central dramatic actions. Furthermore, the first scene in Act II, set in Cyprus, raises the possibility of emotional chaos grounded in *natural forces,* the *same* natural forces discussed by Iago and Roderigo in the opening scene of Act I. Act II, scene i, set in Cyprus, foreshadows the commencement of the unleashing of "natural" forces (though "unnatural" to the Venetians) that will dominate the remainder of the play:

> *Montano:* Methinks the wind hath spoke aloud at land;
> A fuller blast ne'er shook our battlements.
> If it hath ruffianed so upon the sea,
> What ribs of oaks, when mountains melt on them,
> Can hold the mortise? *What shall we have of this?* (emphases
>   mine)

Although the raging sea has destroyed the Turkish fleet, it has also separated Othello from his lieutenant, Cassio, Othello's only official link with Venice. Even Cassio says, "The great contention of sea and skies parted our fellowship." While the Venetians await Othello's arrival at

Cyprus, the "pure" products of the Venetian court—Desdemona, Cassio, Iago, Emilia, Montano, and a second gentleman—reconstruct their courtly manners, their wit, and their sense of "breeding." Othello's absence from this scene may be of great symbolic significance to the play. When he does appear on the stage at Cyprus, he carries in his speech to Desdemona an echo of the storm from which he has emerged, as well as a foreshadowing of his own emotional fate:

> If after every tempest come such calms,
> May the winds blow till they have wakened death.
> And let the laboring bark climb hills of seas
> Olympus-high, and duck again as low
> As hell's from heaven.

Of his return to Cyprus, Othello says:

> How does my old acquaintances of this isle?
> Honey, you shall be well desired in Cyprus;
> I have found great love amongst them. O my sweet,
> *I prattle out of fashion, and dote*
> *In mine own comforts . . .*
> Once more, well met at Cyprus. (emphases mine)

Once again we see Shakespeare searching for a connection between Othello and the Cyprus landscape. Deeper than this, there is an implication that Othello's "own comforts," whatever they are, are now merged with his bond with Desdemona, as well as with her own connection with the Signoria of Venice. A third suggestion that Othello's "own comforts" in Cyprus are becoming alien to the ways of the Signoria is conveyed in two subsequent speeches, after Othello departs with Desdemona. The first is Iago's discourse on unfaithful wives, begun on scene i of this same act, and its continuation with Roderigo. Here Iago's descriptions of Desdemona grow even coarser, and he discloses his suspicion that *both* Othello and Cassio have cuckolded him with Emilia, his wife. On one level of this speech, Shakespeare is simply deepening the conventional characterization of the stage villain, a stock character familiar to his audiences. But on another level, this full speech to Roderigo, set against the "Oriental" backdrop of Cyprus, suggests that Iago, too, is being drawn under the influence of the mysterious "Otherness" that will soon claim the public character of Othello.

An additional narrative suggestion that chaos will soon displace order, that Cyprus will soon threaten the order of Venice, comes just after Iago's soliloquy. This is at the beginning of scene ii in the same act, when Othello's Herald reads his proclamation ordering a celebration of the destruction of the Turkish fleet:

> [E]very man put himself into triumph. Some to dance, some to make bonfires, each man to what sport and revels his addiction leads him. For besides these beneficial news, *it is the celebration of his nuptials.* (emphases mine) So much was his pleasure should be proclaimed. All offices [storerooms, or *ranks of order?*] are open, and there is full liberty of feasting.

From within such a context of license, against the backdrop of Cyprus, the drama moves toward its tragic end.

Within such a context, against such a backdrop of what Shakespeare and his audiences would view as an "irrational" world, the subsequent contrasts between Iago's ethic and Othello's obscure one may well be viewed with greater insight and understanding. It should be recalled that it has been Iago's intention all along to have his revenge on Othello for preferring Cassio as his lieutenant, as he announced to Roderigo in Act I, scene i:

> Preferment goes by letter and affection.
> And not by old gradation, when each second
> Stood heir to the first.

Iago has also made clear in this speech that he knows both sides of Othello's nature, both the courtly and Christianized self, displayed at the Signoria, and the "pagan" side exhibited in other places:

> And I, of whom his eyes had seen the proof
> At Rhodes, at Cyprus, and on other grounds
> Christian and heathen, must be belee'd and calmed
> By debitor and creditor.

It is no accident, I think, that Shakespeare chose the Island of Cyprus and its heathen implications, and not the rational, ordered world of the Signoria, for Iago to act out his will against Othello. On Cyprus, Iago is merely pressing his own case, but against a backdrop that, given Othello's "own comforts" in that landscape—the "pagan" nature of which Cyprus is the symbol—will help further his designs.

Within the specific context of such a perspective, Othello's handkerchief becomes of essential importance. If, as has been speculated earlier, it represents a linkage between Othello and his lineage, as well as with the lineage of Desdemona, the deeper importance of this symbol can be revealed only against the Cyprus landscape, the landscape that best connects Othello with his place of origin. As noted before, there is no mention of the handkerchief while Othello and Desdemona are in Venice. But at Cyprus, when Othello and Desdemona enjoy "the celebration of his nuptials," the handkerchief surfaces and is moved to the exact center of the dramatic action of the play. There is, in Act III, scene iii, a fundamental ambiguity, one that might support this specific reading of Othello's ethic. This is the scene in which Iago is insinuating to Othello a hidden love affair between Desdemona and Cassio. Othello doubts it. Then Desdemona and Emilia enter. Othello complains of "a pain upon my forehead."

> *Desdemona:* Let me but bind it hard; within this hour
> It will be well.
> *Othello:* Your napkin is too little;
> [stage directions: He pushes the handkerchief away, and it falls.]
> Let *it* alone. Come, I'll go in with you. (emphasis mine)

Whether "it" refers to Othello's forehead or to the handkerchief is the fundamental ambiguity in this important scene. As a number of critics have suggested, it makes a considerable difference in the interpretation of later events whether "it" refers to Othello's forehead or to the handkerchief. Given the symbolic importance of the handkerchief to Cinthio's original version of the story, and given the care that Shakespeare took to create Cyprus as the dominant backdrop for most of his play's dramatic action, and considering also the handkerchief's importance to the remainder of the play, it might be suggested that it is the *ethic* represented by the handkerchief itself, and not so much Iago's increasing insinuations and plots, that concerned Shakespeare in all the scenes after the handkerchief is introduced. It becomes the first symbol that binds, on the Island of Cyprus, *all* the major characters in the play—Othello, Desdemona, Emilia, Iago, Cassio, Bianca, and Roderigo. In this reading, the handkerchief, on Cyprus, is an "ordering" force, a symbol of emotional integration, comparable to the reason and courtly manners that bind together all the people in the Signoria of Venice. But in the context of the Island of Cyprus, the handkerchief binds the characters to the "Oriental" or unknown mysteries of Egypt, Arabia, Turkey, the Ottoman

Empire—all the potent emotional powers of the mysterious "East." A comparison could be made here between the rational, unifying intentions of the Western territorial state, in which individuals are bonded by common language, common blood, and common borders (such as Venice), and a Levantine "sect nation," in which a shared belief in a "sacred script," blood and borders notwithstanding, constitutes membership. In this reading, the new emotional order introduced by Othello's handkerchief on the Island of Cyprus threatens to undermine, if not to destroy, the hold of the rational powers of the Signoria. It is almost as if two *different* models of social organization are being brought into focus, and into conflict, by Shakespeare. The less familiar, or alien, model of bonding is symbolized by the introduction of Othello's handkerchief into the very center of the drama. The linkage it imposes on the participants in the tragedy also introduces a counterstructure, or an uneasy emotional order, that threatens the traditional order about to be imposed on Cyprus by the rationalizing power of the Venetian State.

On a personal level, to Othello the handkerchief has something more than organizational meaning. It is the symbol of his own emotional investment, both as an individual man and as a husband, in the continuity of his own version of personal honor. It represents his own pledge to his ancestors and to Desdemona. Also, I suggest, it is Othello's attempt to honor his sworn obligation to the Duke and to Brabantio, Desdemona's father, as well as his obligation to the ethic represented by the handkerchief, that leads him to kill himself.

The handkerchief comes "alive" as an additional actor in the play only after its casual introduction in Act III, scene iii. Emilia first recognizes its importance as Desdemona's "first remembrance from the Moor":

> My wayward husband hath a hundred times
> Wooed me to steal it; but she so loves the token
> (For he conjured her she should ever keep it)
> That she reserves it evermore about her
> To kiss and talk to. I'll have the work ta'en out
> and give't Iago. What he will do with it,
> Heaven knows, not I; I nothing but to please his fantasy.

Emilia discloses that, to Desdemona, the handkerchief *is* Othello. But to Emilia it is something to be copied and also a gift for Iago, her husband.

To Iago, the handkerchief has no spiritual or ethical content. To him it is a *thing* that can be used to trap Othello:

> *Iago:* I will in Cassio's lodging lose this napkin.
> And let him find it. Trifles light as air
> Are to the jealous confirmations strong
> As proofs of Holy Writ.

Once the handkerchief passes from Emilia to Iago, it is increasingly debased and cheapened, losing its original meaning, until it becomes only a trifle for Bianca, Cassio's whore. It would be an instructive exercise to trace the incremental *increase* in Othello's suspicion and "madness" and correlate this with each stage in the debasement of the handkerchief, with each *decrease* in the valuation of the beloved symbol. It is obvious that something changes abruptly in Othello in the very scene (Act III, scene iii) in which Desdemona drops the handkerchief. Emilia picks it up and gives it to Iago just after Othello and Desdemona go off-stage. Othello returns almost immediately, but his mood has clearly shifted from the trusting lover of Desdemona to an attitude of deep suspicion. He says to Iago, "Ha! ha! False to me?" Nothing else can account for this abrupt shift in Othello, from doubt in Iago's insinuations to absolute belief in Desdemona's unfaithfulness, unless it is the debasement of the handkerchief that is now beginning. It is significant to note that Othello's deep suspicion begins *even before he knows* that the handkerchief has been stolen by Emilia and passed on to Iago. It is almost as if Othello senses some spiritual loss inside himself. From this point onward in the play, Othello's language becomes debased and angry. He moves away from the courtly language in earlier sections of the play and begins to employ "low" physical images, rage, and vows of retribution.

I suggest that the handkerchief is, to Othello, a symbol of his entire lineage and reason for existence. It moves from being a symbol of self, to a symbol of his love for Desdemona, to a symbol of their bond, *in his own ancestral terms*. It then becomes a simple trifle with a variety of uses and meanings imposed on it as it passes from hand to hand among an alien people. By losing the handkerchief, and through its cheapening, Othello has lost the symbol of his own election, or predestination, to noble rank. This reading might make much deeper sense of his brooding soliloquy at the beginning of scene ii in Act V, where Othello is torn between his loss of self and his remaining love for Desdemona. For him *two* essential concerns—his loss of his symbolic self, the handkerchief, and his dread of losing Desdemona—are *merged* in this speech. Othello is speaking here to the heavens, from which he once expected protection and salvation, and to himself, both at the same time.

"It is the cause (causality? Loss of the
ethical meaning of the symbol?)
It is the cause, my soul.
Let me not name it to you, you chaste stars.
It is the cause. *Yet I'll not shed her blood,*
Nor scar that whiter skin of hers than snow,
And smooth as monumental alabaster.
Yet she must die, else she'll betray more men.
Put out the light, and then put out the light.
If I quench thee, thou flaming minister,
I can again thy former light restore,
Should I repent me; *but once put out thy light,*
Thou cunning'st pattern of excellent nature,
I know not where is that Promethian heat
That can thy light relume. When I have plucked the rose
I cannot give it vital growth again;
It needs must wither. . ." (emphases added)

If Othello's speech is read in this way, as a meditation on *both* his own soul's face and his love for Desdemona, something essential may come into clearer focus. Both this speech and Othello's recollection of the handkerchief's spiritual importance in Act III, scene iv, contain references to the inextricable integration of the material and the spiritual. The handkerchief is a physical object which contains great spiritual significance for Othello. His speech in Act V, scene ii recapitulates this same close integration. Here, Othello now believes that Desdemona has betrayed him with Cassio, which is the accepted reading of the scene. But which is the *causal* fact beneath his wish to kill her? Is it because through Desdemona the handkerchief has been debased, and through that debasement Othello's own spirit; or is it only that her betrayal has been proved by her loss of the handkerchief? If the latter, then the handkerchief becomes a mere stage prop. But if it is the former, then the handkerchief symbolizes a much deeper causative principle, one that the genius of Shakespeare, despite the intellectual limitations of his historical time and place, was struggling hard to reach and to comprehend.

Othello's handkerchief has passed from Egypt through all the mysteries of the "Orient" into the very "heart" of a European nation-state, as the symbol of a bond between a Venetian senator's daughter and a "pagan" with claims to a comparable nobility. In that handkerchief both the material and the spiritual are merged. Within the confines of Venice, it is only a material item. But against the Cyprus landscape, Shakespeare shows that the handkerchief is of essential importance to Othello as a symbol of spiritual linkage both to his personal past and to Desdemona. But in the hands of Emilia, Iago, Cassio, and Bianca, it is only a material trifle. Its movement from the spiritual plane to the material one coincides, as has been argued, with Othello's increasing jealousy and "madness." But, in Shakespeare's view, is Othello truly mad, or is he trying to resolve a spiritual problem that is essential to the life of his own soul, the fate of Desdemona notwithstanding? It is being suggested here that Shakespeare was trying to *imagine* his way toward an ethical basis for Othello's behavior, one far removed from the outward conformity to both the Christianity and the veneer of manners of his adopted Venice. Shakespeare possibly was contemplating evidence of a form of ethical behavior, and therefore personal transcendence, that historically has always been at odds with the material ethic of the West, and most especially the ethic of personal will dramatized by the plots of Iago.

Read in this context, it might be helpful to observe how Shakespeare treated another "alien" caught up in the ethical structures of this same Venice. This other "alien" is Shylock, the Jewish merchant in Shakespeare's "comedy" *The Merchant of Venice* (1598). Like Othello (1604), Shylock is torn between two competing ethical systems, his own Jewish tradition and the Christian tradition of the Venetian State. Perhaps this play is called a "comedy" because Shylock, the Jew, is shown to be unable to prevail against the expression of personal will, under the guise of Christian ethics, dramatized by Portia. Perhaps the most moving line in the play is Shylock's response to his friend, Tubal, when Tubal tells him that his own daughter, Jessica, has sold a ring to Antonio's creditors for a monkey. Shylock responds, in Act III, scene ii, with the most heartfelt emotion:

> Out upon her! Thou torturest me, Tubal. It was my turquoise; I
> had it of Leah when I was a bachelor. I would not have given it
> for a wilderness of monkeys.

The parallel between Shylock and Othello concerns the value each alien man places on a material item that links each man to a personal past. In each case, Shakespeare seems to be suggesting, the value invested in the symbol is much deeper than its surface appearance.

The world to which both Shylock's turquoise and Othello's handkerchief symbolically link them, in Shakespeare's view, is that unknown and unknowable Levantine world, which enters the known historical world only at specific times and places. These times and places were those chosen by Europeans, selectively, to construct their ideas about the line of progress of history. Shakespeare explored the points at which the Western and Levantine traditions met in some of his historical plays; for example, he used Egypt and Rome in *Julius Caesar* and *Antony and Cleopatra*. Historically, the two worlds met when the sacred texts of Christianity were translated by Greeks and Jews from their original Hebrew. They met again, as has been stated before, when the cult of romantic love, the courtly love tradition, infiltrated western Europe, by way of Levantine influences, during the tenth and eleventh centuries. There are references to this alien world in the histories of the Crusades and in the French epic poem *The Song of Roland*. Limiting the knowable landscape to only these few encounters between the Levantine world and western Europe creates a "blind spot" in the understanding of cultural traditions that are non-European. This is the geographic place, *the psychological border,* at which reason and unreason, rationality and irrationality, meet and confront each other. The ancient Greeks, those first grand masters of reason, resolved this problem by attributing to the action of the gods a "psychic intervention," or *ate,* which would "rationalize" irrational actions on the parts of their heroes. To the Greeks, *ate* was a state of mind—a temporary clouding or bewildering of the normal consciousness, a temporary insanity—brought on by external "daemonic" agencies. Later European societies rationalized the movement of spiritual forces in a variety of other ways. To Christians of the Middle Ages, the *strigla,* or irrational demonic forces, gave rise to beliefs in witchcraft as well as to anti-Semitism. In Shakespeare's day, the sources of the irrational became associated with nature itself. But in *Othello,* Shakespeare seems intent on exploring this intellectual problem through his treatment of the major character. The great writer could only intuit a philosophical system, or an independent ethic, at the basis of Othello's struggle.

To bring into closer focus evidence of what so troubles Othello after his handkerchief is lost, it might be helpful to quote a Mohammedan theologian, almost a contemporary of Cinthio's, who suggests the dualistic nature of the Levantine outlook on the world, its system of symbolic meanings. This is the Sufi philosopher Al-Ghazzali, who, in his *Mishkat Al-Anwar (The Niche for Light)*, speaks of the meaning of the symbolic language of Levantine tradition, a language that enters Western tradition in the allegory called "The Gospel of John," in the stories of *The Arabian Nights,* and, possibly, through Othello's handkerchief:

> The annulment of the outward and visible sign is the tenet of the Spiritualists, who looked, utterly one-sidedly, at one world, the Unseen, and were grossly ignorant of the balance that exists between it and the Seen. This aspect they failed to understand. Similarly, annulment of the inward and invisible meaning is the opinion of the Materialists. In other words, whoever abstracts and isolates the outward from the whole is a Materialist, and whoever abstracts the inward is a Spiritualist, while he who joins the two together is catholic, perfect.

This insight suggests that, to Shakespeare, and therefore to Othello, the handkerchief might have had this same symbolic meaning.

If the above speculation is accepted, Othello's speech in Act V, scene ii, might take on much more significance. Here Othello is trying to reclaim his old ethic, a balance between the "light" once provided by his handkerchief for both himself and his bond with Desdemona, and Desdemona herself, who symbolizes his linkage with the Signoria of Venice. This is the terrible "cause" he must contemplate, and this is the foreshadowing of all his subsequent actions. In such a horrible situation, Othello must struggle to remain true both to sources of self-definition, the spiritual and the physical, and to the traditions of *both* his places of origin.

> *Othello:* It is the cause, it is the cause, my soul.
> Let me not name it to you, you chaste stars.
> It is the cause. *Yet I'll not shed her blood,*
> *Nor scar that whiter skin of hers than snow,*
> *And smooth as monumental alabaster,*
> *Yet she must die, else she betray more men.*
> Put out the light, and then put out the light.
> If I quench these, thou flaming minister,
> I can again thy former light restore,
> Should I repent me; *but once put out thy light,*
> *Thou cunning'st pattern of excelling nature,*

I know not where is that Promethean heat
That can thy light relume. When I have plucked the rose
I cannot give it vital growth again;
It needs must wither. (emphases mine)

It is in the very last scenes of the play, after Iago's last trick has been disclosed and after Othello has killed Desdemona, that a *balanced* nobility in Othello does come out. He now recognizes that his "mistake," made when he allowed himself to be manipulated by Iago, resulted from his *unchanging* belief in the rightness and the purity of his own soul, his own source of motivation. But now he has committed murder, has broken the laws of Venice, and has also broken his vow to Brabantio, Desdemona's father, who, we learn in the same scenes, has died. The unifying power of the handkerchief has been destroyed by being cheapened. The "sect" on Cyprus that has grown up around it has now been supplanted by the authority of the Venetian State. The State has reintroduced its old hierarchy on Cyprus, and Cassio is put in the place of Othello. Othello is stripped of everything except what in him is literal and irreducible. At this point, Othello's true heroism, his natural nobility, emerges. He has judged others according to his own ethic, and now, to maintain a sense of his own old nobility of purpose, he must judge himself—but in *two different scales of justice.* In Act V, scene ii, Othello repeats, in an ironic way, the vow he made in Act I, scene iii, to Brabantio.

Act I, scene iii:

Brabantio: Look to her, Moor, if thou hast eyes to see;
She has deceived her father, and may thee.
Othello: My life upon her faith.

Act V, scene ii:

Othello: But why should honor outlive honesty?
Let it all go.

It is only after the acceptance of his fate that Othello reverts to his old "high" speech, the courtly type of speech of personal bravery, such as the one he gave before the Duke back in Venice. He speaks to Gratiano, recently come from the court:

Behold, I have a weapon;
A better never did itself sustain
Upon a soldier's thigh. I have seen the day

> That with this little arm and this good sword
> I have made my way through more impediments
> Than twenty times your stop. But O vain boasts:
> Who can control his fate?

In this same speech, he says to Desdemona:

> When we shall meet at compt [Judgment]
> This look of thine will hurl my soul from heaven,
> And friends will snatch at it.

But Othello still insists on his nobility of intention when accused by Lodovico:

> *Lodovico:* O thou Othello that was once so good,
> Fall'n in the practice of a cursed slave,
> What shall be said to thee?
> *Othello:* Why, anything;
> An honorable murderer, if you will;
> For naught I did in hate, but all in honor.

There seems to be a contradiction in these two speeches. On the one hand, in terms of the Christian ethic essential to Desdemona's fate, Othello sees himself as a sinner whose soul will be hurled from heaven on Judgment Day. But still, in terms of his own ethic, he sees himself as acting honorably. This double set of scales, I suggest, is at the basis of Othello's last speech. It is a great speech, in the courtly style of the Signoria. Its images integrate the divided loyalties of a noble warrior whose services to the State have always been based on a belief in the rightness of his actions. But much more important than this is Othello's ambiguous reference to the symbolic meaning of the handkerchief:

> Of one not easily jealous, but, being wrought,
> Perplexed in the extreme; *of one whose hand,*
> Like the base Judean, threw a pearl away
> Richer than all his tribe. (emphases mine)

The conventional interpretation is to consider this part of Othello's speech as a reference to Desdemona. But, considering the importance of the handkerchief to the tragic development of the play, and considering also that this speech contains a summary of Othello's life, Shakespeare would have been remiss as a dramatist not to have integrated its meaning into Othello's last speech. As said before, the handkerchief represents Othello's *self*. Also, the term *base Judean* is ambiguous. It could refer to Judas Iscariot, or to an "Indian"; but the implied allusion is to *infidelity,* to the unbeliever. In this reading of the scene, Othello seems to be saying that he has brought this fate upon himself by throwing away (Act III, scene iii) the symbolic item that had sustained both his life and his life's meaning, as well as his bond with Desdemona. This is the "recognition," in traditional dramatic theory, of the tragic hero's moral flaw. A reversal of fortunes always comes after this tragic moment of truth.

In Othello's case, the solution is once again to declare his loyalty to the Signoria, by shifting his images abruptly from "the base Judean" and "Arabian trees" to the history of his past loyalty to the State:

> Set you down this;
> And say besides that an Aleppo once,
> When a malignant and a turbaned Turk
> Beat a Venetian and traduced the state,
> I took by th' throat the circumcised dog
> And smote him thus.

In offering up his own life, Othello affirms his continuing loyalty to the Venetian State. The reference to "a malignant and turbaned Turk" whom he killed is clearly that part of himself that has violated the ethics of the Signoria. Yet, if the pearl that has been thrown away is accepted as Othello's symbolic self, and not Desdemona exclusively, another complexity arises. Is Othello's self-negation so total that he chooses to die to appease *only* the Venetian sense of justice, or has the personal ethic that has sustained Othello all his life, his "perfect soul," his belief in his own election, found a way to be sustained? I speculate that it is at this extremely important point, and not in the speech that precedes his suicide, that Desdemona again becomes central to the action. As he dies, Othello says to Desdemona:

> I kissed thee ere I killed thee. No way but this.
> Killing myself, to die upon a kiss.

Here Othello seems to be renewing his loving bond with Desdemona. But this final kiss, a recollection of the intimacy they once had, in Venice as well as on Cyprus, may well be a symbolic reconciliation with Desdemona, and through her with the bond Othello has made with Brabantio, her father. By killing himself, rather than being killed by the

Venetians (as was the case in Cinthio's story), Othello has *maintained* his sense of personal honor and has possibly also kept alive his old sense of personal rightness, if not predestination. He honors the vow he made to Brabantio back in Venice: "*My life upon her faith.*" This is the other scale of values, his own, that Othello affirms by killing himself. In the act of self-negation, he affirms two sets of loyalties—the one owed to the Venetian State and the one Othello owes to himself.

In this imaginative reading of Shakespeare's great character, Othello grows even more complex. He is brought closer to our human understanding because he possesses an ethic—a philosophical solution to the fact of death and what should survive it—that is comparable to the Christian ethic ostensibly held by Desdemona. Othello's suicide might well be, at the same time, an affirmation of his deepest beliefs. If part of his ethical sense originated, with the handkerchief, in Arabia, among the Islamic peoples of the old Levantine world, then Othello's final action might have been a redemptive one, and also an affirmative one, implying that Othello's soul has earned, after all, the transport into the community of the faithful in Paradise. If his ethical sense originated, along with the handkerchief, in Egypt, then Othello's action might have caused his *ka,* his spiritual double, to attain this same afterlife. On this latter point, it might be helpful if we examined two comparable deaths in another of Shakespeare's tragedies—the double suicide in *Antony and Cleopatra* (entered in the Stationer's Register in 1608), which also puts into contrast the known world, Rome, and the unknown or "Oriental" world, Egypt. By the last scene in the tragedy, Antony has killed himself, and Cleopatra is to be taken as a prisoner to Rome. Cleopatra determines that she will die by her own hand to escape being degraded by the Romans *but also to rejoin Antony.* Her speech to Iras, her maidservant (Act V, scene ii), states the nobility of her intention:

> Give me my robe, put on my crown; I have
> Immortal longings in me. Now no more
> The juice of Egypt's grapes shall moist this lip.
> Yare, yare, good Iras; quick. Methinks I hear
> Antony call; I see him rouse himself
> To praise my noble act; I hear him mock
> The luck of Caesar, which the gods give men
> To excuse their after wrath. Husband, I come:

Now to that name my courage prove my title;
I am fire and air; my other elements
I give to baser life.

Through a comparable action, by kissing Desdemona as he dies, Othello achieves the same nobility and, it is suggested, the same joy "the gods give men to excuse their after wrath." In this reading of the play, Othello and Desdemona are reunited, at least in the terms that are at the basis of Othello's ethic, after their tragic deaths.

Antony's and Cleopatra's deaths took place in Egypt. Othello died a prisoner of the Signoria of Venice. But Shakespeare's Charmian, an Egyptian, might have said the best final words for both sets of lovers:

Guard: What work is here? Charmian, is this well done?
Charmian: It is well done, and fitting for a princess
Descended from so many royal kings.

Shakespeare's *Othello* still has very powerful lessons to teach. Recently, the novelist Scott Turow called the O. J. Simpson murder trial "the *Othello* of the twentieth century." Turow was focused exclusively on the tragic bond between Othello and Desdemona, between Orenthal James Simpson and Nicole Brown Simpson. Perhaps, in a superficial sense, Turow is right. But what else does the play have to teach? For one thing, it provides an understanding of the psychological tension between the Signoria of Venice and the Island of Cyprus; between rationalized authority and "irrational" chaos; between "us" and "them"; between suburb and inner-city; between black and white. The old unstated emotional language of Shakespeare's day still speaks, though in very subtle ways, from the deepest levels of this culture. Also—and this is a political point—this ancient emotional language is likely to resurface, in hysterical ways, as the evolving global economy, structured by communications technology and the movement of money, information, and peoples, threatens to undermine traditional concepts of nation-state sovereignty. The advocates of sovereignty will increasingly find themselves confronting ethical systems that are radically different from their own and far more different than the Signoria of Venice was from the Island of Cyprus.

These are the growing tensions of this century's end. With regard to "the trial of the century," only one thing can be said with clarity and certainty. Having made a good living through the commercialization of thin and fashionable images, there was no ancestral handkerchief, either in Simpson's background or in the trust of a beloved, that could keep alive for him a higher meaning in life.

This is the true tragedy.

From Japanese by Spring[1]

ISHMAEL REED

[Puttbutt, "a low man on the lecturer pole," undergoes
a reversal of fortune when his Japanese instructor becomes acting president of Jack London College where
he teaches. In this scene Professor Crabtree, a pompous
English professor, has to deal with Puttbutt, whom he
has slighted for many years.]

His picture was on the cover of the *California Voice*.
Puttbutt named special assistant to the acting President of Jack London College, the story announced.
People were lined up outside of his office door. Matata Mu-
soni who said on some resumes that he'd attended Oxford,
and on others that he'd attended Cambridge, was there; he
looked up from the newspaper *European* at Puttbutt with
sarcasm in his eyes. Charles Amistad brought his greasy smile
and Professor Crabtree. Professor Crabtree gave him a watermelon grin. He took Crabtree first. If Crabtree had been a hat
wearer he would have had his hat gingerly in hand. The cor-
ners of his mouth pushed back into a huge smile, revealing
some very expensive dental work.

He looked around the office. He must have been im-

---

1. This excerpt, from an early version of the novel, is reprinted with
the permission of the author. It was submitted to the editor in January 1992.
Originally numbered Chapter X it appears as Chapter 27 in the published
novel. There are other minor variations such as the change of name from
Shigoto to Yamato.

pressed. The sleek Japanese furniture. Japanese paintings on the wall. The view of the Pacific. The grand light shafting in. "What can I do for you Professor Crabtree?" Puttbutt said, leaning back in his chair, his hands supporting his head. He tried not to rub it in, considering the reversal of fates. Professor Crabtree paused for a moment, before speaking. Finally, with a good deal of effort: "I know you must be surprised that I came in today. After the rude way I've always treated you."

"You have been rude, Professor."

"I . . . I'm not the most pleasant person in the world, but once you get to know me I—I play a good game of poker. You play poker?"

"Come to the point, Professor, Dr. Shigoto has a great deal of work for me to do. He wants all of us to husband our time. He feels that Americans waste too much time."

"You heard about what happened over in the Department of Humanity. Seems to have been a big shakeup. I understand that the English and Poetics Departments have been moved to ethnic studies. Anglo Saxon Studies. From Chaucer to the Beatles."

"That's right."

"A lot of my colleagues, including myself, are, well you know, concerned about our status."

"I did hear something to that effect, Professor, what do you want me to do about it?"

"I . . . well it seems that you have some pull with that Japanese chap."

"Dr. Shigoto."

"Yes, that's his name."

"Dr. Shigoto and I decided that it would be wasting money to keep people on the staff whose courses were drawing only a few students. Your Sir John Suckling seminar and the course in Old Norse. There are only three students attending. The Japanese don't like to waste money." The Professor didn't say anything.

"And you haven't published a book or an article in fifteen years, and the articles that you have published show considerable borrowing."

"I . . . just haven't had the time, I—"

"I know. Going to these humanity conventions which provide you with an opportunity to meet women other than your wife, and to sample exotic cuisine. Why, last year, your professional organization's program included more information on the restaurants in Chinatown than on the topics when it met last year. I also found out, Professor, that it was you who was instrumental in getting my tenure denied."

"Who told you that? That's supposed to be a secret."

"I took the liberty of looking at my confidential files."

"But you're not supposed to look at those files! They're off limits." He began to rise from his chair until it apparently occurred to him that he didn't have the clout he once had.

"Your article on *Othello*, I felt wasn't first rate. Your thesis that race relations in this country haven't changed since Shakespeare's time. The play was written in sixteen three. That's preposterous. And to call Shakespeare a racist is really overdoing it, don't you think? What claptrap!" Crabtree squirmed in his chair as he said "claptrap."

"I wrote it during my Black Power days."

"Cocamamy detritus."

"O, is it now?" Puttbutt didn't feel like defending a paper he had written years before, but he was irritated by the imperious tone now creeping into Crabtree's voice. He stood and leaned on the table, staring right into Crabtee's eyes. Crabtree recoiled. "The only thing that has changed is that thick lips are in now. All of these white women desiring lip enhancement operations," Puttbutt said. Even saying that gave him relief.

"Come now, Prof. Puttbutt." Crabtree smiled wryly.

"Shakespeare makes Othello into a primitive. He's warlike. His moods change rapidly. His anger is always on the surface, ready to burst. It arises from a 'hollow' hell. And the character, Othello, is always down on himself.

"He says in Act II, scene iii, 'I am black / And have not those soft parts of conversation / That chamberers have.' Why would a General, a man of war, especially an African, be so down on himself? African warriors see themselves as the cock of the walk. They have these griots who follow them around like Bundini Brown, telling them how great they are.

"Shakespeare also promotes a common belief among white men that they can have any woman of any background, but when a black man and a woman of another race get together the motive has to be perverse. You white men can have all of the women you want, while anytime a black man and a white woman fall in love it's because, according to Shakespeare, she's enchanted by him. The black has put some kind of spell on her, or that she is fascinated by his oppression. What incredible ego. The only uncorrupted interracial relationship can be that between a white man and a colored woman."

"William Shakespeare didn't have a racist bone in his body. Surely you're projecting." Puttbutt rose and went to the window. He looked down. A white fraternity had set up a platform. Some of the pledges had painted their faces black. One large white boy had put on the Mammy attire. Red and white polka dot dress. Huge pillows for breasts. The "slaves" were being auctioned off to the older brothers. This was the fraternity's annual Slave Day. Despite Dr. Shigoto's memo to all of the departments and to the students that racism would be punished severely, the overt racist acts were continuing with broad support from the media who were insisting that these young bigots be allowed to "express themselves." It was the targets of their abuse, the media and the corporate financed Think Tanks were saying, who were the real oppressors. They were insisting that everyone be politically correct.

"You blacks are always complaining about racism. Racism this racism that. You use racism to explain away your failure. All of this talk about racism on the campuses of Jack London. I've been teaching here for thirty years and have never found a single instance. Do you hear? A single instance. And now you have to reach back and drag Shakespeare into it. Is there no end to your peoples' paranoia? Now you have some sort of code that makes it an offense to call someone a nigger. Why that word doesn't bother me at all." While Crabtree was speaking, Puttbutt was thumbing through a copy of *Othello* that had been left behind in Witherspoon's hurried attempt to clear his former office.

"Scene III, Othello's speech, 'She loved me for the dangers I had passed, / And I loved her that she did pity them.' "

"Doesn't prove a thing."

"He paints Othello as a noble savage."

"Where? Where did you find evidence for that?"

" 'The Moor is of a free and open nature / That thinks men honest that but seem to be so; / And will as tenderly be led by the nose / As asses are.' When's the last time you read the play, Professor?"

"I—I."

"And if you don't think that Shakespeare's play can be applied to contemporary situations, what about the character of Emilia, a racist feminist?"

"Feminism in Shakespeare's time. You are stretching things, Puttbutt."

"Act III, Scene Four, Emilia says, speaking of men 'Tis not a year or two shows us a man: / They are all but stomachs, and we all but food; / They eat us hungerly, and when they are full, / They belch us.' Certainly some misandry reflected in that speech, Professor Crabtree. As for racism, in Act V she calls Othello a 'black devil.' There are many feminists on Jack London's campus who could be Emilia."

"But I thought you were on their side."

"I'm on my side, Mr. Crabtree. My side." He studied Crabtree's face. His countenance flagged for a moment before reassuming the supercilious demeanor. Like many Eurocentric Professors, as they were being called in the newspapers, he regarded Shakespeare as little more than a cultural hammer to be used to intimidate the infidels. So busy counting iambic pentameter, they'd never taken Shakespeare at his word. They could read *The Merchant of Venice* and *Othello* without taking into account what some of the characters and the language meant to Jews and to blacks.

"You've been here thirty years, Crabtree. That counts for something. Maybe we can work something out. It's not like the old days, when you only needed to know English and French. Dr. Shigoto is requiring that every faculty member study Japanese." Crabtree turned from his usual chalk white to red. He wished that he could read his thoughts. He threw one of the copies of *Japanese by Spring* that lay in a stack on his desk at Crabtree. Crabtree caught it, examined it and then threw it to the floor as though it were a wasp.

"How about teaching a course in Freshman Composition."

"Composition. That's preposterous, a man of my rank."

"Suit yourself."

"You'd better respect your betters young man. I was teaching the Milton seminar, when you were in high school. Don't you forget." Puttbutt glanced at a sheet of paper on his desk. "Two students."

"What?"

"You had exactly two students enrolled in that course on middle English. Dr. Shigoto believes that such courses constitute anglo saxon ethnic cheerleading and feelgoodism. It has to be Freshman composition or nothing."

Crabtree rose. He stood there staring at Puttbutt for a moment. The anger contorted his face. He finally spun around and left the room in a huff. Puttbutt shrugged his shoulders.

[The fact that Puttbutt is not expressing the author's ideas becomes clear as the novel progresses beyond this point. For one thing, Ishmael Reed himself enters the text as a character. Puttbutt forces Crabtree to teach Freshman Composition in Yoruba, and while Crabtree becomes enlightened as a result of his studying Yoruba culture, Puttbutt is revealed increasingly as a self-serving individual willing to do and say anyting that will promote his interests. This reinforces the suggestion that his interpretation of *Othello* is not meant to be accepted at face value.]

"Nèg Pa Bon"
("Nigger No Good")

MARYSE CONDÉ

When I was a child, brought up in little Guadeloupe, going to the theater was virtually unknown. Of course, some French companies used to visit the island once a year before Christmas and present *Le Misanthrope*, *L'Avare*, or any other play by Molière in the *Salle des Fêtes* of Pointa à Pitre, brilliantly decorated for the occasion. However, these performances were reserved for the enjoyment of the adults, and we children were excluded from them. For us, what came close to theater were the wake ceremonies on the eve of the funerals of friends and relatives. For a highly sensitive child like me, a wake ceremony was a strange event. My fear of the dead person, who was stretched on a funeral couch looking so different from the familiar figure I used to see, kept me at a considerable distance from the bedroom. From a distant point of observation, I caught glimpses of the female mourners saying endless prayers throughout the night, or reading whole pages from the Bible, pausing from time to time only to empty their bowls of odorous and spicy soup. I also avoided the kitchen where the women of the family noisily lamented the departed while preparing food. I stayed with the men who smoked their earthenware pipes and stretched their legs in the dining room or on the veranda. Around them, the atmosphere was entirely different. There, praying and sobbing gave way to heavy drinking. As the night grew darker and bottles of rum passed from one hand to another, the jokes became dirtier and dirtier and the peals of laughter louder and louder. Suddenly a man would jump to his feet, sing for a while, and then yell:

> Ye krik, ye krak!
> Ye mistrikrik, ye mistrikrak!
> Mwen voye sevant o pin, pin rive avan sevant.
> (I sent my servant to buy bread, the bread came back before the servant.)

The other men would yell back, "Koko!" ("A coconut!"). And the story would begin to unfold. It was really a play in which the storyteller mimed and assumed various characters for the pleasure of the audience.

Storytelling used to be an old and revered tradition in the Caribbean, and only the invasion of television has managed to put an end to it. In my young days, the art was still flourishing and the names of some storytellers were more highly respected than those of some politicians.

To experience theater in its real form, I had to wait for my adolescent days. When I was fourteen, my parents sent me to a boarding school in Paris. Paris was not an unknown city to me. Every three years my parents, who were civil servants, were entitled to long summer vacations in France. My new life started out in a monotonous though studious fashion. I spent my days apparently immersed in scholarly pursuits while my mind roamed along the hills and paths of Guadeloupe. How I missed Guadeloupe! A place I used to think of as narrow and suffocating became a land of wonders. My mother who was so strict, so obsessed with the notions of good education and proper behavior, became the symbol of Tender Motherhood! I even missed my father and my elder brothers whose aloofness and machismo I used to suffer from so greatly.

At the boarding school, we enjoyed few forms of entertainment. Apart from dutiful visits to museums once a week, clad in navy blue uniforms, walking two by two and hand in hand, we were taken to one of the parks or gardens of Paris such as the Luxembourg, Montsouris, or Bois de Boulogne, where we were allowed to spend one hour in the rowing boats. Once a month, the ten best students of the class were taken to a matinee performance at the *Comédie-Française*.

The first time I entered *La Maison de Molière*, my heart was pounding. I remember the occasion was a performance of Corneille's *Le Cid*, a tragedy that we were about to study in class. I looked in awe at the high ceilings so magnificiently gilded and carved and at the elaborate candelabras dripping with lights. As we were seated rather high up in the house, I could hear the muffled sound of voices mingled with cries and laughter emanating from the boxes and the orchestra below. I had the feeling that once the heavy red curtains parted, a magical new world would be discovered and I would be involved in an experience that would change me for ever after. Slowly the lights were subdued. Three strokes sounded and the curtains parted.

How can I possibly describe my disappointment! Was that the theater? Fake Greek columns, faded scenery, hideous costumes. The booming voices of the actors sounded artificial. For almost two hours, they exchanged their repartee and moved on the stage as in a too well-rehearsed ballet. I was expecting a warm flow of communication between the actors and the audience, shouts, laughter, the stamping of feet. Instead, I heard discreet applause. Even at the end of the play, the encores seemed part of an empty ritual. Strangely enough, for the first time in my life, I consciously measured the distance between French culture and myself.

I belong to a generation of West Indians who have been forced to recite dutifully "Our ancestors, the Gauls." My middle-class parents believed in the "civilizing mission of France" and in the dogma of its cultural superiority over all other nations. They were proud to be French even with black skins. A sullen and difficult child, I had never openly questioned their beliefs, although I had done everything in my power to displease and contradict them. That night it was obvious to me that my identity was an ambiguous construction. Was I supposed to identify with the heroes and heroines in *Le Cid*? Was not this French theatrical convention utterly alien to me? I partly voiced my feelings to the French Literature teacher. He certainly did not sense my nascent rebellion and ruefully admitted that "the classical repertory needed a good dusting." He promised to take the class to the Théâtre *National Populaire* where Gerard Philippe, the well-known French actor, was giving another interpretation of *Le Cid*. The year went on, however, and he did not keep his word. We returned to the *Comédie-Française* for more performances of Corneille and Racine's tragedies.

During the summer of that very year, I made my first trip to England. The girls at the boarding school who had spent previous holidays there had come back with stories about infinite boredom and loneliness. The weather was awful, and so was the food. The language was incomprehensible. As for cars, they were driven on the wrong side of the road. The Busby family with whom I was sentenced to spend nearly one month lived in a small town in Kent whose name I have fogotten by now. Their house, which did not lack charm, was a one-story building built of dark red bricks. The garden was full of azaleas and sweet peas. The family itself was composed of two girls the same age as myself and a baby boy who started crying immediately when he saw me descending from the ferry. (We eventually became friends.) The father and mother were both primary school teachers. They were a strange pair. Mrs. Busby used to wear long flowery dresses and large straw hats. Mr. Busby was entirely bald, a broad-shouldered giant with striking blue eyes. As a hobby, Mr. and Mrs. Busby acted with and directed a small theatrical group. On the very evening following my arrival, I was taken to a performance of *Othello, the Moor of Venice*.

Dare I say that the name *Shakespeare* was almost unknown to me, although I was very conversant with Greek as well as French theater? The performance was to be the major event of a parish fete. A few banners were hanging on the trees of a park near St. Mary's Church with the messages "Confide in Jesus" or "Jesus the Saviour." When we arrived at the theater, the house was already full of people laughing and chatting. Teenage girls were showing off their Sunday dresses. Toddlers were running in the aisles. We waited for a very long time. Then the curtain opened on a nearly empty stage surrounded by a few cardboard columns. Just as I was about to be turned off by this scenery and incomprehensible dialogue, a black man draped in a toga suddenly appeared on the stage. I should rather say Mr. Busby appeared painted as a black man, his blue eyes shining in his darkened face. I was shocked. I was seeing a black man on a stage, and he was not even a real black man. Why? Were there no black actors? Was the art of the theater forbidden to blacks? In spite of this grotesque disguise, my interest was aroused. For the first time, to my knowledge, a black person was a theatrical object. I listened avidly, trying to find my way through the labyrinth of Shakespearean English.

> I fetch my life and being
> From men of royal siege.

Was it a black man who was uttering such words? The oral tradition of Guadeloupe revolves around slavery. It presents a succession of rogueries, dirty tricks, and underhanded deeds committed by the two animals (who symbolize the slaves) in their search for survival. At the wake ceremonies, the men interspersed their stories with obscene jokes and songs full of double entendres that made them unfit for children's ears. What I was hearing was in striking contrast. Othello was saying:

> My parts, my title, and my perfect soul
> Shall manifest me rightly

And later he declared:

> She loved me for the dangers I had pass'd
> And I lov'd her that she did pity them.

I clapped my hands loudly at Desdemona's words:

> I saw Othello's visage in his mind;
> And to his honours and his valiant parts
> Did I my soul and fortunes consecrate.

I spent the whole of the play in a state of excitement that I had hardly experienced before even when reading one of my favorite novels (since I was a passionate devourer of books). Iago's betrayal filled my heart with impotent anger. Like the audience in the movie house in Guadeloupe, which participates so much in the action that it warns the heroes against any possible danger, I would have liked to have protected Othello against Iago. Why was he naive enough to doubt Desdemona, a "most exquisite lady" in Cassio's words? Witnessing his transformation into a brute through the workings of the "green-eyed monster," I was in a rage and felt as if he himself had brought about his own perdition. Why was he so easily victimized?

Looking back at those so distant days, I cannot say that I immediately understood the reasons for the cult of Shakespeare in England and why the complete leatherbound edition of his plays on display in every home was as revered as the Holy Bible. I was not impressed by his dramatic artistry or by his mastery of language, although some lines sent shivers throughout my body:

> Whip me, ye devils
> From the possession of this heavenly sight!
> Blow me about in winds! roast me in sulphur!

Wash me in steep-down gulfs of liquid fire!
O Desdemona! dead, Desdemona! dead! O!

I could not tell whether the actors were well trained by their director or
whether Mr. Busby himself, in what he supposed to be good black manners, did not gesticulate and grimace too much. What struck me was the
intrigue. I was simply stunned by the power of the story and saw the
characters as if in real life. Surprisingly enough, I was almost completely
indifferent to Desdemona's plight and did not heed her pathetic cry: "Kill
me tomorrow! Let me live tonight!" Our common womanhood was no
bond because she was white and I was black. In those adolescent years,
race transcended gender.

Although I felt a certain measure of sympathy for Othello, I was
above all fascinated by Iago's character. Iago seemed to me the sole hero
of the play, exercising his powers in order to unleash the shameful forces
otherwise hidden within the black man's self. I saw him as the symbol of
those who, from time immemorial, cunningly using the weaknesses of
the black man's soul, have brought about the downfall and enslavement
of the black race. In spite of everything Othello said and did, in spite of
the apparent nobility of his heart and the gentleness of his manner, Iago
was convinced that he remained nothing but a savage and goaded him
to be just that. The noble Moor who declared at the beginning of the
play, "My parts, my title, and my perfect soul / Shall manifest me
rightly," ended by murdering his wife, gnawing his lips, his whole frame
shaken with "some bloody passion."

In Iago I recognized the incarnation of racism, although I had never
directly experienced it. The education that I received as a child was
somewhat disquieting. I was brought up to believe that, as a black person,
I was fatally marked by Our Maker and possessed a terrible ugliness of
soul. A proverb that family and friends constantly repeated summed it
all up: "Nèg pa bon. I mové tou bonnman." ("Nigger No Good, totally
no good.") Although France was the most generous of motherlands, it
nevertheless sheltered hideous creatures lurking in the dark and bent on
bringing into the open this painfully concealed ugliness. In order not to
fall prey to them, I had constantly to watch my step, my words, and my
very thoughts. This was the price I had to pay to become a true human
being. Education was but a struggle against one's inner self. Iago demonstrated to me how this struggle could be pointless in the face of a
superior and malevolent willpower. I felt miserable. I felt threatened. For

the first time, I understood and thanked my parents who, even at the cost of my exile, were doing everything in their power to ensure for me the best of educations. But in spite of all their efforts, would they be able to protect me from possible Iagos? Suddenly, life seemed to me an arduous and mountainous road, strewn with pitfalls that I would never be able to avoid.

At the end of the play, I accompanied the Busby family into the dressing room. Surrounded by his admirers, Mr. Busby was cleaning off his makeup, and gradually the pinkish color of his skin showed through. He smiled and asked me, "Little Maryse, did you enjoy it?" To my surprise, I burst into tears.

Did Shakespeare Intend Othello to Be Black? A Meditation on Blacks and the Bard

PLAYTHELL BENJAMIN

In a *New York Times* article of June 16, 1991, "Looking Inside That Outsider, Othello the Moor," the Irish director Joe Dowling tells critic Richard Bernstein: "*Othello* is not about racism. . . . And I think that's one of the dangerous things about it in terms of contemporary ideas." Among the thing he says in defense of this curious thesis is that Brabantio's rage over Orthello's elopement with his daughter, the beautiful Desdemona, is not movitated by racial considerations but because the Moor "is an outsider."

In his attempt to eradicate racism as a central theme of the play, Dowling argues: "Of course there's racism here. Brabantio and the other Venetians talk about him in the language of racism. 'Thick lips' they call him. They talk about the 'sooty bosom.' The language is the language of racism, but the attitude towards him is not, because Othello is of value to the state and it uses him." And finally, Dowling offers this explanation of the drama's tragic essence: "Iago does not simply gull the Moor because his is black. He gulls him because he himself needs the satisfaction of the motiveless malignancy." To his credit, Bernstein observes: "There is a touch of revisionism in this view, since Othello has generally been played, at least in recent decades, as Shakespeare's treatment of race and racism." But then he tells us: "Laurence Olivier, for example, used to play Othello in black face, as though he were a Subsaharan African, but Mr. Dowling claims that that is a well-intentioned present day inaccuracy. Othello was a Moor, a North African, which would have made him somewhat darker-skinned than a Venetian but not much more so"—a view of Othello echoed by the *Voice* critic Michael Feingold.

These attitudes embody all the convoluted inanities that character-ize the arguments of those who have sought to deny that Shakespeare intended Othello to be a black man, or that the play is fundamentally about sex and race, specifically the conflict that is likely to result when a black man woos and wins a beautiful, high-class white woman. And, like all such arguments, Dowling's argument has no factual evidence (textual or historical) to support it. It is, therefore, that he has recourse to the spurious and anachronistic argument, first advanced by Samuel Taylor Coleridge, that Iago's treachery toward Othello and Desdemona is spurred by "motiveless malignity." For if racial and sexual jealously are excised from the play, Iago's actions became inexplicable. When Wilford Cartey, a Trinidadian, who teaches English literature at Columbia Uni-versity and City College, read Dowling's comments on the play, he con-cluded, "Either the man cannot read or he wishes to rewrite the text." I agree with Cartey and am not impressed by Dowling's arguments. To fathom Shakespeare's intentions, I would like to rely on the evidence of the text and the history of race relations in Elizabethan England.

Let us first consider the question of Iago's relationship to Othello, the relationship on which the dramatic power of the play turns. As in all Shakespeare's plays, several themes are explored in the course of the story, a reflection of his profound understanding of the complexity of human behavior. In the conversation between Iago and Roderigo that opens the play, it is easy to discern the professional and sexual jealousy, blind ambi-tion, and, yes, racism, by which Iago is motivated. And these three coalesce to produce a virulent enmity toward Othello. The jealously first becomes clear when Iago complains about Othello's refusal to make him his lieuten-ant. He knows his "price," he is "worth no worse a place," but Othello, "loving his own pride and purposes," has already chosen his officer:

And what was he?
Forsooth, a great arithmetician, one Michael Cassio, a Florentine,

> A fellow almost damn'd in a fair wife;
> That never set a squadron in the field,
> Nor the division of a battle knows
> More than a spinster; unless the bookish theoric.

His ambition thwarted by Othello's choice of Cassio, Iago decides on a path of deception to undo the noble and trusing Moor who constantly refers to him as "honest Iago." He is clear in his purpose:

> Were I the Moor, I would not be Iago;
> In following him, I follow but myself;
> Heaven is my judge, not I for love and duty
> But seeming so, for my peculiar end.

And he concludes this commentary with "I am not what I am." Roderigo replies, "What a full fortune does the thick lips owe, if he can carry't thus." This clear reference to Othello's racial characteristics, unflatteringly offered, is quickly followed by more explicit racist epithets when Iago and Roderigo decide to inflame Brabantio against Othello: "Call up her father, / Rouse him . . . / . . . incense her kinsmen." The clue lies in the way in which they choose to incite the passions of Desdemona's family. Most critics take Othello to be a Christian. There is no conclusive proof of his being one, apart from his reference to the "circumcised dog" he "smote" in Aleppo. He may be a Muslim and, therefore, an infidel. But religion is never mentioned. They choose the race issue:

> Your heart is burst, you have lost half your soul:
> Even now, now, very now, an old black ram
> Is tupping your white ewe. Arise, arise;
> . . . .
> Or else the devil will make a grandsire of you.

And race and sex go together: "You'll have your daughter covered by a barbary horse," and "Your daughter and the Moor are now making the beast with two backs."

When Brabantio confirms that Desdemona has married Othello, he accuses him of foul play and denounces him before the Duke and the senators in the most racist terms:

> If she in chains of magic were not bound,
> Whether a maid so fair and happy
> . . . .

> Would ever have, to incur general mock,
> Run from her guardage to the sooty bosom
> Of such a thing as thou.

The racist intent here is so obvious that it is difficult to escape the conclusion that anyone who claims that it is not there either has blinkers on
or is a malevolent obscurantist.

After Othello explains how he won Desdemona with tall tales of
his military adventures, the Duke declares, "I think this tale would win
my daughter too." Because Brabantio brings these charges when the
Duke and the senators want Othello to devise a strategy to repel the
invading Turks, they are more than happy to get his complaint behind
him. This does not, however, prove Dowling's argument that they are
not racist. The facts of the text suggest otherswise. They use his services
in spite of their racism, much as the Bush administration used Colin
Powell. And, I suspect, the Duke's comment to Brabantio, "If virtue no
delighted beauty lack, / Your son-in-law is far more fair than black,"
also explains the way many whites view General Powell.

The most perplexing thing about the motiveless evil thesis is that
Iago's sexual jealousy of Othello is so obvious. He tells us on two occa-
sions that he thinks Othello has seduced his wife; first in an internal
monologue in Act I, scene iii:

> I hate the Moor:
> And it is thought abroad that 'twixt my sheets
> He has done my office:
> I know not if't be true;
> But I, for mere suspicion in that kind,
> Will do as for surety.

and then in Act II, scene i:

> For that I do suspect the lusty Moor
> Hath leapt into my seat; the thought whereof
> Doth, like a poisonous mineral, gnaw my innards;
> and nothing can or shall content my soul.

The fact that in critical commentary, dominated by white males, this
irrefutable evidence of Iago's fanatical obsession with "black" Othello's
sexuality goes virtually unremarked is cause for suspicion, not of Iago's
motives but those of critics! For it is this obsession with Othello's alleged

sexual prowess—he does not know for sure—that inspires Iago to conspire with Roderigo—who has, to put it colloquially but forcefully, "the hots" for Desdemona—to cuckold Othello: "Let us be conjunctive in our revenge against him: if thou canst cuckold him, thou dost thyself a pleasure, me a sport."

Those who persist in the argument that Shakespeare did not intend Othello to be a Negroid type, a genuine black man, take on a burden of proof that cannot be supported by the text. Here myriad ignorances converge in an unholy alliance that provides license for uninformed prattle to masquerade as scholarly discourse. There is ignorance of the geography and ethnography of Africa; the racial characteristics of the Moors who invaded southern Europe and occupied the Iberian peninsula for over seven centuries; the history of black–white relations in Shakespeare's England; and the literary nuances employed by Elizabethans to distinguish between blacks and mulattos. All are pressed into service to support the baseless argument that Othello was not conceived as a black man, and blackness is an intellectual fashion of modern contrivance, the handiwork of literary do-gooders. Yet to argue that Othello was not a black man because he was "not a Subsaharan African" is to offer no proof at all. Minute Bol of the National Basketball Association is a North African, and he is blue-black, a color common to many ancient indigenous peoples of that area. Hence, to say that Othello was a "North African Moor" when Moorish complexions ranged from light bright, near-white Arabs, to coal-black Sudanese is to say nothing. Moors looked very much like Afro-Americans.

One need only examine the text of *Titus Andronicus*, Shakespeare's early tragedy, to discover how language was employed to distinguish between light- and dark-skinned Moors. In Act V, scene i, the Goth recounts his discovery of Aaron, described in the text as a "coal black Moor," cradling his son begotten of Tamora, queen of the Goths and empress of Rome:

> I heard a child cry underneath a wall.
> I made unto the noise; when soon I heard
> The crying controlled with discourse:
> "Peace, tawny slave, half me and half thy dam!
> Did not thy hue bewray whose brat thou art,
> Had nature lent thee but thy mother's look,
> Villain, thou mightst have been an emperor."

The reference to the mulatto child of Aaron and Tamora as "tawny" is characteristic of the age. Dark-skinned Moors were called "blackamoors," and light-skinned Moors were called "tawny" Moors, just as there are "black" and "yellow," or "ebony" and "sepia" Afro-Americans. Indeed, black American artists have often celebrated the range of hues among their people. Witness Langston Hughes's poem "The Girls of Sugar Hill," or Duke Ellington's "Black, Brown, and Beige Suite." The difference in skin color among the "Moors" of Shakespeare's time must have been much the same as that among the "Negroes" of modern America.

Most ignorant of all, however, are those who argue that Shakespeare could not have intended to create a black character because he had seen no blacks. As is now well known, there were so many black people in Elizabethan England that on August 11, 1596, Queen Elizabeth's Privy Council observed, "there are of late divers blackamoors brought to this relm, of which kind of people there are already too many, considering how God hath blessed this land with many of our own nation," a statement issued around the time Shakespeare was writing *Titus Andronicus*. But in spite of the Privy Council's reservations, the black population continued to increase because of increasing British involvement in the African slave trade. The late Sidney Kaplan, professor of English at the University of Massachusetts, argues that Shakespeare did intend *Othello* to address the problem of race relations: "Because Shakespeare was a genius, with a rare insight into human motivation, he rose above the racial conventions of his time and created this magnificent drama as an intentional statement against racism." All the antiblack dialogue, he points out, is put in the mouths of "defective" characters: Roderigo, a fool; Iago, a villain; and Brabantio, a silly old man.

After a period of servitude, mostly of the domestic variety, many of these Africans were on their own. Edward Scobie of City College tells us in his book *Black Brittania*: "Some blackamoors then fell on evil days. Others contracted diseases like tuberculosis and died. But many of them became absorbed into English life, marrying, raising families, and becoming permanent residents in Britain. A small, very talented handful, even gained fame and prominence and were accepted into the highest circles of the land." One such blackamoor who "gained fame and prominence" was "Lucy Negro" or "Black Lucy," the most famous courtesan in London. Described by Shakespeare scholar Leslie Hotson as "a beautiful harlot, black as hell," this lady was an actress in a form of street theater

called "The Gray's Inn Revels," in which the participants were common-
ers and nobility, as well as an entrepreneur who ran a sporting house in
the Clerkenwell district. G. B. Harrison suggests that Shakespeare was
smitten by this ebony Aphrodite but lost her to the Earl of Southampton,
and states, "This Lucy Negro I would identify as the Dark Lady of the
Sonnets."

But whether Black Lucy was Shakespeare's lover or not, a careful
reading of the Sonnets reveals that he was enchanted by some dusky
woman. Consider these lines from Sonnet 127:

> In the old age black was not counted fair,
> Or if it were, it bore not beauty's name:
> But now is black beauty's successive heir.

In Sonnet 131, he says, "Thy black is fairest in my judgment's place." In
Sonnett 132, he writes, "Then will I swear beauty herself is black / And
all they foul that thy complexion lack."

Whatever life experiences brought him to it, Shakespeare shows a
definite interest in the exotic charms of interracial sex. We encounter this
in three major plays: *Othello*, *The Tempest*, and especially *Titus Andronicus*, his first tragedy. Although there has been much argument whether
Othello and Desdemona have a physical relationship at all, there can be
no such argument about Aaron and Tamora in *Titus*. There is also no
doubt that Aaron, Tamora, and the characters with whom they interact
are acutely aware of Aaron's blackness. Actually, it is in Aaron that we
first observe the attraction–repulsion syndrome that has come to characterize the black experience in Western civilization. Whereas Tamora
finds his blackness enticing, white males see it with fear and loathing.

When Tamora encounters Aaron alone in the forest in Act II, scene
iii, while her husband, Saturninus, emperor of Rome, is out hunting, she
greets him with: "My lovely Aaron, wherefore look'st thou sad / When
everything doth make a gleeful boast?" A few lines later she invites him
to do the "wild" thing:

> Let us sit down . . .
> And after conflict such as was suppos'd
> The wandering prince and Dido once enjoy'd
> . . . .
> We may, each wreathed in the other's arms,

> Our pastimes done, possess a golden slumber:
> Whiles hounds and horns and sweet melodious birds
> Be unto us as is a nurse's song.

And still later she calls him her "sweet Moor, sweeter to [her] than life." Though Aaron is, to all outer appearances, the empress's man-servant or slave, in reality, as he tells us, she is *his* slave:

> Then, Aaron, arm thy heart, and fit thy thoughts,
> To mount aloft with thy imperial mistress,
> And mount her pitch, whom thou in triumph long
> Hast prisoner held, fetter'd in amorous chains.

The fascination with the "sexual vibrations" between this black man and white woman, Aaron and Tamora, is expressed in many ways throughout the text. Consider the catty comments of Lavinia, Titus's daughter and Prince Bassianus's betrothed, when they discover Aaron and Tamora in the woods: " 'Tis thought you have a goodly gift in horning [cuckolding]; / And to be doubted that your Moor and you / Are singled forth to try experiments." She tells Bassianus, "I pray you, let us hence, / And let her joy her raven-coloured love; / This valley fits the purpose passing well." Bassianus's admonition to Tamora is typical of the white male: "Believe me, queen, your swart Cimmerian / Doth make your honour of his body's hue, / Spotted, detested, and abominable."

The response of the Western literati to this play has been, to say the least, curious. It ranges from denial of Shakespeare's authorship to statements that it is a bad play because it is unrelieved tragedy. The first has been disproved by recent scholarship, and the second would be true of almost all the tragedies that are regarded as masterpieces. Aaron, methinks, is the fly in the bowl of milk. I have seen *Titus Andronicus* performed and find it to be one of Shakespeare's most engaging dramas. Two years ago, the New York Shakespeare Festival mounted a fabulous version of it at the Delacort. It featured Keith David as Aaron, and Kate Mulgrew as Tamora. Keith David, a muscular, milk-chocolate Afro-American, cut a striking figure beside the alabaster skin and long flaming red mane of Kate Mulgrew. Both are fine actors, and together they set the stage afire with their passion. It only confirms my argument that, for the maximum dramatic effect, real actors, by which I mean black actors, should be cast in the roles of Othello, Aaron, and Caliban in *The Tempest*.

The statement that Othello has been played by a black man only in the last few decades shows an ignorance of the brillant career of Ira Aldridge. A black American actor born and raised in New York City, Aldridge received his early training in the African Grove Theater, an all-black company founded by black thespians at the corner of Mercer and Grover Streets in Greenwich Village. The son of a West African prince who became a Presbyterian minister, Aldridge had an ebony black complexion. Shakespeare was common fare at the African Grove. But after being jeered and threatened with bodily harm from flying objects tossed by racist white ruffians incensed by Negroes presuming to play the bard, the company closed and Ira set out for Europe to seek his fortune in the theater. After a few years study at the University of Edinburgh in Scotland, Aldridge began his professional career on the English stage. Under the *nom de plume* "Mr. Keene," he made his debut on the English stage playing the title role in *Oronooko*, a play by Thomas Southerne, adapted from a seventeenth-century novel by Aphra Behn, the first English woman to find fame enough to earn her living from writing. The play opened on December 16, 1825, at the Theatre Royal in Brighton, and Aldridge received highly favorable notices.

On the very next evening, Aldridge gave his first performance as Othello on the English stage. The reviews, however, were not as enthusiastic. The comment in the *London Morning Post* was typical: "He was not as much at home in the character, however, as he had previously been in that of Oronooko." Nevertheless, within a year he was being hailed in the British press as "the celebrated Mr. Keene" and "the African Roscious," after the Roman slave whose virtuosity as a thespian won him freedom and who later became a tutor to Cicero. But the accolades heaped on Aldridge in 1826 were only the beginning. He went on to become one of the greatest tragedians of the nineteenth century, as his chair at Stratford-on-Avon testifies. Those familiar with his career argue that he was the quintessential Othello of the past century. His critical notices throughout Europe certainly support this claim. By the 1850s, Aldridge had matured in the role and reached such a state of artistic perfection that a critic in Vienna declared, "It may well be doubted whether Shakespeare himself had ever dreamed for his masterpiece, *Othello*, an interpretation so masterly, so truly perfect."

On January 3, 1853, as the debate over slavery heated up and America approached civil war, Aldridge opened at the Italian Opera House in Berlin as Othello. The critic for the *Preussische Zeitung* had this to say of his performance: "His face is the mirror of his soul. After this Othello it would be an anticlimax to have to see an ordinary Othello again! A Negro from the African West Coast had to come to show me the real Othello, the great one and only, the most beautiful male artist that one can imagine. If Shakespeare were to present this play himself, as he had written it, he could not have presented it better." Theophile Gautier, the celebrated French author and drama critic for *Le Presse* of Paris, witnessed Aldridge's performance of Othello in St. Petersburg, Russia, the night a group of students unhitched the horses and pulled Aldridge's carriage through the streets in homage to his performance.

Gautier describes Aldridge's performance at the Alexandrinski Theater thus: "His first entry was magnificent, he was Othello himself as created by Shakespeare, his eyes half closed as though dazzled by an Africa sun, his manner orientally carefree with that negroid grace of movement which no European can imitate." He characterized Aldridge's style as "majestically classical" and said of the great Russian actor Samoilov, who had played Othello in the same theater, "His impersonations were popular but not as popular as those of Aldridge . . . for, to be frank, Samoilov could not make himself into a Negro." Aldridge's virtuoso performances in Shakespeare's tragedies—though Othello was his favorite role, he played in most of them at one time or another—won him not only the praise of critics, but numerous decorations from the crowned heads of Europe.

On February 1, 1853, King Frederick Wilhelm IV of Prussia presented him with the Gold Medal for Arts and Sciences. Emperor Franz Josef of Austria later presented him with the coveted Medal of Ferdinand, and on January 31, 1858, two years before the outbreak of the war that overthrew slavery in the United States, Aldridge was made a Knight of Saxony with the title of "Chevalier." Aldridge's fame made him much sought after as a friend as well as a performer by the European elite. Alexander Dumas and composer Otto Goldschmidt were friends, Richard Wagner was a "fan," and Aldridge was widely admired by other artists, among them the renowned "Swedish Nightingale" Jenny Lind, who called him "the greatest Othello of them all." When Aldridge died on August 7, 1867, in Lodz, Poland, he was given a state funeral and buried in the Evangelical Cemetery. Meanwhile, in the United States, Congress was debating whether or not Afro-Americans should be considered citizens and extended basic human rights!

The high standard set by Aldridge in the nineteenth century was continued by Paul Robeson in the twentieth century. Robeson, an Afro-

American renaissance man who was an outstanding athlete, scholar, and performing artist, may well be the preeminent Othello of this century. He certainly had all the physical gifts for which Aldridge was celebrated as well as great intelligence. Robeson was the valedictorian of his class at Rutgers in 1919, graduating Phi Beta Kappa while distinguishing himself in four sports. Three years later he graduated from Columbia Law School after being subjected to shamefully racist treatment. He taught himself to sing in twenty-four languages. He possessed a cultivated bass voice that was magnificent in rendering the spoken word. The *London Spectator's* description of Aldridge after his Covent Garden performance of April 10–11, 1833, was also true of Robeson. "His person was tall and well framed, and his action free flowing and graceful. His voice is rich and melodious, and sonorous withal."

When Robeson opened on the British stage in his first performance of *Othello* in 1930, ninety-seven years after Aldridge's English debut, he was greeted, as Aldridge was, with mixed reviews. According to his recent biographer Martin Duberman, "The virtues of his performance were sharply contested." At one extreme, he was hailed as "great," "magnificent," "remarkable," at the other decried as "prosaic" and "disappointing." One participant observer was swept away by his performance: the great British thespian Peggy Ashcroft. A newlywed at the time, she nevertheless fell madly in love with her co-star who was also married. Fifty years later, Aschroft confessed that "what hapened between Paul and myself" was "possibly inevitable." And she wondered, "How could one not fall in love in such a situation with such a man?" Ashcroft's remarks parallel Dame Madge Kendall's recollections of playing Desdemona to Aldridge: "He had some species of well I will not say genius because I dislike the word as used nowadays—but gleams of real intelligence." And she observed, "Though a genuine Negro, he was quite the prix chevalier with the ladies."

The *New York Times* music critic, photographer, and bon vivant Carl Van Vechten, saw Robeson's performance in London, and, according to Duberman, wrote to publisher Alfred Knopf, "He is magnificent, unbelievable," and to the early twentieth-century Afro-American renaissance man James Weldon Johnson, "Paul is simply amazing. . . . He completely bowled me over with surprise. I did not expect such a finished and emotional performance." The English production ran for six weeks in London, then toured the provinces for a few more weeks. When talk first began about bringing the production to the United States in 1931,

Robeson told the *New York Times*: "I wouldn't care to play those scenes in some parts of the United States. . . . The audience would get rough; in fact, it might become very dangerous." In the racist milieu of his time, Robeson had been wary of romancing a white woman on stage even in England. He recalls his first scenes with Ashcroft: "For the first two weeks in every scene I played with Desdemona that girl couldn't get near to me, I was backin' away from her all the time. I was like a plantation hand in the parlor, that clumsy."

As in the case of Aldredge, white critics and admirers were constantly fascinated with Robeson's physical gifts. When Robeson returned to London to do Eugene O'Neill's *The Hairy Ape*, Duberman tells us that the "*Graphic* critic devoted a fifth of his review to waxing eloquent over Robeson's physique: 'That Mr. Robeson should be stripped to the waist is my first demand of any play in which he appears. Perhaps one of the disappointments of his *Othello* was its encumberance with the traditional dress gown.' " But this admiration, although flattering, no doubt contributed to Robeson's skepticism about the response of white American audiences, particularly white males, to his playing the heroic Moor opposite beautiful white actresses. Indeed, one southern editor warned that should Robeson play Othello in his neck of the woods: "He knows what would happen and so do the rest of us. That is one form of amusement that we will not stand for now or ever." In my view, it is the persistence of similar attitudes that prevents more directors from realizing the obvious dramatic power of casting, say Avery Brooks and Meryl Streep, or some comparably talented look-alikes, as Othello and Desdemona, or Aaron and Tamora.

Finally, in 1943, twelve years after his London debut, Robeson got his chance to play Othello in his native land, and on Broadway no less. Playing opposite Uta Hagen, Robeson's "black" Othello set a record for performances of Shakespeare on the "Great White White Way." Ms. Ehrenfeld, who now teaches reading at Public School 84, remembers seeing Robeson as Othello while standing backstage with her parents, who were Jewish radicals: "He came out in costume, and he was so big and magnificent looking I thought he must be a god, if there were such things." Professional critics were effusive in their praise. Robert Garland of the *Journal-American* confessed, "In all my nights of attendance on the world of make believe, there has been nothing to equal it." The *World Telegram*'s Burton Rascoe echoed Garland in his panegyric: "one of the most memborable events in the history of the theater. . . . It is unbelievably magnificent." *Variety* declared him "a great Othello," and *Billboard* said he gave "a tremendous performance."

Newsweek described the audience's response on opening night: "For twenty minutes, and half as many curtain calls, the applause and the bravos echoed from orchestra pit and gallery to give Forty Fourth Street the news of something more than just another hit." Margaret Webster, who directed the play, recalls, "They yelled at us through a long succession of calls and fairly screamed at Paul." And Burton Rascoe reported, "Never in my life have I seen an audience sit so still, so tense, so under the spell of what was taking place." The impact, as several critics realized, was due to the fact that a black actor was playing the lead role. The *Variety* critic summed up the general reaction when he declared that after Robeson "no white man should ever dare presume to play Othello."

It is uncanny how closely the comments of American theater critics regarding Robeson echo those of European critics regarding Aldridge, a century and an ocean away. I think the reason is obvious. Not only is there dramatic tension inherent in a powerful black man and a beautiful white woman on stage together as lovers, but black actors relate emotionally to the role in a way unavailable to white actors. For, as the lone black character in the play, the black actor's situation in the cast approximates Othello's in Venetian society. And, given the persistence of racism in America as well as Europe, the black actor on opening night feels some of the same ambivalence and hostility, real or imagined, that Othello experiences in Venice. Aside from these factors, black actors relate to both Shakespeare's Moors as fellow black men trying to negotiate their way in a hostile white society. For instance, Robeson said of his interpretation of the role that he "listened carefully to directors and Shakespearean authorities, but in some cases their Othello didn't think and act exactly as I believe a great Negro warrior would do, and in those cases I played it in my way."

Ira Aldridge also felt an identification with Aaron, who was as devious as Othello was noble, which is why he revived the role in the 1850s after it had not been performed on the English stage for two hundred years. White women also feel the role of Desdemona more acutely when Othello is black. Peggy Ashcroft recalled that playing Desdemona to Robeson's Othello was "a lesson to me in the power of the drama to encourage a portrayed emotion to become a fantasy of one's own." Interestingly, not only she but also Uta Hagen fell very much in love with their "black" Othello. The straight-laced Hagen stated, years later, that for "Big Paul's" love she would have "gone anywhere and done anything." With all that fire between them, it is no wonder they set a Broadway record for Shakespeare of 296 performances and close to a million dollars at the box office! Since Robeson's days of glory, many black actors have distinguished themselves in the role: James Earl Jones, William Marshall, and recently, Avery Brooks and Samuel L. Jackson.

It is unreasonable to believe that William Shakespeare, the premier dramatist of the English language, would not have recognized the great dramatic power that results from pairing a magnificent black warrior with a beautiful white woman of delicate sensibilities and elegant manners, especially because he had convincingly demonstrated such understanding in *Titus Andronicus*. Sidney Kaplan, who saw both Robeson and Olivier as Othello, observes: "The performance of Robeson, which was compelling, provides the best argument for why even the greatest white actors should not play the role. This becomes especially obvious when compared to the performance of Laurence Olivier, who was simply awful. The only way Olivier could conceptualise the character was as a madman." Thus, to conclude—as Dowling, Bernstein, Feingold, and others have done—that the bard did not intend Othello to be black strikes me as a desperate exercise in wishful thinking. It is another case of narrow-minded, intellectually arrogant, racially conscious people airing their racial/sexual anxieties and substituting their contemporary racial provincialism for the cosmopolitan vision of Shakespeare.

Hello, Othello

Hello, Othello:
Now, let's get down to things!
You probably wouldn't recognize the credit-fat Venice of today. After all, it *has* been four hundred years since the Old Bard set you down in smart, rich Venice to die so senselessly in that tragic story. The Venice I presume you to have served so valiantly has gone through some changes. But you know the old French saying. Actually, when I last checked, present-day Venice was prospering as much as the Venice of your day; a perfect model for what it's chic to call a "market economy."

Now that I've been hanging around for decades with you and thoughts of you, I figure it's high time I wrote you my mature reactions to *Othello, the Moor of Venice*. Naturally, I'd love to be able to say I've finally fooled around and figured you out, my man. But, as Ira Gershwin puts it in his opera *Porgy and Bess*:

> The things that you're liable
> To read in the Bible
> It ain't necessarily so.

So, Othello, I'm going to come right out and ask: "Just between us, tell me, how did you feel about playing such an unreal role? How did it feel to be constantly reacting to Iago's schemes and maneuvers? Wasn't it all calculated to undermine you, your professional authority, your personal happiness? Did you feel manipulated, or what?

Although Shakespeare's language and the English of the King James Bible are drawn from the same Elizabethan well, some of his plots and characterizations—maybe it's just me—are barely swallowable. It's tough, for instance, to swallow his cartoonlike depiction of you as an exotic; the foreigner, a colorful menace, a Moor. But then there are some unbuyable things in the Bible itself that trouble and puzzle readers and non-readers.

Trouble and puzzlement seem to dog your heels and hover all around you, Othello. It was during the troubled Dark Ages of the early 1950s, when I was just arriving at my teens and opening to the greater world around me, that your name first caught my attention. By then the Cold War was in full force. The infamous Senator Joseph McCarthy was virtually heading the House Un-American Activities Committee, and witch-hunting and witch-burning had once again become the order of the American day. It was open season on Communists, Socialists, pacifists, intellectuals, and artists in general, and their so-called sympathizers, affiliates, and "fellow travelers."

Having traveled to Detroit, my family, Mississippians all, had gradually managed the jump from 4641 Beaubien on the eastside to 1632 Pingree on the westside—half a block from the 12th Street that would eventually become Rosa Parks Boulevard. Like you, presumably a born Muslim, abruptly parachuted into Venice, we woke up to find ourselves installed in a neighborhood still mostly Jewish and working class.

Exploring the new neighborhood, staking out the turf, I discovered right away a few wonderful drugstores and newstands that would get to be hangouts. At those magazine racks and bins, I first laid hands on such left-wing publications as the *National Guardian, Mainstream,* and the *Daily Worker.* At first these dangerous-looking periodicals puzzled me; they were like pickled herring, eggplant, Yiddish, and the blueslike moaning I'd hear seeping from the corner synagogue on Fridays.

It was Paul Robeson, perhaps the most memorable of Othellos, whose name kept turning up alongside yours in articles and columns I read. I read about him, too, in newspapers I was delivering; the straight, safe dailies—the Detroit *Free Press,* the *News,* the *Times.* Reading about this American scholar, athlete, singer, and actor who seemed to be up to his chin in the very Deep River he sang about so soulfully, I came to understand that he was—in classic African American parlance as well as in the eyes of disapproving white folks—a Bad Nigger. Then, too, there were those who saw Robeson as a good nigger gone bad.

Robeson tended to do things his way. I learned, for example, that in his 1930 London debut as you—with lovely Peggy Ashcroft his Desdemona—all hell broke loose. It seems that in their roles as husband and wife, the two had put far more passion into hugging and kissing one another than the British audience could handle. New York drama critic Burns Mantle had written: "If Peggy Ashcroft comes to New York to receive and return Othello's kisses frankly and eagerly in character, a furor would result. But if Lillian Gish accepts the role, things could become quite terrible."

Terrible and terrifying might also describe the Renaissance mentality—or, in any case, the Anglo-Saxon mentality—that gave birth to you, Othello. Surely you'd have to be deaf or blind not to pick up on the kind of terror Mr. Mantle was warning his readers to expect. Lillian Gish— in case that name slipped past you—played the lead in D. W. Griffith's controversial, big-grossing 1915 film, *Birth of a Nation*. And you think you had problems!

One scene in *Birth of a Nation* depicts the plight of a lily-white damsel so determined to keep out of reach of a fierce black brute, dead set on raping her, that she leaps from a cliff to her death to save honor. Griffith even has scenes showing reconstruction Negro officials jammed into the state legislature with their feet up on desks, chomping on fried chicken and watermelon. So it was up to the Ku Klux Klan (the film is based on *The Clansman*, the Reverend Thomas Dixon's novel) to protect southern womanhood. President Woodrow Wilson even brought Griffith to the White House, for a special screening, shook his hand, and saluted Griffith's invaluable contribution to American history.

And, Othello, that's pretty much the way it's been going, too. But let's go back yet again to that 1604 play written by Shakespeare, who deftly lifted its storyline from a 1565 collection, *The Hundred Tales* by Cinthio, that prolific Italian writer. Even though it's entitled *Othello*, the script doesn't seem to be so much about you as about Iago. And if you've stayed with me this far, you won't be surprised to hear me say that Iago comes off as the personification of seventeenth-century England.

We're talking ambitious, outward-looking island culture here. Japan springs to mind. Manhattan, even. Places where everything is so spatially cut and dried that people, finding themselves piled all on top of one another, work out elaborate social systems and politeness codes to keep things straight. They build empires with emperors and Empire State Buildings. And, man, can they talk and write and dream and scheme!

By the time Shakespeare introduced you, Europe had revised history so thoroughly that her debt to African civilization had been virtually erased. Only by reading the works of early Greek and Roman writer-historians—Thucydides, Plato, Cicero, Pliny—do we discover the origins of what came to be called Europe. But by Shakespeare's time, Othello, they were coming up with such names for you as Thick-Lips, Sooty Bosom, Old Black Ram, and Barbary Horse.

Those old-time Venetians, according to the Bard, knew how to hurt a guy with names, didn't they? And they could hurl some sticks and stones as well. Even today Venetians and Florentines are busy getting up petitions and ordinances to limit the number of licenses issued to African-born street vendors, street artists, and entertainers in tourist areas. It appears Africans are becoming both popular and numerous.

As a kid, I didn't altogether grasp what Robeson had done to turn the powers-that-be so vehemently against him. Yet even then I knew it had something to do with his being black *and* brilliant. Black *but* brilliant—that's the way Christians in your day might have put it in the King James Bible. "I am black but comely, O ye daughters of Jerusalem," is what our nubile narrator tells us in *The Song of Solomon*. After poet–translator Marcia Falk went to Israel to take a fresh look at the ancient Hebrew text, she ended up restoring the original line: "I am black *and* comely." Evidently, those King James translators, unable to deal with their own color hangups, had fudged the words.

"But," I can picture you asking, "what does all this have to do with anything Desdemona and Iago and Roderigo and Cassio and I did? Or didn't do?"

Oh, Othello, things on earth do not change all that much. They were a mess then, and they are still a mess. Sure, the situation's a little different from what it was when you made your debut and then went your way. So-called white people aren't running the whole show the way they thought they were back around 1600. Even then, the Ottoman Turks were giving the Europeans a hard time. Or would it be more accurate to say the Muslims were giving the Christians hell? From the schoolbook histories they had us reading, you would never figure out what was going on and why. To this day, people here in the United States have no idea how close Europe came to embracing Islam. After all, the Mediterranean for the longest time was pretty much a Muslim lake. And there's something even a lot of Spaniards no longer know: that from the time the Moors got to Spain from North Africa until the time they left, seven hundred years had slipped by. And now we know from reading Ivan Van Sertima and other anthropologists and historians that the Moors brought a high level of culture and technical know-how to Spain. I'm talking about mathematics, urban development (street lighting, for instance), libraries, scholarship, science.

A military scientist—that was you, Othello, right? Even though I have trouble trying to figure out what in the world you were doing in Venice in the first place, I find it difficult to understand why Shakespeare didn't allow you to carry out more of your soldierly duties than he did.

General Othello, isn't it true that the Signiory, the Venetian Senate, commissioned you to serve as their protector? And with the Turks, the French, the Spaniards, and the imperial Britons all at each other's throats, Venice and the rest of the Italian peninsula must have been one endless war zone! Venice considered you bright, skilled, professional, and noble enough to ask you to lead their armies in battle, and yet they must have also seen you as the very "general enemy Ottoman" against whom, as the Duke makes clear in the opening act, "we must straight employ you."

But, no, you couldn't just do the job and leave well enough alone; you had to get mixed up with the boss's daughter. I suppose even that would've been okay had you not come in there looking the way you couldn't help looking. Forgive me, Othello, but I can't help chuckling when I think about another counterpart of yours: Sidney Poitier who plays a handsome, thoroughly trained and educated professional named John Prentice in Stanley Kramer's 1968 movie, *Guess Who's Coming to Dinner*. For all his impeccable credentials, this colored gentleman has to jump through hoops of flame to prove himself worthy of the hand of Spencer Tracy and Kathryn Hepburn's no-big-deal of a daughter.

Let us put it another way: Was Desdemona such a big deal, such a big social catch that the Bard decided to hang the whole play on society's determination to destroy this interracial romance? But you were a convert, yes? A Christian, yes? Isn't that what you mean in Act V, scene ii, just before you plunge the dagger into your own guilt-ridden heart?

And say besides that in Aleppo once,
Where a malignant and a turbaned Turk

Beat a Venetian and traduced the state,
I took by th'throat the circumcised dog
And smote him—thus.

With that you lay one last kiss on stone-cold-dead Desdemona, then check out forever, leaving the scene to Iago and Lodovico to complete.

Your odd goodbye troubles me even now, here at this crowded gateway to the twenty-first century. Why? Because your creator whisked you away before I fully got the chance to know you at all. In one sense you're like that "Promethean heat" of which you speak at the sleeping Desdemona's side. That is, you're like a sun that never shows its face but whose hot light shines and bounces off everything it can reach or touch. In another sense, though, you yourself are "the very error of the moon." What was the line? Oh, yes:

It is the very error of the moon.
She comes more nearer earth than she was wont
And makes men mad.

Yes, you simply got too close to where those people lived—those upper-crust Venetians. So you had to be prepared for ambitious, ignoble types like Cassio and Iago who didn't have much use for you. Neither did the senators. Presumably they had only hired you to do a job; they never meant you to stick around town weekends and weeknights, too. Like a police chief, an athlete, a boxer, a football or baseball or basketball player, a musician, or an entertainer, you were hired to do a job. Once you fought the war or won the game or played the gig you were supposed to leave. Go away. Go back home. Go back to your "community," back into your box. Go back to wherever your kind is expected to repair, or, better yet, disappear.

But you didn't do that, Othello. Instead, you did exactly what your own mother probably warned you against. Probably. It's hard to say. Your past has been so spotlessly eradicated. Somehow you went up north and tangled with white folks. Big white folks—Desdemona, Senator Brabantio's daughter, who must have been irresistible: pale, perfumed, big-eyed and shapely, her liquid locks falling and flipping and flying. I love Shakespeare. You have to hand it to the gentleman. When it comes to turning a phrase and making a play he is hard to beat. D. W. Griffith was also a brilliant filmmaker. However, that doesn't mean I have to like everything their works openly tell us. They don't come much whiter than

Shakespeare, do they? He wasn't exactly soft on that other Venetian, either. I'm talking about the Jewish merchant Shylock, who came a little before your time. Did your paths ever cross?

Down across the centuries, books and plays and other works of art have been burned. Addison Gayle, the late African American literary critic, once told me that, if he had his way, he would burn several hundred works of Western literature because of the way they either distorted or maligned the image of persons of African descent. Not surprisingly, the play that bears your name was high on Mr. Gayle's list. But so were works by Tolstoy, Herman Melville, Mark Twain, and William Faulkner.

I told Mr. Gayle at the time that I found his attitude saddening and wrong-headed. He responded by keeping good his promise never so much as to mention me or any writings of mine in his compendious critical histories of black American literature.

How do I feel? Thankful, of course, just as I am thankful to Shakespeare for sitting down and putting pen to paper to let us know exactly what was on his own mind and what sentiments quivered in the hearts of those for whom he wrote. By doing so, Shakespeare left us with a fairly useful record of how the battle of Them versus Us was shaping up in England around the time the sixteenth century was melting into the seventeenth.

Still, I'm eager to find out your feelings and insights on all this. Do let me hear from you, Othello, even if it has to be with the aid of a crystal ball gazer, or some other crazy go-between.

Hello?

Who Is Desdemona?

JOHN A. WILLIAMS

I
n his novel *Explosion in a Cathedral*, which covers the
French Revolution and some of the little-known reper-
cussions of that event on the Caribbean colonies of the
European powers, Alejo Carpentier remarks:

> The white man, whose aberrations in dependent terri-
> tories were viewed with indulgence, lost nothing of his
> prestige by making love to a black woman. And if a
> brood of quadroon, octoroon, or mulatto children re-
> sulted, this proliferation gained him an enviable repu-
> tation as a fertile patriarch. The white woman, on the
> other hand, who lay with a colored man—cases were
> few and far between—was looked on with abomination.
> There was no worse role one could play, between the
> shores of the Natchez and the shores of the Mar del
> Plata, than that of a colonial Desdemona.

In the almost two centuries *before* the French Revolution, close to the time when *Othello* was written (1604), not
much had happened to alter this universal opinion of sex and
race. And in Carpentier's own time (1904–80), almost two
hundred years *after* the Revolution, the opinion had changed
little. Every performance of *Othello* anywhere in the world is
literally colored by its themes of sex (more projected than

actually played) and race rather than by its equally important themes of displacement (leading to Iago's envy, malice, and betrayal) and irony (Othello, the "Barbary horse," the "old black ram," of "sooty bosom," being called on to save the State, that is, civilization).

Discussions of the play as a racial–sexual tragedy focus on Othello, however, rather than Desdemona. Seeming contradictions in his behavior strike us, whereas those in her pass unnoticed. Yet Desdemona is more crucial than Othello to a "black" perspective on the play—which is the point I would like to make in this essay.

The original plot of *Othello* is believed to have come from *A Hundred Tales* (1565) by Giovanni Battista Giraldi Cinthio (1504–73) of Ferrara, Italy, via the translation attributed to George Whetsone (1544–87).

Extratextually, the black presence in Italy, if not documented in most histories, is well recorded by painters such as Veronese, Monaco, Herlin the Elder, Weyden, Memling, Montegna, and Carapaccio (one of whose paintings, "Scenes from the Life of St. Ursula," 1494, depicts black men working on the quays of Venice). *Moretto* and *moretta* were terms for young black males and females found in the language of late fifteenth-century Venice. Black people, although rare in various locations around the Mediterranean, were found serving in a variety of occupations, sailing perhaps being the most favored. Some were gondoliers in Venice.

Shakespeare brings us a Moorish prince in *The Merchant of Venice*. The Prince of Morocco speaks proudly, even boastfully, of his color as he attempts to win Portia at the opening of Act II; he, like Othello, speaks of battles won and courage great. Indeed, the Prince seems to be the parent of Othello, a character neatly and splendidly done, but quickly dismissed. It may be, as is often the case with writers, that a minor character in one work lingers on in creation and eventually becomes larger than when first drawn in a later venture by the author. The Prince of Morocco does not marry the white woman he comes to woo. Othello does. And the stark fact of an interracial marriage stares the audience literally in the face when a black actor plays Othello.

Ira Aldridge was the first known black man to play the role of the Moor. Paul Robeson, the second, is the actor most well-known as Othello. Fine as the performance of subsequent black actors in the role has been, they have not been able to make people forget Robeson. He played the role three times: London, 1930; New York, 1943; and London again, 1959. He practically owned the role. It is with Robeson, as his New York producer Margaret Webster wrote in the playbill of the 1943 (October 19) production, that:

> One fact stands in sharp relief. The difference in race between Othello and every other character in the play is, indeed, the heart of the matter. This is the cause of Othello's terrible vulnerability on which Iago fastens so pitilessly; because of this, the conduct of which Desdemona is accused seems to Othello only too horribly possible; this is Iago's first and most powerful weapon, twisted to every conceivable use.

Robeson played the role with this vulnerability to racism, which he himself personally felt, as the crucial motivating force; most actors did, or tried to, even though in black or tawny face, from Edmund Kean (whose son, Charles, once played Iago to Aldridge's Othello), through various other actors to Godfrey Tearle (1948), Anthony Quayle (1954), Orson Welles (in film, 1955), Richard Burton, and John Neville (1956). Laurence Olivier in his 1964 production played a "Leavis" Othello, as Duberman puts it, "a self-dramatizing narcissist," or in F. R. Leavis's own words, a man of "heroic self-dramatisation." (It is difficult to imagine a black man in Othello's position devoid of the self-confidence needed to bring him there. But this self-confidence usually is mistaken for arrogance or demagoguery if displayed by a person of color.)

The 1989 Stratford-on-Avon production starring the black opera singer Willard White as Othello was done "traditionally." Ian McKellen's Iago, however, was viewed as a departure from the actively scheming, blatantly evil character we have come to know. McKellen's Iago is the contemporary bigot, smooth, quiet, and matching the furniture; he does not stand out, and he is the complete soldier.

Thus, even stage performances have centered on Othello and Iago. Desdemona hardly comes into the picture. But to me she has always been an unanswered question, so much so that I used some of her lines to Iago (in Act II, scene i) in my novel *Mothersill and the Foxes* (1975):

> I am not merry, but I do beguile
> The thing I am by seeming otherwise.
> Come, how wouldst thou praise me?

Brabantio's parting words forewarn us of the events to come when he tells Othello:

Look to her, Moor, if thou has eyes to see
She hath deceived her father, and may thee.

We understand his anger. His daughter has slipped off and married a "stranger" instead of marrying the "wealthy, curled darlings" of the Venetian nation, or even Roderigo. He feels betrayed. He feels also that he has been mistaken in her character. His warning to Othello is in keeping with his new concept of her character. She obviously never was the "maiden never bold" whose "spirit" was "so still" that "her motion blushed" at itself; who modestly "shunned" any kind of courtship and would not be wooed even by the cream of Venetian society. The Duke, to whom Brabantio complains, however, does not incline to his side and accepts Othello's tale of the way in which he wooed and won Desdemona—but then he must if he is to have this general save the State.

The extensive word play between Iago and Desdemona in Act II, scene i, has always seemed odd to me. Othello is a general, Iago but an ensign. Light banter between Cassio and Desdemona seems acceptable because the class division between them is not marked as it is between, say, Falstaff and Hal. We know certain rules obtained between classes, some codes of conduct, even as they do today. They existed in Cinthio's time and in Shakespeare's.

Further, the idea of play itself is punctured by Iago's constant use of the term *fair*:

Iago: If she be fair and wise, fairness and wit—
The one's for use, the other useth it.
Desdemona: How if she be black and witty?
Iago: If she be black, and thereto have a wit,
She'll find a white that shall her blackness fit.
Emilia: How if fair and foolish?
Iago: She never yet was foolish that was fair,
For even her folly helped her to an heir.

Twice more Iago uses the term before Cassio joins them. It seems clear that *fair* and *black* are double entendres that play on the relationship between Othello and Desdemona, a game that is not suitable for a "maiden never bold." It is a game that "betters" do not play with "lowers"; it exists, of course, for a purpose, but that purpose eludes me. I cannot understand why she permits this. She says she is pretending to be other than what she is. But is it only pretense?

Desdemona and Iago are "signifying"—that is, they are engaging in double-talk, indulging in innuendo. Are they making fun—of whom? of what? They are delving into states of mind and physical characteristics. Such a quick mind, such perception, seems utterly out of character for Desdemona who, in Act III, scene iii, prattles insistently about Cassio while Othello requests repeatedly that she bring him his mother's handkerchief. This is the same woman who requests Emilia to lay her wedding sheets on the bed in the hope that they will bring back love between Othello and herself or, the sense is communicated, serve as her shroud.

Perhaps the real problem I have with the play is time. We do not know how much of it has elapsed since Brabantio, in Act I, scene i, discovers the marriage, and his death, news of which is brought by Gratiano in Act V, scene ii. The curious, unfixed time serves to help Iago develop the plot against Othello but leaves Desdemona's development—her mood swings, her alternating sharp perception and incomprehensible blindness—a mystery on which Othello's behavior revolves. This can be placed in perspective and understood only if we know who, or what, Desdemona truly is.

III

Academic Critics

"A Round Unvarnished Tale": (Mis)Reading Othello or African American Strategies of Dissent

JACQUELYN Y. McLENDON

O brothers mine, take care! Take care!
The great white witch rides out tonight.
Trust not your prowess nor your strength
Your only safety lies in flight;
For in her glance there is a snare
And in her smile there is a blight.
—James Weldon Johnson, "The White Witch"

Crazy niggers turning their backs on sanity. When all it
needs is that simple act. Murder. Just murder! Would
make us all sane.
—Amiri Baraka, *Dutchman*

n teaching an introduction to African American literature,
I choose clusters of texts to develop various thematic
patterns of inquiry. One such cluster includes a number
of texts by male writers whose central narrative, like that of
William Shakespeare's *Othello*, is the tragic story of a taboo
relationship between a black man and a white woman.[1] The

---

1. Although the list is too exhaustive to include in its entirety, among
the better known, Richard Wright, Ralph Ellison, James Baldwin, Chester
Himes, Amiri Baraka, and David Bradley, have all treated the subject of
miscegenation either centrally or peripherally. For a thorough survey and
discussion, see Anna Maria Chupa.

allusions and direct references to *Othello* in some of this literature, the
popularity and importance of the character as a black "hero" before the
twentieth century,[2] made me realize that Shakespeare's play could be
useful as a paradigmatic representation of narratives of miscegenation
against which to read twentieth-century African American literature, specifically Chester Himes's novel *The Primitive* (1955) and Amiri Baraka's
plays *Dutchman* and *The Slave* (1964).[3] I argue that African American
male writers' treatments of miscegenation revise dominant narratives that
interpret the psychology of the black male in white male terms. I argue
further that these refigurations, these (mis)readings, told from various
perspectives of black men most often reveal themselves in radically op-
positional relationship to Shakespeare's perspective. These writers offer
their own critical versions in order to challenge the construction of
(black) masculinity in dominant discourse and to assert the specificity of
a black male psychology. This revisionary intervention, then, is one of
the reasons why black male writers use race relations in their works to
examine issues such as I have described above. It is also why much of
their writing suggests that, as the protagonist in Himes's *The Primitive*
says, "Race relations is the study of black man, embracing white woman"
(111). Finally, this gesture of reading African American texts against
Othello as master narrative has enabled me to explore the ways in which
black writers critique the content of works by precursory white writers
as well as received literary forms and discourses of exclusion. Thus,
approaching *Othello* from this critical direction not only illuminates readings of the play but also explores how black male difference is inscribed
in the later writings.[4]

Refigurations of *Othello* by black writers retain several essential
aspects of its plot: relationships between black men and white women
are usually formed amid the objections of family and friends; white
women, though objectified, are in positions of power over black men;
violence is the means by which black men attempt to remedy or reconcile

---

2. Anthony Gerard Barthelemy discusses the popularity of the play and argues that
"no other play until the twentieth century offered a black hero of Othello's stature. . . .
The importance of Othello as the dominant representation of an African on the stage
cannot be overestimated" (161–62).

3. At the time of publication of these plays, Baraka was still known as LeRoi Jones.

4. I am indebted to my colleagues, Rhonda Gobham-Sander, P. Gabrielle Foreman,
Reinhard Sander, and Zita McShane, for their thoughtful readings during various stages of
this essay and to both David Bradley and Richard Cody for their critical insights.

unequal power relations; and the narratives end in literal or symbolic deaths or both. Further, both *Othello* and the works of the black writers suggest that their protagonists' fates are overdetermined by their blackness. *Othello*, however, implies that this dilemma is the result of racial and cultural deficiencies within Othello himself, whereas the other works insist that it results from racist and oppressive conditions without. Thus, more complex, experientially based feelings, shape the protagonists of the African American texts, especially the need to de/reconstruct the socially established interpretation of black male sexuality.[5]

Although *The Primitive, Dutchman*, and *The Slave* reflect in numerous ways the contradictions and ambivalences of such complex feelings, their basic plots are quite simple. Briefly stated, Himes's *The Primitive* centers on the lives of Kriss Cummings, a middle-aged white woman of fading beauty, and Jesse Robinson, a black man with "sepia" skin, "semi-caucasian" features, and "nappy" hair. Both have once been married, and they engage in a parasitic relationship with each other out of fear. Kriss is obsessed with the fear of waking up alone, Jesse with failing as a writer and as a "man." The plot develops along the lines of an exploration of their relationship but only insofar as it figures in the larger issue: Jesse's (the black male's) search for self.

Baraka's two plays, *Dutchman* and *The Slave*, also depict parasitic relationships between its characters but ultimately depend even more than *The Primitive* on racial and sexual stereotypes that evoke mythical and historical materials in order to show the timeless and overreaching effects of racism. In *Dutchman*, Lula is the white liberal pawn of white American patriarchy whose job it is to seduce the naive, young, black, middle-class Clay. They meet on a subway train where Lula simultaneously entices and insults Clay, uncovering the potential killer beneath a facade of middle-class respectability (in the simultaneity of her actions, she plays out the roles of both Desdemona and Iago). Once exposed, Clay poses a threat that must be destroyed; thus, Lula kills him and then searches out her next victim, another young black man "of about twenty [who] comes into the coach, with a couple books under his arm" (37).

---

5. This distinction between Shakespeare and black writers is not meant to be essentialist but simply to point out that the latter are keenly aware that "the unique experience of the black writer should not be reduced to a vague human problem with universal application." See Chupa, 25. Also see Chester Himes, "Dilemma of the Negro Novelist in the USA."

The ending implies a perpetual recurrence of the plot and "demonstrates that Lula is caught in a situation of compulsive repetition" (Sollors, 121–22).

The Slave inscribes a similar perspective of the perpetual effects of racism with its movement between—indeed, its collapsing of—the future, a revolutionary race war, and the past. The recent past of the play is represented by a nostalgic and antagonistic encounter between the black protagonist, Walker Vessels, his white ex-wife Grace Easley, and her present white husband, Bradford; the distant past is represented by the play's opening monologue of an old field slave and by the direct references to *Othello*. Although the action concerns all three characters, the central conflict concerns the individual psychomachia of the black protagonist.

The inner struggle of the black man is what Shakespeare does not depict. Although he makes Othello a great general—noble, honest, courageous—and gives to him, as critics argue, the richest language in the play, he undermines these gestures by having him succumb to the passions of excessive jealousy.[6] That is, he finally deals with Othello in terms of the prevailing negative images of blackness, giving in to the stereotypical views concerning the "lust and jealousy of Moors" (Barthelemy, 155). For instance, Othello's speech requesting that Desdemona be allowed to accompany him to Cyprus is eloquent and convincing. He says when he allows pleasure to "corrupt and taint my business, / Let housewives make a skillet of my helm, / And all indign and base adversities / Make head against my estimation" (I.iii.267–70). Yet once Iago's plot takes hold, this kind of language disappears, and "lust and jealousy" do, indeed, become the discursive terrain on which he deals with Desdemona, thereby moving him closer to the stereotype of the villainous Moor (Barthelemy, 154).[7]

Othello goes to great lengths to convince Brabantio and the others that sex is not the primary reason for his relationship with Desdemona, that his desire is not "[t]o please the palate of my appetite, / Nor to comply with heat the young affects / In my defunct and proper satisfaction; / But to be free and bounteous to her mind" (I.iii.258–61). Barthe-

---

6. Edward Berry points out, "The threat of miscegenation is the play's hidden nightmare, and it cannot be overcome by arguments about virtue or service to the state" (324).

7. Also see Eldred Jones, who surveys the portrayals of blacks in Shakespeare and his contemporaries.

lemy reminds us that Iago is the one who is obsessed with sex and not Othello (151); yet, Othello's rage is ignited by his belief that he has been cuckolded. Once he becomes suspicious of Desdemona, his pleasing speech, full of compliments for her, abounds with derogatory epithets like *strumpet* and *whore* and with sexual innuendo: her moist hand "argues fruitfulness and a liberal heart. / Hot, hot and moist" (III.iv.34). He speaks of being weakened in his resolve to kill her by her "*body* and beauty" [emphasis mine] (IV.i.199). Gamini Salgado glosses the phrase "[g]oats and monkeys!" (IV.i.254), which seems to be spoken involuntarily when Othello is welcoming Lodovico to Cyprus, as a "suggestion of uncontrolled lust, show[ing] what Othello has been really thinking about while his conscious mind has been struggling to attend to official matters" (136). Finally, the murder scene, which I will discuss in detail later, subverts narrative intent, since it focuses on Othello's loss almost exclusively in sexual terms.

Unlike Shakespeare whose intent, even though unsuccessful, seemed to be to decenter sex as motivation for Othello's relationship with Desdemona, Himes emphasizes the sexual relationship between a black man and white woman as the only significant one by politicizing it. That is, Himes explicitly depicts sexuality as the primary arena of power struggle. He makes clear that love is not among the many reasons why Kriss and Jesse become involved. Their relationship is inextricably tied to their lack of options in a hegemonic society that dehumanizes blacks and objectifies women. Jesse sleeps with white women because, shaped within the psychodynamics of a racist society, he believes he "wouldn't be human if he didn't" (136–37). Kriss believes white men "threw her to the niggers" (107). Feeling used by white men and thereby "lowered" to the status of blacks, "only when sleeping with a Negro could she feel secure in the knowledge that she wasn't dirt . . . with them she never felt ruined [because] they never thought of her as ruined" (86).

In *Dutchman*, too, Clay and Lula communicate on a sexual level that has nothing to do with love. In fact, Lula describes their communication aptly as "exchanging codes of lust" (23). They are clearly racial and sexual types:

> Popular symbolic interpretations of *Dutchman* have Lula representing a white America that abides Negro America as long as Negro America respectfully accepts whiteness as the norm. . . . [and] have Clay representing a Negro America that wears a mask

of respectability and non-violence, a schizoid Negro America that
tries on one hand to accept America on white terms and on the
other to accept its own identity. (Hudson, 149)

As representative of white America, Lula thinks she knows all about
Clay, even though she's never seen him before—she says he's "a well-
known type" (12). Her mission is to lead him "[i]nto my dark living
room" to "sit and talk endlessly, endlessly . . . [a]bout [his] manhood"
(25). The sense that she, like Kriss, is being used by white patriarchy is
revealed in her references to the eternal and "compulsive repetition" of
her actions: for example, "My hair is turning gray. A gray hair for each
year and type I've come through" (13).

Since many of the later texts stress that relationships with white
women are not always motivated by love, what then is the motivation?
What does the white woman have to do with the black man's position
in society or, at least, what he perceives his position to be? Why is the
black male/white female relationship so often at the center of critical
inquiry of black male self-definition? Frantz Fanon and others argue that
in a society in which the white male is the only recognized frame of
reference for humanity, to possess what is his is, for the black man, to
become human.[8] In "The Man of Color and the White Woman," Fanon
describes this attitude as follows:

I wish to be acknowledged not as black but as white. Now—and
this is a form of recognition that Hegel had not envisaged—who
but a white woman can do this for me? By loving me she proves
that I am worthy of white love. I am loved like a white man.
I am a white man.
Her love takes me onto the noble road that leads to total reali-
zation. . . .
I marry white culture, white beauty, white whiteness. When my
restless hands caress those white breasts, they grasp white civilization and dignity and make them mine. (63)

Fanon does not attribute the above attitude to all or even most black
men but discusses it as one possible manifestation of "a wish to be
white"or "a lust for revenge" (14).

---

8. Also see Sandra L. Richardson, 70–71.

The complex interplay of issues of identity involving the black man/ white woman is not fully addressed in *Othello*. Shakespeare does not foreground the notion that Othello's marriage to Desdemona is his way to gain entry into Venetian society. But even though Othello boasts that "I fetch my life and being / From men of royal siege" (I.ii.20–21), nowhere else in the play is there any evidence that he feels connected with his African heritage.[9] On the other hand, black writers explicitly examine such issues in their writing. In *The Primitive*, Jesse Robinson sees his need for a white woman as analogous to a boy he knew who felt "normal" only when he was high on marijuana: "Jesse wondered, half-amused, if a white woman had the same effect on him. 'Get a white woman and go from schizophrenia to homogenia . . .' " (60). In the beginning he, like Othello, internalizes white society's racist views of blacks. He hates himself for wanting to sleep with Kriss, whom he doesn't love, but he believes it "[l]ogical enough, though. Unavoidable really. Nigger got to want to have a white woman. Got no choice the way they got it set up. Wouldn't be human if he didn't" (136–37). The implications of Clay's behavior, in *Dutchman*, also suggest that it is "logical" to want a white woman. He accepts the advances of Lula, a stranger, without question. As the stage directions tell us, his is "[a]lmost an instinctive though undesirable response" (4). Even more telling is that in answer to Lula's "Would you like to get involved with me, Mister Man?" he says, "Huh, I'd be a fool not to" (11). His and Jesse's, like Othello's, is the quintessential paradox of the black man in a racist society: it is "normal" and "logical" that he should desire a white woman, but the attainment of his desire is considered unnatural.

The frustrations resulting from this dilemma manifest themselves in black men's texts often in forms of violence against white women— including rape or murder or both. And here is one of the most significant ways in which black male writers revise *Othello*. Just as many of their texts stress that love is not necessarily a motivation for black men's involvement with white women so do they also stress that violence is not necessarily motivated by jealousy. Rather, rape and murder become

---

9. Caryl Phillips observes: "There is no evidence of Othello having any black friends, eating any African foods, speaking any language other than theirs. . . . From what we are given it is clear that he denied, or at least did not cultivate, his past." Also see "Othello's Alienation," in which Berry argues, "The most rootless of Shakespeare's tragic heroes [Othello] has no geographical or cultural anchor to his being" (323).

tropes through which these texts show sexual relations between black men and white women as an essential dimension of the power relations between black men and white *men*.

Such rhetorical strategies suggest that women's bodies—black and white—provide the locus where sexism and racism intersect.[10] However, black male inquiry, while inscribing sexism, also seeks to deconstruct the "myth of the Black rapist," to borrow a term from Angela Davis, who describes the conception of the myth as it figures in American history (172–201). Similar to this myth are myths concerning the "lust and jealousy of Moors," which Robert Burton, in *The Anatomy of Melancholy*, says were reported by "every geographer of them [Moors]." Barthelemy argues that although Burton's book was not published until 1621, it "codifies opinions that were in currency long before its publication" (155), and Edward Berry argues that the "linkage between hot climates and hot passions was an Elizabethan cliche" (321–22). Black writers' (mis)reading of *Othello* heightens an awareness of the ways in which these myths are inscribed in the earlier texts. If we consider Shakespeare's work alone, we find in *Titus Andronicus*'s Aaron the obvious manifestation of them. Or just as obvious, in *The Tempest* we find what Fanon describes as the "Prospero complex":[11] "Prospero assumes an attitude that is well known to Americans in the southern United States. Are they not forever saying that the niggers are just waiting for the chance to jump on white women?" (107)

Less explicit but perhaps more insidious are the manifestations of these myths in *Othello*. In Iago's warning to Brabantio, "Zounds, sir, y'are robbed . . . / . . . an old black ram / Is tupping your white ewe" (I.i.86–89), the accusation of rape is implied by the use of *robbed* and *tupping*, the evocation of bestiality, and the integration of black and white.[12] A second instance is Brabantio's question to Roderigo: "Is there not charms / By which the property of youth and maidhood / May be

---

10. Bell Hooks cites Eldredge Cleaver's *Soul on Ice*, reminding us of the point in the text when he, "writing about the need to 'redeem my conquered manhood,' described raping black women as practice for the eventual rape of white women" (58). However, although many black male writers have used "sexualized metaphors to talk about the effort to resist racist domination," as Hooks argues, not all of them have used them to justify rape and other forms of violence against women.

11. As the point of departure for his own discussion, Fanon uses O. Mannoni (40).

12. Winthrop D. Jordan states that Iago's accusation was not "merely the language of . . . a 'dirty' mind: it was the integrated imagery of blackness and whiteness, of Africa, of the sexuality of beasts and the bestiality of sex" (38).

abused?" (I.i.172–74). Here the word *charms* implies trickery and there-fore a lack of consent on Desdemona's part as well as a much harsher image of force evoked by the description of an "abused" virginity. A third is implicit in Brabantio's confrontation with Othello:

> O thou foul thief, where hast thou stowed my daughter?
> Damned as thou art, thou has enchanted her!
> For I'll refer me to all things of sense,
> If she in chains of magic were not bound,
> Whether a maid so tender, fair, and happy,
> So opposite to marriage that she shunned
> The wealthy, curled darlings of our nation,
> Would ever have, t'incur a general mock,
> Run from her guardage to the sooty bosom
> Of such a thing as thou—to fear, not to delight?
> Judge me the world if 'tis not gross in sense
> That thou hast practised on her with foul charms,
> Abused her delicate youth with drugs or minerals
> That weaken motion. I'll have't disputed on;
> 'Tis probable, and palable to thinking.
> I therefore apprehend and do attach thee
> For an abuser of the world, a practiser
> Of arts inhibited and out of warrant. (I.ii.61–78)

The binary opposition that informs the larger structure of the play—black as evil and white as good—informs Brabantio's speech as well. Like Aaron in collusion with the demons of hell, and Caliban the off-spring of a witch, Othello, through compounding references to magic, charms, drugs, and minerals, is painted not simply as inferior to "the wealthy, curled darlings" but as frightening and "otherworldly" as well. Against the many arguments that Shakespeare emphasizes stereotypes only to explode them, we clearly see a *pattern* of inscribing blacks as devilish, suggesting that Shakespeare himself could not move beyond racial clichés.[13] Here the image of the "tender, fair, and happy" Desde-

---

13. For some examples, see Martin Orkin, 59–60, and Berry, 316. See also Jones's discussion in which he argues that "a comparison between [Shakespeare's] Aaron in *Titus Andronicus* and his noble Moor shows two extremes of his work. In the earlier play, he is the young dramatist exploiting the tastes of the times; in the later play he is the mature dramatist flying in the face of tradition" (132). Jones's argument loses validity, however, when we consider the portrait of Caliban in *The Tempest*, which was Shakespeare's last play.

mona, "chained," "weakened," and "abused" by "such a thing" as the "sooty bosom[ed]" Othello effectively reinforces the associations with the black man as rapist.

A fourth instance is Othello's own speech as he watches the sleeping Desdemona. The lines "Be thus, when thou art dead, and I will kill thee, / And love thee after" (V.ii.18–19) capture valences that are discernible only if this scene is read in the context of physical love. The lines "hint" at necrophilia, as Barthelemy argues, as well as suggest rape. The distance between Shakespeare and the three white villains of the play is lessened by this description of Othello colluding with hegemony and the suggestion that uncontrollable passion and sexual perversion have always been part of his nature. Othello, then, becomes a more subtle version of the villainous Moor.

Even when the white woman consents, as apparently Desdemona does, the sexual act between a black man and white woman is considered rape as we have seen above and also as African American signifying strategies demonstrate. Baraka's *The Slave* signifies on such a reading of Othello during a confrontation between Walker Vessels, Grace, and Bradford. Grace accuses Walker of "playing the mad scene from *Native Son*. A second-rate Bigger Thomas," but Walker identifies more closely with Shakespeare's Moor, saying, "[R]emember when I used to play a second-rate Othello. . . . I was Othello . . . Grace there was Desdemona . . . and you were Iago . . ." (57). After a short exchange with Bradford, Walker threatens to "stay here and rape your wife . . . as I so often used to do . . . as I so often used . . ." (59). His reference to raping Grace while they were married implies that he understands how even the sanctity of marriage does not protect him from the black rapist myth. Although clearly women can be raped within marriage, the sense here is that the politics of consent are always overdetermined by race, and therefore this passage constitutes a significant critique of traditional ways of seeing and thinking about black male sexuality.

That the black man is haunted by this rapist image is also evident in a scene in *The Primitive* in which Jesse is chasing his landlord's errant dog in order to punish it for urinating in his bedroom:

He [Jesse] pursued, and got in another good lick before he slipped again and knocked over the white marble statue of a nude that blocked the passage. He made a desperate lunge and caught the statue before it hit the floor, breaking its fall, then fell on the top of it. He got up bruised and shaken and restored it to the table. "Good thing you're not in Georgia, son," he told himself. "Open and shut case of rape." (103)

Although Jesse, at this moment, alludes to the southern conceptualization of the myth, his direct reference to Othello at the time of Kriss's murder fuses narrative histories, in the way the "Prospero complex" does for Fanon, to imply the pervasiveness and the perpetuation of racist ideology.

These explanations of the ways in which African American men refigure *Othello* are most certainly not an attempt to argue the absence of sexism in the later texts. Noticeably, although they revise negative images of black men, they often do little to revise sexist images of women. For example, the murder scene in *The Primitive* parodies the murder scene in *Othello*, but Jesse's perception of women seems not to be parody but an expression of the sexist view of women similar to that found in the play. The implications that Desdemona is less threatening when asleep, that if she lives she will only "betray more men" (V.ii.6), that only through death can her former light (innocence, virtue) be restored, are alluded to in Jesse's contemplation of Kriss, who he believes is sleeping but who is in fact dead. As he bends over her, he thinks her face "serene and astonishingly beautiful" at the same time that he thinks, "Too bad they [women] can't function in their sleep. When you wake up their brains the trouble begins" (150). Chupa argues, "Identifying with William Shakespeare's Moor [Jesse] reveals his dependency on Western myth, which informs his objectification of Kriss as Bitch Goddess" (23). Yet, Himes's depiction of Kriss, even though sexist, must also be seen as an attempt to revise the portrait of the white woman as always the innocent, virginal victim (Davis, 177, 196–98).[14]

The otherwise parodic thrust of Himes's murder scene seems to be necessitated by his attempt at self-inscription. A number of parallels signal a reference to *Othello*, but by virtue of the differences between the two situations, Himes destabilizes dominant images of black masculinity and sexuality. Sex pervades the murder scene in *Othello*, whereas the

---

14. Davis contends, "Racism has always served as a provocation to rape, and white women in the United States have necessarily suffered the ricochet fire of these attacks." However, she also cites specific cases in which white women have testified falsely against black men, causing their imprisonment or death or both. Because the "myth has sometimes been legitimized by white women," she argues, "it is wrong to portray the women as innocent pawns, absolved of the responsibility of having collaborated with the forces of racism" (198).

murder scene in *The Primitive* is devoid of sex. When Jesse climbs into bed with the dead Kriss, as if to act out the necrophilia only implied in *Othello*, he goes to sleep instead. When he awakens from sleep, the room is freezing cold. Ironically, because at this point he doesn't remember having killed Kriss, he asks, "Damn, aren't you cold, Kriss-baby?" When he finally touches her, "her ice-cold flesh burned his hands" (157). Besides evoking the image of death, these descriptions of coldness evoke the view, albeit stereotypical, of the white woman as frigid, and thereby qualify, if not completely reverse, the suggestion of the black male's sexual perversion.

Unlike Othello, who feels remorse over having murdered Desdemona, Jesse feels vindicated when he discovers that he has murdered Kriss. He says it was

> Not only natural, plausible, logical, inevitable, psychiatrically compulsive and sociologically conclusive behavior of a human being, but mathematically and politically correct as well. Black man has got to have some means of joining the human race. Old Shakespeare knew. Suppose he'd had Othello kiss the bitch and make up. Would have dehumanized him. (159)

The comments about Shakespeare are ironic because Himes's (mis)reading of *Othello* implies that "Old Shakespeare" really did *not* know. It is as if Himes not only anticipates the question Bell Hooks poses in *Yearning* by almost forty years, "What does it mean when primarily white men and women are producing the discourse around Otherness?" (53), but also attempts to answer it. It means, he seems to say, that the "Other's" relationship to self is mediated by configurations of hegemonic power, racism, sexism, and classism. Shakespeare *could not* know. Thus, defining and inscribing the black self necessitate not only critical interrogation of images of the "Other" within the dominant tradition but also critical intervention and, finally, revision.

For Othello, the murder of Desdemona is the decisive act in destroying his humanity. Othello's final words are indicative of the state to which he has degenerated:

> And say besides that in Aleppo once,
> Where a malignant and a turbaned Turk
> Beat a Venetian and traduced the state,

I took by th'throat the circumcised dog
And smote him—thus. (V.ii.355–59)

As Terence Hawkes points out, "Reduced to a level quite below that of genuine humanity, the 'dog' he melodramatically stabs to death is appropriately himself" (142). Also relevant is Madelon Gohlke's discussion of "Othello's appalling pun, relating his suicide to an act of sexual consummation," which is evidenced by the lines "I kissed thee ere I killed thee. No way but this, / Killing myself, to die upon a kiss" (V.ii.355–56).[15] The "appalling pun" reduces Othello to a perverse sexual animal, emphasizing his lack of humanity, his movement from the civilized to the barbarous. Evocative of the act of sexual consummation, these last words also recall the earlier lines "I will kill thee, / And love thee after" (V.ii.18–19) and reinforce Shakespeare's depiction of Othello's uncontrollable passion as an inherent racial characteristic.

Jesse's movement from primitive to human, then, as an ironic reversal of Othello's movement from human to primitive (worse, animal), functions to displace dominant cultural codes and assumptions. It articulates, ironically, an indictment against a society that does not accept differences, that assumes superiority because of those differences, that uses its women for its own evil purpose:

> Black man kills white woman. All the proof you need now. Absolutely incontrovertible behaviorism of a male human being. Most human of all behavior. Human beings only species of animal life where males are known to kill their females. Proof beyond all doubt. Jesse Robinson joins the human race. . . . Knew they'd keep experimenting on us until they made us human. The Christian way . . . Went in the back door of the Alchemy Company of America a primitive, filled with things called principles, integrity, honor, conscience, faith, love, hope, charity, and such, and came out the front door a human being, completely purged. (159)

Himes associates those attributes generally considered noble and good with "primitiveness" instead of "humanity." Through this protagonist,

---

15. Gohlke's argument centers on a comparison of men and women in *Othello* and other Shakespearean tragedies. She argues: "While the tragic hero typically undergoes a process in which his initial sense of self is fractured or broken down, a process which may involve a brush with madness, but which culminates in a reassertion of a coherent self, the major female figures move from an initial position of strength to one of reticence or madness, characterized by silence or a highly enigmatic speech" (105).

Jesse, Himes implies that the black man's attempt to assimilate, to become white, is his undoing but that both the desire and the consequences
are inevitable in a racist society.

Baraka's *Dutchman* similarly indicts assimilation in its claim that
"primitive" is better. Lula voices Baraka's condemnation of the black
bourgeoisie in her accusatory appraisal of Clay: "You look like you live
in New Jersey with your parents and are trying to grow a beard. That's
what. You look like you've been reading Chinese poetry and drinking
lukewarm sugarless tea" (8). It is not surprising that the antagonists in
the play are a black man and a white woman since, as Baraka himself
says, Clay is a "boy trying desperately to become a man" and "*Dutchman*
is about the difficulty of becoming a man in America" (187–88). Lynne
Segal argues, "For four centuries the relations between Black and white,
Othello and Desdemona, have been overlaid by Black sexual imagery"
(176). This presence of the interconnectedness of assimilation, sexuality,
and man/selfhood in *Dutchman* signals that it stands in an intertextual
relationship with *Othello* even though Baraka makes no explicit reference
as in *The Slave*. The critical difference between Baraka's texts and *Othello*
is that Baraka articulates a more complex politics of identity. The play
presents a powerful symbolic enactment of the perennial psychological
dilemma facing black men in white America.

In the same way that Othello is stripped of the Venetian facade of
extreme self-control to uncover his latent violent passion, Clay is stripped
of the three-piece suit, the proper speech, the middle-class respectability
facade to uncover the potential murder. Lula pleads with Clay to "rub
bellies," to "do the thing," and "The Nasty." Her words are an ugly
accusation: "You middle-class black bastard. Forget your social-working
mother for a few seconds and let's knock stomachs. Clay, you liver-
lipped white man. You would-be Christian. You ain't no nigger, you're
just a dirty white man" (31). Lula succeeds in provoking Clay, causing
him to leap up and yell at her to "shut up and let me talk" (33), losing
his self-control and thereby the controlled speech of the middle-class
intellectual, a degeneration of speech as in *Othello*.

Othello's speech deterioration defines the extent to which he has lost
his humanity. As Hawkes notes, by the end of the play, "Othello no longer
speaks well," and "all that remains is a fumbling attempt to reach back to
his former identity, his former humanity" (141). For Clay, however, the so-
called degeneration of speech is a good sign. Clay's giving up the refined,
controlled speech and actions of the middle-class black man he represents

is a sign of increasing consciousness and of growing self-respect. As he tells Lula, "I'm the great would-be poet" (35). But it is not a poetry of words; it is "a simple knife thrust" (35). Clay explains that

> Bird [Charlie Parker] would've played not a note of music if he just walked up to East Sixtyseventh Street and killed the first ten white people he saw. Not a note! And I'm the great would-be poet. . . . Just let me bleed you, you loud whore, and one poem vanished. A whole people of neurotics, struggling to keep from being sane. And the only thing that would cure the neurosis would be your murder. Simple as that, I mean if I murdered you, then other white people would begin to understand me." (35)

Clay threatens Lula by saying, "I *could* murder you right now" (emphasis mine), but he doesn't. The speech is eloquent; his understanding is heightened, but he doesn't act. Thus, Lula has the chance to kill him. She "brings up a small knife and plunges it into Clay's chest. Twice" (37). This act is simultaneously a symbolic castration and, as in *Othello*, Clay's suicide. In *Dutchman*, committing murder would have made Clay a true poet; in *Othello*, the greatest poet of them all is undone by committing murder.

As perhaps Othello seeks to define himself in terms of Venetian society so Clay (like Jesse and Walker) seeks to define himself in terms of white American society from which he is equally alienated. Unlike Shakespeare, Baraka suggests that through violence one might gain a sense of manhood. In *The Slave*, the notion of gaining manhood through violence is exemplified by Walker's confrontations with the white characters. On one occasion he screams at Grace, "Believe me, self-righteous little bitch, I want to kill you" (83), and on another, "I could have killed both of you [Grace and Bradford] every night of my life" (85). Walker's violence is directed toward the husband through his relations with the wife. He finally kills Bradford in self-defense, saying that Bradford "thought he ought to kill me" (82). That he has left the larger war in order to confront this white man in a private war over his own black manhood is evidenced in his threats to Bradford that he will rape his wife and in his constant references to him as "fairy," as "closet queen," as "Professor No-Dick."[16] In this case, the confrontation clearly suggests

---

16. In "An Interview with LeRoi Jones by Sidney Bernard," Baraka's condemnation of individuals who forsake the greater good for the individual good is evident in his

that some black men share with white men "the patriarchal belief that revolutionary struggle was really about the erect phallus, the ability of men to establish political dominance that could correspond to sexual dominance" (Hooks, 58). This latter idea is implicit in *The Primitive* as well and is made explicit in Jesse's last words to the dead Kriss: "Now we're all even" (160).

Although the moral implications differ from text to text, these black writers seem to argue that "murder . . . [is] the only act of self-assertion possible, the only route out of a lifetime of enforced, child-like submission and powerlessness" (Segal, 183). Further, with regard to sexism, whatever the narrative intent, the persistent tendency to present objectivized and idealized women is motivated by and structured around the male gaze. The difference is that Shakespeare depicts Desdemona as an innocent victim, whereas Baraka, like other black writers, depicts his white woman antagonist as complicit in "racist-inspired" violence.[17]

One final dimension of Baraka's and Himes's revisionary modes of inquiry bears consideration here. That is, all three black texts explore the position of the black male artist in relation to the world of white (male) art. Othello's description of himself as "rude . . . in speech," not "blessed with . . . soft phrase[s]" (I.iii.81–82), is a manifestation of his struggle to overcome the constructed identity of the Moor. In *The Slave*, however, Walker gives up being a poet to be a revolutionary and thereby denounces Western literary traditions. As he says, "Didn't St. Thomas say that? Once a bad poet always a bad poet . . . or was it Carl Sandburg as some kind of confession?" (50) and "the worst thing that ever happened to the West was the psychological novel" (70). Likewise, Clay, in giving up the restrictive speech of the bourgeoisie in favor of vernacular forms of communication—not only in speech but in music—reaffirms his black identity.

In *The Primitive*, as Jesse gains a heightened sense of self, he begins making up absurd rhymes:

---

comments about the play. He states that "Walker Vessels is hung up in his own ego syndrome, his individualism. That's why I call the play 'The Slave.' . . . He has no business there talking to these people. He is supposed to be out leading his brothers. He is supposed to be fighting, he's not supposed to be sitting there bullshitting with white people. And this is why, essentially, Walker is a weak man."

17. For the purposes that I have outlined in this essay, however, if we can view these depictions as not always reflective of real women but of men's fears being projected onto women, it may increase our understanding of the texts under consideration.

Be happy—Go nappy. . . . Feel low? Lynch Negro! Banned from the Hierarchy? Shack up with a darky! When all your Money affords you No Ease—Then Sambo will Please! (158)

This language shows his lessening desire for his literary works to be acceptable in the world of white art. Himes also disrupts received generic modes by structuring some parts of his novel like a play, simultaneously parodying and, by virtue of the hyperbole of the rhymes, deconstructing the master narrative of *Othello*. Both Himes and Baraka revise not only traditional ways of seeing black masculinity and sexuality but also traditional discursive styles of Western culture. In short, they challenge and reject the reductionist language of white male hegemony.

Segal argues, "Some Black men have seen only too clearly that fighting racism is also about fighting dominant images of masculinity, about rejecting racist fantasies of Black sexuality" (203). As Clay screams at Lula, "You fuck some black man, and right away you're an expert on black people. What a lotta shit that is" (34). These writers decry the socially established interpretation of black male sexuality, the limiting force of the white gaze, through their various strategies of dissent. It isn't enough that Shakespeare did not have Othello "kiss the bitch and make up." These writers clearly suggest that one cannot make a unique relationship such as Othello's and Desdemona's the focal point of a text and then try to deflect attention away from it by arguing, either implicitly or explicitly, for human essences or universal despair. Contrary to Robert Heilman's opinion that "Othello's scope is lost sight of if we can understand him only by racial psychology" (138), the narratives of Himes, Baraka, and others suggest the very great danger of sacrificing the particular for the universal. Thus, these writers construct alternative narrative histories that interrogate, subvert, and disrupt structures of racist domination. In the process, they articulate new narrative space as well as new personal freedom.

"Haply, for I Am Black":
Othello *and the Semiotics of Race and Otherness*

ELLIOTT BUTLER-EVANS

I

A s I approach a critical "reading" of *Othello*,[1] I become aware that I do not address a singular text but the numerous encounters with a largely heterogeneous body of texts designated as *Othello*. My earliest experience with the play as literature was in an undergraduate English class, when I, like so many of my contemporaries, read the play as part of the English canon, particularly those aspects of the canon that celebrated everything British. A subsequent and more ironic encounter with the play involved my playing the role of Brabantio in a production of the play by an exclusively black university. Equally significant were my seeing the title role played by the American black actor William Marshall; reading of Paul Robeson's and Ira Aldridge's handling of the role; discussing it as a graduate student in a seminar at

---

1. "Reading" here should be understood to denote any of several different acts of decoding. It refers to a broad application of any communicative process that involves the existence of an authorial agent, a "text," and an addressee. Hence, viewing a play can be said to constitute a form of "reading."

the University of Chicago in which the critical and interpretive strategies employed became containment strategies by which ideological issues, such as race and imperialism, were excluded; and viewing the film, as well as following the controversy, related to the screen portrayal of the protagonist by Sir Laurence Olivier.

Although I will have reference to a specific text in developing my argument, my approach will be to focus on the several "Othellos" as units of a larger text *Othello*, whether a theatrical or performance text, or a written or literary text. I shall subject that text to semiotic scrutiny. I am particularly interested in the manner in which insights arrived at from a critical approach structured by work in social semiotics, that branch of applied semiotics primarily concerned with the ideological issues endemic to sign production,[2] might be useful in illuminating and deconstructing the underpinning ideology of the text.[3] My argument is that at the subtextual level of the drama *Othello* there is discursive exploration of ethnic and racial issues in which contradictory and conflicting representations of race and Otherness are explored but left largely unresolved.

Drawing on the research of scholars who have explored the issue of racial representation in sixteenth- and seventeenth-century cultural production, and reframing that research within theoretical issues raised in semiotics, I hope to show that there is a gradual unfolding of an ideological text on race that remains somewhat unresolved at the end of the drama. Specifically, I will show that characterization of Othello as Moor and outsider is overdetermined. Only when one situates that characterization within discourses of Otherness and emerging discourses of race of the period does one gain insight into the production of that character. Moreover, the resonances that the characterization has with a racial discourse that has characterized Western writing greatly determine how we read that character even today.

---

2. Arthur Asa Berger provides a concise definition of *sign*: "The sign is a central concept in semiology and semiotic analysis. For Saussure, a sign is a 'combination of concept and sound image.' The linguistic sign, said Saussure, 'unites not a thing and a name but a concept and a sound image.' For Peirce, a sign is 'something which stands to somebody for something in some respect or capacity.' For Eco, 'a sign is everything which can be taken as significantly substituting for something else,' on the basis of a previously established social convention" (191).

3. Ideology here should be understood in the Althusserian sense of "the representation of the imaginary relationship of individuals to the real conditions of their existence" (162).

In my approach, therefore, I shall consider how the specific representational strategies in the play are consonant with similar strategies of other writing of the period. My approach will be somewhat similar to that used by Robert Hodge and Gunther Kress in their focus on the ideological issues generated by sign production—a concern central to their mapping out a social semiotics. They declare their departure from a structuralist or "mainstream" semiotics and situate their work within the "famous formulation" proposed by Karl Marx and Frederick Engels:

> Men are producers of their conceptions, ideas, etc.—real, active men, as they are conditioned by a definite development of their productive forces and of the intercourse corresponding to these, up to its furthest forms. Consciousness can never be anything else than conscious existence, and the existence of men is their actual life-process. If in all ideology men and their circumstances appear upside-down as in a *camera obscura*, this phenomenon arises just as much from their historical life-process as the inversion of objects on the retina does from their physical life-process. (47)

Hodge and Kress further frame the discussion of their enterprise within the context of the relationships that exist between dominant and dominated groups. Although there is significant disagreement in the United States about the value of a Marxist–semiotic approach, one can argue that some of the basic tenets of semiosis, the process of transmitting and receiving signs, readily lend themselves to political application. This becomes evident when one considers the pioneering scholarship of Charles Morris. Adopting the Charles Sanders Peirce formulation, Morris in *Signification and Significance* describes the semiotic process as follows:

> Semiosis (or sign process) is regarded as a five term relation—v, w, x, y, z—in which v sets up in w the disposition to react in a certain kind of way, x, to a certain kind of object y under certain conditions, z. The v's, in the cases where this relation obtains, are *signs*, the w's are *interpreters*, the x's are *interpretants*, the y's are *significations*, and the z's are the *contexts* in which the signs occur. (2)[4]

---

4. In an earlier work, *Signs, Language and Behavior*, Morris directly addresses the political implications of semiotic study and practice: "[S]haring a language with other persons provides the subtlest and most powerful of all tools for controlling the behavior of these other persons to one's advantage—for stirring up rivalries, advancing one's own goals, exploiting others. Modern propaganda is the witness to this within existing nations; a world language would make the same phenomena possible over the earth as a whole.

Morris goes on to identify three dimensions of signs. Framing his description of those dimensions within a paradigm similar to George H. Mead's analysis of an act, he argues:

> A sign is *designative* insofar as it signifies *observable* properties of the environment or actor, it is *appraisive* insofar as it signifies the consummatory properties of some object or situation, and it is *prescriptive* insofar as it signifies how the object or situation is to be reacted to so as to satisfy the governing impulse. In these terms, usually "black" is designative, "good" is primarily appraisive, and "ought" is primarily prescriptive. (4)

This focus on the properties of the sign, particularly its appraisive, designative, and prescriptive dimension, can provide a useful theoretical foundation for our discussion of *Othello.* I would argue that the representational strategies involved in the creation of the character Othello are largely a part of a broader and more generalized discourse in which "Moorishness" and "blackness" constitute a form of Otherness. This discourse, in all probability determined by economic and political interests of the moment, invites "readers," or viewers, to respond in a specific manner. However, because the development of racial ideology was still in process at the time of the initial production and performance of *Othello,* it is presented as unresolved.

II

A starting point for an ideological reading of *Othello* would be investigation into the rather complex tropological swerves in the representation and self-representation of the central character. In the list of dramatis personae, where others are described in terms of kinship and other forms of interpersonal relationships, Othello's identity is couched in racial or cultural terms: "Othello, a noble Moor; in the service of the Venetian state." This particular strategy of objectification and reification is sustained throughout the drama by the repeated references to him as Moor. Hence, we can assume that for the Elizabethan audience the term signified Otherness or difference, and the same may be said of an audience today, albeit perhaps with less specificity.

And semiotic itself, as it develops will be subject to the same kind of utilization by individuals and groups for the control of other individuals and groups in terms of self-interest" (214).

Moor, as a sign, however, was somewhat indeterminate for a seventeenth-century audience and would in all likelihood signify a generalized and vague exotica for general European and American audiences even today. The polysemous and indeterminate nature of the signifier *Moor* is addressed by Barthelemy when he comments on the difficulty endemic to attempts to define it:

> Like the words *Turk*, *Saracen*, *Oriental* and *Indian*, *Moor* is difficult to define precisely. In the fifteenth, sixteenth, and seventeenth centuries, the word meant different things to different people. All these words, however, shared a common connotation: alien, or foreigner. Because these words were used so imprecisely—frequently they were used simply to identify any non-Christian—they came to denote a rather general category of alien. (6)

Barthelemy continues by examining attempts to establish an etymology for the word:

> The *OED* cites the 1390 *Confessio Amantis* of Gower as the earliest example of *Moor* meaning Negro. The second meaning of *Moor* offered by the *OED* focuses on religion, while it identifies yet another ethnic group: A Mohammedan, esp. a Mohammedan inhabitant of India. 1588 is cited as the earliest examples of the meaning, although evidence in *Mandeville's Travels* suggests this is somewhat late. The layers of qualifications given in the first definition allow us to include under the word *Moor* many people who are neither Berbers nor Arabs, as well as to exclude many who are Negroes. If we consider the second meaning, we can identify by the word *Moor* people of many different races and different religions. *Moor* can mean, then, non-black Muslim, black Christian, or black Muslim. The only certainty a reader has when he sees the word is that the person referred to is not a European Christian. (7)

It is clear that the term *Moor* could not evoke a specific interpretant but clearly carried with it a prescriptive or appraisive dimension. Therefore, one might argue that although the sign *Moor* is lacking in specificity, it elicits a generalized concept of Otherness in audiences, constituting them as "interpreter families" who experience a shared interpersonal understanding of the sign (Morris, 21). Othello, then, becomes the symbolic embodiment of the non-European outsider.

The references to race dramatically foreground Othello's difference.

The signifier *Moor*, as I have indicated, need not necessarily evoke racial difference. Its interpretant remains largely undecidable and multivalent. In *Othello* we see a specific racialization of the term, in which *Moor* signifies not only Otherness but blackness and the various negative associations culturally signified by blackness. Othello's "thick lips," "sooty bosom," and so forth all become signs, or more significantly signemes, of his "Negroness."[5] This becomes further reinforced through the range of references to excessive sexuality and bestiality that are identified with *Moor*, particularly black Moors. This construction and understanding of blackness as undesirable and repulsive is perhaps most directly expressed in Brabantio's expression of outrage. Arguing that Othello has exercised supernatural powers over his daughter, he states:

> For I'll refer me to all things of sense,
> If she in chains of magic were not bound,
> Whether a maid so tender, fair, and happy,
> So opposite to marriage that she shunn'd
> The wealthy curled darlings of our nation,
> Would ever have, to incur a general mock,
> Run from her guardage to the sooty bosom
> Of such a thing as thou; to fear, not to delight.
> Judge me the world, if 'tis not gross in sense
> That thou hast practis'd on her with foul charms,
> Abused her delicate youth with drugs or minerals
> That weaken motion: I'll have't disputed upon;
> 'Tis probable, and palpable to thinking. (I.ii.64–76)

This conflation of the two concepts—Moorishness and blackness—problematizes the characterization of Othello. Previously, he is narratively constructed as the "noble Moor," and although difference is stressed in that characterization, the qualifier *noble* has an ameliorating effect. Brabantio, however, associates blackness with traits that would evoke negative appraisive responses. This marks the surfacing of a body of signemes that came in later years to be understood as the elements of blackness, as a general sign of lack of humanness. The articulation of explicit and implicit bodies of binary oppositions used to identify Oth-

---

5. Arthur Berger defines signemes or sign elements as "fundamental elements in a sign, elements that cannot be broken down further. They are the most simple signs. A bubble in a glass of champagne would be a sign element or signeme. So would the light yellow color champagne has" (114).

ello—European/African, Christian/Moor, fair/dark, civilized/primitive—
establishes the textual instance in which Moorishness and blackness are
fused to complete a broader and more focused discourse of racial difference and Otherness.

It may rightly be argued that the concepts "racist" and "racism"
did not enter the English language until three centuries later. Further, the
specific racial discourse of the play is confined to only a few problematic
characters. I would argue, however, that particular constructions of race
are normalized in the universe of the play and are, in fact, reproductions
of other discourses of race in Western culture. In fact, what we have here
is the recoding of a discourse of race that has long been a part of Western
thought. Of particular relevance is the symbolic significance of blackness.
In his study of the representational strategies that characterized the production of the image of the black man on the English stage during the
sixteenth and seventeenth centuries, Elliot Tokson argues:

> Studies have shown quite clearly that in western culture "black"
> has "been connected with thoughts of hell, sin, death, and other
> manifestations of what is gloomy and forbidding. . . ." The signif-
> icance is explicit in expressions such as blacklist, blackmail, black-
> guard, to look black, blackout, but its understood inferiority to
> white can be recognized in subtle and unconscious expressions such
> as this from the learned Thomas Browne, who arranges colors, it
> seems, vertically: "the inhabitants of America are fair; and they of
> Europe in Candy, Sicily, and some parts of Spain, deserve not prop-
> erly so low a name as Tawney." And again in the same passage,
> Browne reflects the subtle negative attitude towards "black": "there
> are many within this zone whose complexions descend not so low
> as unto blackness." (7)

Equally significant, however, is what Tokson identifies as an apparent
contradiction, or at least ambivalence, in these representations:

> There were, however, some special meanings attributed to black
> color in the Renaissance. Don Cameron Allen has pointed out that
> black could signify not only sorrow and mourning, but disap-
> pointed love, constant love, a love that extends beyond the grave
> and constancy. (7)

Citing Winthrop Jordan and other scholars as support, however,
Tokson argues that the characterizations of blackness as negative were

most consistent and dominant, not only in the "literature" of the period, but also in the written texts produced by numerous travelers, traders, and ethnologists that characterized blacks, inter alia, as bestial, devoid of reason, sexually permissive, and extremely jealous, and at the same time, ingenuous and of a free and open nature. It is within these general discourses of race and Otherness, with all their contradictions, that the character of Othello is to be understood. As a Moor, he is clearly presented as Other, but not necessarily an offensive Other; the qualifier *noble* Moor does not extricate him from the realm of the exotic, yet it undermines the perception of him as evil. The association of him with blackness and its numerous signifieds, however, clearly locates him in the world of the undesirable. This blackness is articulated in a culture in which black is the color of degeneracy and damnation.

What is most striking in this development of the discourse of Otherness is the strategy of self-representation that Othello employs. Othello's primary approach to self-construction in his earlier appearances is through storytelling or self-narration. This strategy may be said to have two major dimensions: a narrative construction of the self, through storytelling, reinforced by aestheticizing strategies and a focus on literariness that represents and elaborates his character as noble and exotic; and an appropriation of the discourse of cultural Otherness that allows him to identify with the dominant group (Venetians) and suggests difference from Moors and blacks. This is dramatically represented in the scene in which he defends himself against Brabantio's charges:

> Her father lov'd me; oft invited me,
> Still question'd me the story of my life
> From year to year, the battles, sieges, fortunes
> That I have pass'd.
> I ran it through, even from my boyish days
> To the very moment that he bade me tell it;
> Wherein I spake of most disastrous chances,
> Of moving accidents by flood and field,
> Of hair breadth 'scapes i' the imminent deadly breach
> Of being taken by the insolent foe
> And sold to slavery, of my redemption thence
> And portance in my travel's history;
> Wherein of antres vast and deserts idle,
> Rough quarries, rocks and hills whose heads touch heaven

It was my hint to speak, such was the process;
And of the Cannibals that each other eat,
The Anthropophagi, and men whose heads
Do grow beneath their shoulders. (I.iii.128–45)

The first part of this narrative unit simply consists of a mode of self-presentation in which the signifier *noble* is given substance or embodied. The narrative process is one that arguably would indicate an excessive aestheticizing or foregrounding of literariness and contribute significantly to the representation, or in this instance the self-representation, of Othello as exotic or different. The primary function of the details is to elaborate Othello's bravery, which the text addresses both implicitly and explicitly. The narrative elements of the second part of Othello's speech, however—"the Cannibals that each other eat," the "Anthropophagi, and men whose heads / Do grow beneath their shoulders"—have significations that echo some of the racial ideological positions that are beginning to emerge. Othello, in this utterance, simply ventriloquizes the descriptions of non-Western others that characterized the discourse of the West. Tokson points out that the image of the wild man, or man as beast or monster, can be traced to the Middle Ages as a feature of Western discourse, and that such a trope eventually became associated with blackness. He suggests that Shakespeare may have been acquainted with these images (9–10). What is possibly presented in Othello's speech, then, is an "othering" of the self, both distancing from and negating of blackness. This act of self-defacement makes Othello less the "Other" and more an outsider whose epistemological stance toward non-Westerners does not differ from that of Venetians. James L. Calderwood argues this point rather convincingly when he states:

> [It] is made quite clear that the Moor is at least somewhat like us in that he is a convert to Christianity. He has crossed spiritual property lines, to be sure, but on a journey that we as Christians not only encourage but demand, especially if we Christians in this case are Venetians and a Turkish fleet is sailing for our property in Cyprus and if the converted infidel is a general whose record of military conquests makes him a likely candidate for doing away with the Turks. (7)

By the end of the first act, then, the racial subtext has unfolded in all of its complexity. The signifier *Moor* has been introduced as designative of a rather generalized and indeterminate Otherness. The concept "black" has been encoded within frameworks that might be said to be both appraisive and prescriptive. Othello as both Moor and black becomes representative of the contradictory cultural attitudes of his observers: he is "noble" yet black.

III

As Iago's influence over Othello becomes more powerful and intense, resulting in the latter's psychological disintegration, the discourse on blackness as negative is more strongly reinforced. The following exchange between the two men is especially telling:

> *Othello*: I do not think but Desdemona's honest.
> *Iago*: Long live she so! and long live you to think so.
> *Othello*: And, yet, how nature erring from itself.
> *Iago*: Ay, there's the point: as—to be bold with you—
> Not to affect many proposed matches
> Of her own clime, complexion and degree,
> Whereto, we see, in all things nature tends;
> Foh! one may smell in such, a will most rank,
> Foul disproportion, thoughts unnatural. (III.iii.225–33)

The exchange clearly evokes Brabantio's objections to the union of Othello and Desdemona on racial grounds, objections that appear normalized. It is striking here that Othello himself introduces the phrase "nature erring from itself," thereby legitimizing racial objections to himself. This self-negation is further reinforced by repeated references to black as deficiency or lack. Hence, when trying to come to terms with Desdemona's suggested betrayal of him, Othello concludes, among other things, "Haply, for I am black, / And have not those soft parts of conversation / That chamberers have" (III.iii.263–65). Similarly, when expressing his anguish to Iago, he again resorts to a color or racial trope: "Her name, that was as fresh / As Dian's visage is now begrim'd and black / As mine own face" (III.iii.387–89).

Othello's distancing and negating of the black self that I addressed earlier have become by the third act of the drama the beginning of a total negation of the self. By internalizing and parroting elements from the linguistic universe by which he is surrounded, he in the earlier "noble" stage makes an eloquent plea for his claim to humanity and in the moments of his gradual deterioration subverts that characterization of himself. The "noble Moor" has been displaced by an irrational and jealous black. That this jealousy itself would have been decoded as a racial sign by an audience at the time of the initial performances of *Othello* is strongly suggested by scholars. Tokson writes, for example, that John Leo Africanus, addressing jealousy among blacks, wrote: "No nation in the world is so subject unto Jealousie; for they will rather lose their lives, than put up any disgrace on behalfe of their women" (17).

From the third act to the conclusion of the play, we witness the total transformation of Othello from "noble" Moor to jealous fiend whose blackness signifies his moral imperfection. Again Othello seems to have internalized such a view of himself. At the moment of his suicide, his final extensive speech in the play suggests this appropriation of the world view of the other when he implores Lodovico, Gratiano, and others to speak of him as "one whose hand, / Like the base Indian threw a pearl away, / Richer than all his tribe" (V.ii.345–47). This self-negation and valorization of the culture of the Other is made even more dramatic in his penultimate utterance:

> And say besides, that in Aleppo once,
> Where a malignant and a turban'd Turk
> Beat a Venetian and traduc'd the state
> I took by the throat the circumcised dog,
> And smote him thus. (V.ii.351–55)

These lines are especially significant in that they reinvoke the image of the "noble" Moor that has been undermined in the last two acts of the play. Yet again they leave intact the language of Otherness that is used to characterize the non-European. Hence, although Othello is transformed at this instant from the degenerate, or evil, to the tragic, the discourse that would identify non-European others as morally imperfect remains the same.

I have argued in this essay that a semiotic reading of Shakespeare's *Othello* would reveal complex strategies of encoding and decoding signs of race and Otherness that are dialectically related to similar narrative strategies used in other discourses of the period. We can, of course, only speculate on the specific relationship of these constructions to actual political concerns of the day, for example, the emergence of British imperialism. Both Tokson and Barthelemy, for example, avoid simplistic or reductionist generalities about the politics of race based on their studies of images of blacks in the literature of the period. I am suggesting, however, that a semiotic approach to *Othello* can begin a new and refreshing dialogue on the play.

Literature and Racism:
The Example of Othello

S. E. OGUDE

I

T S. Eliot once remarked that about "anyone as great as Shakespeare, it is probable that we can never be right." But he was quick to qualify this seemingly profound truth: "[I]f we can never be right, it is better that we should from time to time change our way of being wrong" (126). No play of Shakespeare demands this change of critical direction more than *Othello*. Everyone seems to assume that *Othello* is Shakespeare's least complex tragedy in terms of plot, characterization, and dramatic conflict.[1] Albert Gerard dismisses *Othello* as "a tragedy of *groundless* jealousy," a jealousy that depends on what he detects as a disturbing imbalance in the total makeup of the personality of Shakespeare's coal-black hero: "a character with a high rank in society, with a noble heart and with an undeveloped mind. . . . [T]he fundamental tragic fault in the Moor can . . . be said to lie in the shortcomings of his intellect" (14). In the light of this sort of critical

---

1. M. C. Bradbrook, for instance, writes, "The play is complete, rounded, simple; no subplots, no metaphysical questions" (176).

opinion, Eliot's qualification needs further qualification: that in addition to changing our way of being wrong, we must define the limit of our error. In other words, we must be wrong within the context of the specific play under consideration.

The purpose of this essay is to reassess Othello in the light of contemporary black experience and bring out those peculiar traits of character that make him ill-equipped for survival in Venice. In doing this, I shall draw heavily on traditional European assumptions and prejudices.

Othello criticism began with the classical-minded Thomas Rymer whose *A Short View of Tragedy* (1692) has continued to attract critical side glances but not much respect. Rymer was the first to take note of the comic structure of *Othello* when he concluded his essay with these words:

> There is in this play, some burlesk, some humour, and ramble of comical wit, some shew, and some *mimickry* to divert the specta-tors: but the tragical part is, plainly none other, than a Bloody Farce, without salt or savour. (164)

Rymer, sharing none of the guilt of modern European critics who tend to extenuate the conflict of race and culture in *Othello*, plainly spoke his mind:

> The character of [Venice] is to employ strangers in their wars; But shall a poet thence fancy that they will set a Negro to be their General; Or trust a *Moor* to defend them against the *Turk*. With us a Black-amoor might rise to be Trumpeter; but *Shakespear* would not have less than a Lieutenant-General. With Us a *Moor* might marry some little drab, or small-coal Wench: *Shakespear*, would provide him the Daughter and Heir of some great Lord or privy-councellor. (134)

No critical work of the seventeenth century, or of the eighteenth century, significantly challenged Rymer's essential argument. In the nine-teenth century, Samuel Coleridge and the German critic A. W. Schlegel accepted Rymer's essential objections, although admittedly Coleridge saw literary qualities that might redeem the play if the negroid charac-teristics of Othello could be toned down. He suggested, therefore, that in order to make the relationship of Othello and Desdemona acceptable, or even plausible, Othello should be represented as "a high and chivalrous Moorish Chief" (II.350). Schlegel, in *Lectures on Dramatic Art and Literature* (1815), had earlier expressed similar views, maintaining that Cinthio's unnamed Moor should have been presented as "a baptized Saracen of the northern coast of Africa" but that Shakespeare's Moor was in every respect a Negro:

> We recognize in Othello, the wild nature of that glowing zone which generates the most raging beasts of prey and the most deadly poisons, tamed only in appearance by the desire of fame by foreign laws of honour, and by nobler and milder manners. . . . [His jealousy] is of that sensual kind, from which, in burning climes, has sprung the disgraceful ill-treatment of women and many other unnatural usages. . . . The Moor seems noble, frank, confiding, grateful for the love shown him and he *is* all this and moreover, a hero that spurns danger . . . but the mere physical force of passion puts to flight in one moment all his acquired virtues, and gives the upperhand to the savage in him over the normal man. (*Variorum*, 431–32)

Schlegel's argument is, in a way, linked to Coleridge's. The African he describes is by nature cruel, a creature to whom virtue is unnatural. He is in essence what Coleridge meant by "a veritable negro" (I.47). In spite of his acquired virtues, Othello remains at heart a *Negro*, and thus Schlegel sees in him a fine instance of the tamed savage reverting to type. Thus, in spite of the apparent contradictions, both Schlegel and Coleridge accept the European image of the African and his continent.

There have been some other extreme interpretations, notably but not surprisingly, from America. For instance, Mary Preston writes in her *Studies in Shakespeare*:

> In studying the play of *Othello*, I have always imagined its hero *a white* man. It is true the dramatist paints him black, but this shade does not suit the man. It is a stage decoration which *my taste* discards; a fault of colour from an artistic point. . . . Shakespeare was too correct a delineator of human nature to have coloured Othello black, if he had personally acquainted himself with the idiosyncrasies of the African race. (*Variorum*, 395)

John Quincy Adams denounces Desdemona as a wanton who was shameless enough to marry "a rude unbleached African" (*Variorum*, 391). Yet another American, Lillian Winstanley, sees Desdemona's love for and trust in Othello as "so unnatural that even Othello feels it" and goes on: "Modern critics ignore the intense moral and physical repugnance of Shakespeare's age for Moors. . . . The Moor to Shakespeare's England was like the negro to the southern state Americans today" (II.547). Charles Lamb, though from a less extreme position, makes a clear distinction between reading Shakespeare's *Othello* and seeing the play on stage—between a purely intellectual appreciation and a socially conditioned human reaction to the play as a probable historical fact. He condemns Desdemona's taste in choosing to wed a Moor, a black (*Variorum*, 410–11), a condemnation that underlines the grave moral doubts that underpin Rymer's objections.

Surprisingly, a moral critic like Samuel Johnson ignores Rymer. He emphasizes a purely intellectual response to the play and sees the hero through Desdemona's eyes. Somewhat disappointingly, Johnson assigns appropriate labels to each of the main characters, asking us to view the "fiery openness of Othello, magnanimous, artless, and credulous"; "the cool malignity of Iago, silent in his resentment, subtle in his designs"; and "the soft simplicity of Desdemona, confident of merit and conscious of innocence" (114–15). In the end, Johnson evades the painful moral dilemma that has confronted generation after generation of European critics from Rymer to Eliot when they see the milk-white Desdemona in the sooty embraces of the Moor.

II

The contention, often vigorously expressed, that Shakespeare knew nothing about Africans, and much less about the distinction between Africans and Moors, has been effectively answered by Eldred Jones in the introductory chapter of his *Othello's Countrymen* (1965). Elizabeth I's proclamation (1601) expelling Moors and Negroes from England suggests their presence in large numbers—and suggests also the topicality and relevance of the subject to the Elizabethans.

The evidence thus demonstrates that the black man was not exactly unknown in Shakespeare's England. On the contrary, what Thomas Carlyle called "The Nigger Question" was already vexing the Elizabethans (Jones, 87).

At this time, Shakespeare chooses to present a black hero. It is important to remember that Shakespeare's contemporaries demanded tales about fantastic and extraordinary creatures, demands that sixteenth-century travel books sought to meet. Speaking a century later of the authors of these books, the Earl of Shaftesbury observed that from "monstrous brutes" they moved "to yet more monstrous men" (223). It is instructive to note that Shaftesbury regarded Othello as one of these monstrous creations.

Othello has been seen, quite understandably, in many shapes. Yet he seems to me to illustrate two simple but basic truths: one, that appearances are deceptive and, two, that violation of the rules that held together the well-ordered sixteenth- and seventeenth-century universe of the Elizabethans leads to disaster. The first truth is expressed in the tragic grandeur of the leading ironies that run through the play and, as it were, give it its greatness: honest Iago; the noble Moor. The weight of the irony can best be appreciated by reference to what happens at the end of the play where Othello's own words

That's he that *was* Othello, here I am

(emphasis mine)

are confirmed by Lodovico's

O thou Othello, that went once so good,
Fall'n in the practice of a damned slave,
What should be said to thee? (V.ii.292–94)

The second truth is expressed in the marriage between Othello and Desdemona. Othello recognizes this as his one serious crime: loving outside his proper sphere; upsetting the neatly balanced social order of Venetian society, itself a projection of the Elizabethan society Shakespeare knew so well. Othello sums up his own tragedy: he is one "that lov'd not wisely" (V.ii.344), while Emilia sums up Desdemona's:

She was too fond of her most filthy bargain. (V.ii.157)

Ultimately, the tragedy of Othello results from a number of incompatibilities. There is a strong social and cultural difference, there is a racial difference, and there is an age difference. Iago and Roderigo seize on these differences in Act I, scene i, and Iago manipulates them throughout the play to his own ruin and the ruin of Othello and Desdemona. The text bears this out. Whatever we may think of Iago, it is almost certain that the rich store of abusive language he often hurls at Othello reflects the attitude of the Elizabethans to blacks, be they blackamoors, Negroes, Ethiopians, chivalrous Moors, or plain Moors. Iago's first picture of Othello undercuts the image of the noble Moor because he has turned down the request of some leading Venetians that Iago be promoted:

> But he, as loving his pride and purposes
> Evades them, with a bombast circumstance,
> Horribly stuff'd with epithets of war. (I.i.12–14)

Later in the same scene, Roderigo fills in the portrait of Othello:

> Your daughter (if you have not given her leave,
> I say again) hath made a gross revolt,
> Tying her duty, beauty, wit and fortunes
> In an extravagant and wheeling stranger
> Of here, and everywhere . . . (I.i.133–37)

However prejudiced Iago and Roderigo may be, Othello does show a great love for phrases "horribly stuff'd with epithets of war." Grandiloquence is an invaluable asset that functions as a psychological necessity, a need to reassure himself in his rather insecure and lonely situation.[2] Othello's faith is not so much in himself as in his services to the Venetian State, services that Othello assumes to be indispensable. Thus, when Iago tells him of Brabantio's complaints and reminds him that the old senator is an influential man, Othello replies:

> Let him do his spite;
> My services which I have done the signiory,
> Shall out-tongue his complaints; 'tis yet to know—
> Which, when I know that boasting is an honour,
> I shall promulgate—I fetch my life and being
> From men of royal siege. (I.ii.17–22)

The curious thing is that Othello repeats the spirit of this speech even in his dying words. The speech begins "I have done the state some service, and they know it" and concludes:

> And say besides, that in Aleppo once,
> Where a malignant and a turban'd Turk

---

2. Rymer first observed that "the Moor has no body to take his part," that is, "no body of his colour" (157), a point Helen Gardner develops in "The Noble Moor." The same may be true of the Prince of Morocco in *The Merchant of Venice* whose language is as colorful as Othello's and who boasts of his martial prowess before Portia whom he comes to woo (II.i.24 ff).

Beat a Venetian, and traduc'd the State,
I took by the throat the circumcised dog,
And smote him thus. (V.ii.352–56)

Thus, throughout the play, Othello betrays the self-love and boast-fulness of which Iago complains. Even his description of his wooing of the poor silly Venetian maid is little more than a song in praise of Othello, his hero-worship of himself:

Her father lov'd me, oft invited me,
Still question'd me the story of my life,
From year to year; the battles, sieges, fortunes,
That I have pass'd:
I ran it through, even from my boyish days,
To the very moment that he bade me tell it.
Wherein I spake of most disastrous chances,
Of moving accidents by flood and field;
Of hair-breadth scapes i' th' imminent deadly breach;
Of being taken by the insolent foe;
And sold to slavery, of my redemption thence
And with it all in my travel's history
Wherein of antres vast, and deserts idle,
Rough quarries, rocks and hills, whose heads touch heaven,
It was my hint to speak, such was the process:
And of the Cannibals, that each other eat;
The Anthropophagi, the men whose heads
Do grow beneath their shoulders: this to hear
Would Desdemona seriously incline. (I.iii.128–45)

Othello's projection of himself as a supreme achiever is, as I said earlier, a psychological necessity. He seeks to bury his physical and social disabilities in the myth of his achievements. Thus, whereas all other characters point to his blackness, his race, his culture, or more appropriately, lack of it, he creates a world of illusion and for a time finds satisfaction in it. Only once does the thought of his racial disability cross his mind, but it is a mere flicker of a reality that Othello cannot endure:

Haply, for I am black
And have not those soft parts of conversation
That Chamberers have, or for I am declin'd
Into the vale of years. (III.iii.267–70)

and he dismisses it with "yet that's not much"—and turns his mind elsewhere. But in those four revealing lines, we feel Othello's suffering and the agony that he labors to conceal. We also hear an echo of Iago's description of Cassio, "He has a person and a smooth dispose" (I.iii.403); Emilia's description of Lodovico, "A very handsome man" (IV.iii.37), and Desdemona's "This Lodovico is a proper man" (IV.iii.36); as well as Othello's own admission, "Rude am I in my speech / And little blest with the set phrase of peace" (I.ii.81–82). No one could be more aware of his own inadequacy. This sense of inferiority is what makes him rely so absolutely on the self-assured and apparently knowing Iago.

Othello's inferior racial status is underlined by the other characters in the play. Roderigo first brands him "thick-lips," and he and Iago incite Senator Brabantio to action in highly charged, emotive, and racially provocative language:

> Zounds, sir, you are robb'd, . . .
> Even now, very now, an old black ram
> Is tupping your white ewe; arise, arise,
> Awake the snorting citizens with the bell
> Or else the devil will make a grandsire of you. (I.i.86–91)

and even more explicitly:

> [Y]ou'll have your daughter cover'd with a Barbary horse; you'll have your nephews neigh to you; you'll have coursers for cousins and gennets for germans. (I.i.110–13)

While Iago continues with his animal imagery ("[Y]our daughter and the Moor are now making the beast with two backs" [I.i.116–18]), it is the less extravagantly imaginative Roderigo who tells the story in plain language:

> [Y]our fair daughter,
> At this odd-even and dull watch o' the night, [is]
> Transported with no worse nor better guard,
> But with a knave of common hire, a gondolier,
> To the gross clasps of a lascivious Moor. (I.i.122–26)

The intent of these inflammatory speeches is clear. Both Iago and Roderigo state that the match between Desdemona and Othello is unnatural, that there is something not quite right about it: an old black ram . . . a white ewe; your fair daughter . . . a lascivious Moor. The pairs do not fit. To Brabantio, too, Desdemona's falling in love with Othello seems wholly unnatural. Hence the theory of witchcraft, the only natural explanation for a most unnatural act:

> To fall in love with what she fear'd to look on?
> It is a judgement maim'd and most imperfect . . .
> That will confess perfection so should err
> Against all rules of nature. (I.iii.96–101)

All the ingredients on which Othello's jealousy is nurtured are to be found in the above passage. They constitute Iago's gateway into Othello's mind.

After his fabulous tale, Othello seems reassured by the Duke's unconvincing comment: "I think this tale would win my daughter too" (I.iii.171). One wonders what the Duke's reaction would have been if the Turks were not threatening Cyprus, what the fate of the culprit would have been if he were any person, black or white, other than Othello. For as we may recall, the Duke had given Senator Brabantio the unusual privilege to be both the accuser and the judge in the case:

> Who'er he be, that in this foul proceeding
> Hath thus beguil'd your daughter of herself,
> And you of her, the bloody book of law
> You shall yourself *read*, in the bitter letter,
> After its own sense, though our proper son
> Stood in your action. (I.iii.65–70; emphasis mine)

But when Brabantio reveals the identity of his antagonist, the sympathy of the Venetian Senate evaporates and all he gets is a laconic but unanimous "We are very sorry for it" (I.iii.73). The Duke finds himself in a quandary, his self-assurance falters, and he lapses into meaningless platitudes:

> When remedies are past, the griefs are ended,
> By seeing the worst, which late on hopes depended.
> To mourn a mischief that is past and gone,
> Is the next way to draw more mischief on.
> What cannot be preserv'd when fortune takes
> Patience her injury a mockery makes.
> The robb'd that smiles, steals something from the thief,
> He robs himself, that spends a bootless grief. (I.iii.202–09)

To this Polonius-like piece of wisdom, Brabantio's reply stands as a clear rebuke. The joke is both impertinent and obscene in its insensitivity. Brabantio sees through the Duke's dilemma and makes the point very well:

> So let the Turk of Cyprus us beguile,
> We lose it not so long as we can smile;
> He bears the sentence well, that nothing bears
> But the free comfort which from thence he hears: . . .
> But words are words; I never did hear
> That the bruis'd heart was pierced through the ear:
> Beseech you now, to the affairs of state. (I.iii.210–20)

Brabantio's speech punctures the Duke's mask of self-confidence and has the sting and the crushing force of Hamlet's "these old fools."

At this moment of emergency, the Duke and the senators logically choose to place the interest and security of the State far above a Venetian family's misfortunes. Their natural inclination leads them toward sympathy with Brabantio, but for the moment it is inconvenient to express that sympathy positively. Hence the Duke seeks to offer comfort:

> If virtue no delighted beauty lack
> Your son-in-law is far more fair than black. (I.iii.289–90)

This is another false attempt "to paint the blackamoor white." All Othello's friends are quick to ignore his color, to pass over his physical appearance and praise his virtues and prowess. Even Desdemona refrains from referring to Othello's color and assures the Senate (rather unconvincingly):

> I saw Othello's visage in his mind,
> And to his honours, and valiant parts
> Did I my soul and fortunes consecrate. (I.iii.252–54)

III

Indeed, a striking feature of the Othello–Desdemona relationship that many critics appear to have ignored is the basic contradiction between Othello's and Desdemona's concept of love. Nothing expresses and epitomizes the incompatibility of their doomed union more poignantly. As against Desdemona's idealization, Othello's love is essentially physical and at the height of his jealousy is expressed in coarsely physical terms.

A thorough study of the text clearly shows that Othello is indeed more in love with the whiteness of Desdemona's skin and the sweetness of her body than with her as a human being. This color worship is sharply contrasted with Desdemona's tendency to play down Othello's color and emphasize his heroic achievements. Shakespeare seems deliberately to emphasize this sharp contrast between "the lascivious Moor" and the gentle maiden whose "motion / Blush'd at her self" (I.iii.95–96).

Othello does not see Desdemona beyond her white integument. Most of his references to her are preceded by the words *sweet* or *fair*. And although *sweet* and *fair* are typical of the language of wooing, they do acquire special significance when used repetitiously by a black hero in all kinds of situations, many of which have nothing to do with wooing. Thus he promises to tell the Senate how he "did thrive in this fair lady's love" (I.ii.125). He greets her in Cyprus as his "fair warrior" (II.i.181). Her persistent demand for the recall of Cassio is answered with "Not now sweet Desdemona" (III.iii.56). As her guilt is "established," she becomes "the fair devil" (III.iii.458). He fears that his resolution to kill her will melt because "her body and beauty [will] unprovide my mind again" (IV.i.201–2). His preoccupation with Desdemona's body, with the color of her body, is seen even in his final resolution:

Yet I'll not shed her blood,
Nor scar that whiter skin of hers than snow
And smooth, as monumental alabaster. (V.ii.3–5)

Monumental alabaster is the phrase that sums up Othello's love, or rather, his color-worship. His love, as I have demonstrated, goes no deeper than Desdemona's skin. Desdemona's life, Desdemona's worth, are embodied in her milk-white skin. Even when he believes that the smooth alabaster conceals rottenness and lechery, his worship of the skin appears unchanged. Here is no love of true minds but a love born of the color contrast between himself and Desdemona, which he expresses thus:

Turn thy complexion there;
Patience, thou young and rose-lipp'd cherubin,
I here look grim as hell. (IV.ii.63–65)

This contrast suggests the tremendous gulf between Othello and Desdemona, not only with regard to age but, more crucially, with regard to race and culture. Thus instead of regarding *Othello* as "the realistic tragedy of the man-in-this-world overthrown by limitless evil focussed in the irreconcilable clash between an Othello and an Iago," as John Lawlor does (107), it is perhaps more meaningful to see it as an authentic racial tragedy, a play that relates the "tragic sense" to an uncanny awareness of racial differences and the inherent potentialities of race-related social tensions.

Indeed, the real function of the first act of *Othello* is to establish a basis for the working out of its central theme: the conflict of black and white. Shakespeare realizes that what is essentially a love story is irreversibly altered by the race factor, and we can see how radically that factor alters the attitude of the reader, the actor, the producer, and the audience. The first two scenes are about Othello, but never once is his name mentioned. He is simply the *Moor*, enclosed and made vulnerable by that designation.

This ensures Iago's success. If we examine the ingredients in the Iago magic cauldron, it becomes obvious that Iago is given more credit for originality than he actually deserves. His approach is not foolproof; rather it is the material on which he works that guarantees his success. Othello believes whatever he is told, so that by the end of the first act Iago is able to tell us that the Moor "will as tenderly be led by the nose / As asses are" (I.iii.407–08). The rest of the play merely proves how right Iago is.

Toward the beginning of Act III, scene iii, Iago makes his insinuations, and by the middle of the scene, not only does Othello see Desdemona's behavior as unnatural ("And yet, how nature erring from itself," 227) but he also begins to take note of and denigrate his color:

> Her name, that was as fresh
> As Dian's visage, is now begrim'd and black
> As mine own face. (III.iii.392–94)

Henceforth, Othello sees the devil in his own visage, a fact Emilia emphasizes in the last scene. Thus, when he confesses that he killed Desdemona, Emilia cries, "O, the more angel she, / And you the blacker devil" (V.ii.132–33) and "Thou dost belie her and thou art a devil" (V.ii.134) before pronouncing the final judgment: "This deed of thine was no more worthy heaven / Than thou wast worthy her" (V.ii.161–62).

These lines take us back to the central proposition that the germ of the tragedy is inherent in the union of Othello and Desdemona. Indeed, "What should such a fool / Do with so good a woman" (V.ii.233–34) except to be seen as "making the beast with two backs"—and that is where Iago's perception is so sharp.

Othello suffers from an overwhelming inferiority complex, which is seen as a part of his racial heritage, his lack of social refinement, the absence in him of the fine balance of reason and emotion that comes with true "education." Iago's suggestions have a tremendous effect on him because of his social and racial inadequacies. Shakespeare starts out with the proposition that the black man, even when favored with the hand of a white woman, feels inferior and undeserving. This point is made in the first act and is confirmed in the last act. Between Act I and Act V, Othello is left to commit one folly after another.

IV

In a sense, every production of *Othello* is a reenactment of racial tensions, and Othello is preeminently a caricature of the black man. There is something grotesque in the presentation of Othello. That explains why it is a travesty of Shakespeare for a "veritable negro" to play the role of Othello. A black Othello is an obscenity. The element of the grotesque is best achieved when a white man plays the role. As the play wears on, and under the heat of lights and action the makeup begins to wear off, Othello becomes a monstrosity of colors: the wine-red lips and snow-white eyes against a background of messy blackness.

It is interesting to observe in this connection that both the fierce barbarian of Edmund Kean and the romantic barbarian of Laurence Olivier are simply studies in monstrosity. A "natural" Othello is unlikely to make much impact; not even Paul Robeson could obviate the element of caricature that is an essential part of the makeup of Othello's personality. Leslie A. Fiedler notes that "Othello everywhere comes perilously close to . . . being unintentionally comic" (125). Barbara Heliodora C. De Mendonca argues that the influence of the *commedia dell'arte* on *Othello* can be detected in structure, characterization and conflict, and that "it is a tragedy built on a comic structure" (93).[3]

This comic aspect of the black man goes hand in hand with another point that establishment critics of the *Shakespeare Survey* club have either labored to ignore or at best mentioned only in passing, namely, the white

---

3. Her argument, however, ignores the substance of the comedy, and she goes on to add that "at no point is Othello presented as gauche or in any way socially inadequate" (97).

man's fear of miscegenation—the kind of fear that makes Brabantio wish he had given his daughter to the sentimental gull, Roderigo, and that sends him to his grave before the end of the play. In 1972, Charles Marowitz produced an "offshoot" entitled *An Othello* in which the line between Iago and Desdemona is thinly drawn and Desdemona declares, "I hate the Moor" (276). Indeed, Marowitz's Iago suggests an interesting motive for Othello's desire for Desdemona:

> And did you tell her, when she was givin' up her world of sighs, that when you had your furry black cock into her, it wasn't love you was wantin' but revenge, and when you were on top of her, you were gratifying the urge to kill—for all those centuries the white man killed you—boxed you up, shipped you away like ox, like cattle. . . . Did you tell her that every time she moaned and wriggled beneath you, it was music to your ears 'cause in your heart you were beatin' her, whippin' her, destroyin' her for her whiteness to atone for your blackness. (266)

This is not the "Othello Music" about which G. Wilson Knight wrote so lyrically, but it underlines the latent structure of racial antagonisms in Shakespeare's play, a structure modern writers exploit because its presence in *Othello* is very real.

Thus, the final impression that emerges from the five acts of *Othello* suggests that Shakespeare was acutely aware of and indeed shared some of the deep-seated fears of his contemporaries about black people, foremost among them the fear of miscegenation. In this sense, *Othello* expresses as well as confirms the prejudices behind Elizabeth's decree banishing "negars" from England. In Shakespeare's plays, relationships between black men and white women tend always to portend tragedy. Aaron and Tamora in *Titus Andronicus* illustrate the point, as does the marriage between Claribel and the king of Tunis in *The Tempest*. Sebastian sees the shipwreck as a punishment for Alonso's unnatural choice of husband for his daughter:

> *Sebastian*: Sir, you may thank yourself for this great loss,
> That would not bless our Europe with your daughter,
> But rather lose her to an African;
> Where she, at least, is banishe'd from your eye,
> Who hath cause to wet the grief on't.
> *Alonso*: Prithee, peace.

Sebastian: You were kneel'd to, and importun'd otherwise,
By all of us; and the fair soul herself
Weigh'd between loathness and obedience, at
Which end o' th' beam should bow. (II.i.118–28)

Be it *Othello* or *The Tempest*, white critics, especially those with liberal pretensions, have put on critical blinders to ignore or skirt the issue of racism. This may well be due to the increasingly explosive nature of the racial problem in modern times. Certainly, insofar as *Othello* is concerned, earlier critics were not as uniformly blind to this central issue of the play. The case of Rymer has been mentioned. But even in the nineteenth century, Victor Hugo, for example, in *William Shakespeare* (1864) saw the play for what it is: an undisguised expression of racism.

> Maintenant qu'est-ce qu' Othello? C'est la nuit. . . . La nuit est amoreuse du jour. La noirceur aime l'aurore. L'africain adore la blanche. . . . Il est grand, il est auguste, il est majestueux . . . mais il est noir. Aussi comme jaloux, le heros est vite monstre! le noir devient nègre. (*Variorum*, 452)
>
> (Now what is Othello? He is night. . . . The night is amorous of the day. The darkness loves the dawn. The African adores the white. . . . He is noble, he is dignified, he is majestic . . . but he is black. Consequently when jealous, the hero quickly becomes a monster! the black becomes a Negro.)

And the Negro always ends up a "nigger"! That is the fate of the house nigger. Suddenly the scales fall off his eyes, and he discovers how lonely, how miserably lonely and vulnerable he is. The case of Nat Turner in William Styron's *Confessions* is worth recalling here. Some aspects of the experience of Nat Turner bear interesting parallels to Othello's in many respects. First, there is the basic assumption, generally accepted by the white man, that the black man always longs for the white woman. As I have already suggested, Shakespeare implies that Othello's love is only skin deep. Nat Turner tells us in *The Confessions* how he secretly admired Emmeline, who offered him "quite unawares the rare glimpse, face to face, of her pure, proud, astonishing smooth-skinned beauty." He adds, rather significantly, "In later life, of course, I learned that an infatuation for a beautiful white mistress on the part of a black boy was not at all uncommon, despite the possibility of danger" (177). This feature in the black–white relationship informs Hugo's view that the African is invariably drawn toward the white woman just as darkness loves dawn.

There is another sense in which Nat Turner confirms Othello's experience. The encounter between black and white in an entirely white society invariably leads the black to self-knowledge, to tragic self-knowledge, to a knowledge of his vulnerability. Nat Turner underscores this point graphically, poignantly, when he tells us of the effect on him of Mcbride, the Irish overseer who epitomizes white authority:

> The appearance of his round, heavy face, uplifted to the sun in dreamy pleasure, sickens me inside, and I feel a sense of my weakness, my smallness, my defencelessness, my *niggerness* invading me like wind to the marrow of my bones. (151)

Othello and Nat Turner are both black, the one middle-aged and a distinguished general; the other thirty-one and highly favored for his smattering of learning and his mastery of the Bible. Both are successful in their different ways, but find out, too late, that mere success is not enough to protect them in their respective societies. Worse still, Nat Turner, encouraged by the Old Testament, seeks vengeance on those who have enslaved his race for centuries. He is deceived, and he and his band of rebels have to pay for it. Othello, too, is deceived into the belief that his military successes have made him a Venetian. Both of them misread their success stories; both discover in the end, their *niggerness*. And this leads to loneliness, humiliation, and death.

"At the Door of Truth":
The Hollowness of Signs in Othello

EDWARD WASHINGTON

E ven in this time of diverse, sophisticated, and politically progressive critical methodologies, Kenneth Burke's formalist statements (144, 149) remain a valuable guide for critics of *Othello* who wish to avoid the dubious conclusions that ensue from ill-premised racist ideology. In the first detailed account of racism's influence on *Othello* scholarship, Martin Orkin exposes and denounces the long tradition of racist discourse that pervades even the highest echelons of *Othello* criticism. Several scholars have since taken up the issue of race in *Othello* seemingly in response to Orkin's implicit challenge to critics to construct unbiased (that is, reliable if not precisely "objective") evaluations of the drama's racial dimensions. Although most of these more recent essays strive to establish critical positions that eschew hasty racial prejudgments, no reading of the play has yet emerged that fully sets forth the semantic complexity of Othello's blackness.[1] There are two reasons for this. First, *Othello*

---

1. See Neill, Loomba, Newman, Braxton, Dollimore, Berry, Cantor, and Bartels. These critics, however, almost invariably discuss the issue of race in *Othello* in conjunction with a "related" subject, such as colonialism, Renaissance ideologies of gender, sexual mores of the audience, and psychosocial functions of perversion. In *Othello* criticism, the introduction of such "larger"

scholarship has relied too heavily on historical and anthropological methodologies to explain the significance of Othello's blackness and has neglected available alternative meanings of blackness within the play.[2] Second, critics tend to evaluate Othello's motivations and actions from the delimiting (or delimited) gaze of the dominant white Venetian society, thereby precluding an unsentimentalized view of "the action as a whole" from Othello's perspective—that is, from the perspective of an "all sufficient" (IV.i.261) black figure ascribed a culturally marginal position by white "others." In the effort to address these two critical deficiencies, and to supply the interpretive lacuna regarding racial blackness in *Othello*, this essay will explore the relationship between the play's racial signifiers and the transmutations of convention in the text. More important, given the ways in which the authority of Shakespeare—and by extension that of his critics—continues to shape normative cultural values, this essay will also seek to determine the degree to which Shakespeare's *Othello* reconfigures, rather than confirms, conventional cultural stereotypes of blacks.

The difficulty in defining Othello's blackness as either a conventional or unconventional literary sign (or trope) is illustrated by the sharply varying opinions of critics who question its moral and aesthetic value. Thus, whereas Eldred Jones, Gwyn Williams, and Martin Orkin see Othello as admirable (that is, finally unstereotypical and unconventional) because of his intrinsic but tragically vulnerable honor and nobility, others such as Lemuel Johnson and Anthony Barthelemy see Othello's blackness as an artfully devised ironic mask, a black patina of virtue and nobility that obscures the more conventional meaning of the sign. And although cultural materialist Ania Loomba believes that Othello's "barbarity" is an "ideological construct" rather than a quality "natural" to blacks, she warns against glossing the faults in Othello that do in fact uphold insidious racial stereotypes. This variety of critical opinion leaves unresolved the question of whether blackness in *Othello* is good or evil, literal or symbolic, conventional or unconventional, stereotypical or typically human. As Elliot Tokson laments:

---

issues tends to obfuscate rather than reveal fully the complexities of racial blackness in the play. In this regard, Loomba, Berry, and Bartels are more focused, and many areas of agreement exist between their arguments and my own.

2. Leah Marcus has outlined the essential problem of historical analyses of Shakespeare as follows: "What we call Shakespeare is somehow mysteriously different, impervious to history at the level of specific factual data, the day to day chronicling of events" (xi). See also Graham Holderness.

Arguments have been raised both for and against the view of Othello as a noble Moor ... and the problem of that nobility—or barbarism—unavoidably has turned attention to the question of Shakespeare's racial tolerance or bigotry. Some critics believe that Shakespeare was uninterested in the racial aspects of the tragic situation altogether while others hold that Shakespeare was so deeply concerned with Othello's blackness that to miss that theme is to miss the heart of the play. ... Whether Shakespeare's imagination probed more deeply than any other writer of this period into the possibilities of the black man, or whether he basically followed the stereotyped pattern on which he traced the outline of Othello's character, or whether he combined popular notions with original perspective are gritty questions that one could more fruitfully pursue were there available some suitable materials with which *Othello* could be compared. (xi)

Tokson's frustration with the inconclusiveness of meaning inherent in Othello's blackness is, however, exactly the point: that is, the ambiguous mixture of virtues and deficiencies in Othello is what makes him both more mimetically "human," and tragically complex. This is not to suggest (as many have) that Othello's blackness is simply incidental (or coincidental) to the "larger" meanings in the play. On the contrary, although Othello's blackness is not a one-dimensional emblematic signifier, it does represent an essential element in his dramatic characterization—like Richard III's deformity, Shylock's "Jewishness," Falstaff's rotundity, or Lear's age. That is, blackness in Othello's character provides the rationale for why he thinks and acts the way he does in the given dramatic context.

I

Bernard Spivack, Mark Rose, and Howard Felperin (among others) draw attention to a metaphorical relationship that exists between the play's dramatic realities regarding race and the play's dramatization of blackness as an unconventional Shakespearean literary emblem. They see *Othello* as a struggle between two traditional literary genres—(chivalric) romance and morality drama—each vying with the other for ascendancy in the play.[3] To the extent that Othello knows his "cues" and can play

---

3. Spivack examines the play in relation to morality drama allegory; Rose presents

his part "without a prompter" (I.iii.82–83), he would have us see the play as a romance: more particularly, I would argue, as his version of the romantic fairy tale "Beauty and the Beast." In this tale, Othello plays the part of the black prince, once thought to be beastly, but whose true beauty is revealed through the love of the fair woman whom he marries. Iago, on the other hand, in his role as playwright or stage director, prefers to have us see the play as a morality drama, with himself in the role of Chief Vice. Through deceit and innuendo, Iago seeks to destroy Othello's romance by turning the virtue of the would-be fairy tale into the pitch of tragedy. Taken together, Iago's lies and innuendos make up a false story, a parallel second plot that constitutes a morality drama test for the Beauty and Beast of Othello's plot. As the author of this false second story, Iago strongly resembles the dark tempter Archimago in Spenser's *Faerie Queene*. Like Archimago, Iago deceives his victim into believing that his love has been unfaithful to him. Like Archimago, Iago also achieves his goal by deluding his victim with falsehoods so realistic that the false seems truer than the true. Like the Redcrosse Knight, once Othello is taken in by these potent lies, he loses faith in real love.[4]

In the balance of the struggle between Iago and Othello hangs not only the play's tragic outcome but also the fate of the image that Othello has carefully built up of himself. That is, depending on the outcome of the struggle, Othello's reputation as an "all-sufficient" black soldier will be either furthered or destroyed. Similarly, on the level of metadrama, Othello's (or Shakespeare's) poetic image of unconventional black beauty either will be confirmed through romance or, should Iago prevail, will revert (as many critics argue it does) to stereotypical definitions of beastly blackness.

II

In spite of Othello's relatively secure situation in Venice, his role in the drama is circumscribed (more than has been generally recognized) by the social realities of race-centered marginalization, or racism. This racism

---

a convincing case for his view of *Othello* as a chivalric romance; and more broadly, Felperin asserts that several literary forms (morality drama and romance inclusive) are showcased in *Othello*—varied forms that ensue from the tendency of most of the characters to present, and represent, themselves in an array of conventional literary roles. Most recently, Paul Cantor has described the play as a "generic . . . displacement . . . [of] martial epic . . . into Italian bedroom comedy" (297).

4. Rose cites this analogy (295).

is not always overt (Othello is held in high regard by many); rather it is most often a latent and muted hatred of blackness that surfaces suddenly with vituperative and sometimes destructive force, with or without the necessity of demonstrably "Moorish" behavior by Othello. For example, throughout the play, Emilia either implies or states outright that Othello is unfit for Desdemona because of his blackness; Roderigo glosses over his own unsuitability for Desdemona by denigrating Othello as "the thick lips" or the "gross . . . lascivious Moor" (I.i.66, 126). Iago of course claims to hate the Moor for particular and perhaps for general reasons, and it is significant that he (and Roderigo) incite the ire of Brabantio, the "good" (that is, white) citizen and cheated father, by resorting to race-baiting.

Brabantio himself reflects most sharply the quite real and unpredictable nature of antiblackness in Venice, dangerous even to a black figure as well-situated as Othello. Having once been the charitable host to Othello, Brabantio suddenly becomes not simply a wounded father who has lost his daughter to an "unlawful" suitor but a racist demagogue who would brand Othello a conjuring black witch, to be imprisoned (and burned at the stake, we might imagine, should the accusations be sustained). Thus, although Othello has found some acceptance in Venice, his blackness is nevertheless susceptible to the dangers of white racism that erupt when he transgresses Venetian definitions of racial acceptability.

Although recent critics have begun to acknowledge the role of racism in the play, few have pursued in much depth the degree to which the play shows Othello himself to be keenly aware of forces that stand ready to reject his blackness at the least provocation. It is unlikely that Othello could have achieved the success he has over a period of years without being cognizant of the latent (and overt) racism in society. Despite the fair number of critics who maintain that Othello's tragedy results from his being an outsider in Venice, one wonders how Othello could have not only survived but thrived here, without having understood a good deal about this society's dangerous racial waters. I would suggest that Othello has survived Venice's latent racism by cultivating a reputation and respect strong enough to hold back the tide of antiblackness. The bedrock of this reputation is, of course, military prowess, but Othello is no mere brute soldier. He has the charisma of a commander, and he emphasizes the ceremonial aspects, the pomp and circumstance of the position he holds. But more than this, Othello has established himself socially in Venice: he is well liked, much respected, and welcomed into the homes of Venetian aristocrats like Brabantio. He inspires so much respect in fact that he is able to defuse, without much effort, the racial protest against a marriage that few dominant groups would allow to an outsider. (Even the Jewess Jessica in *The Merchant of Venice* must turn Christian in order to marry Lorenzo.)

Othello achieves this acceptance by his politic behavior. We see it in his conduct of military affairs: in the selection of the highly regarded Cassio as his lieutenant; in the way he halts the impending clash on the streets of Venice; in the "full liberty" he grants his men after the defeat of the Turks (and before they begin their new duties in Cyprus). We also see it in Othello's judicious handling of Cassio's drunken brawling on the island: Othello demotes Cassio, not because he believes him unworthy but rather to "make . . . an example" (II.iii.242) of him to the other soldiers. (As Iago says, the demotion is "a punishment more in policy than in malice" [II.iii.265–66]). We see it again in his timely reminders to Venice of how much it has benefited from his military service. Othello's politic abilities are not limited to war matters, however; in social situations, too, he uses his intelligence and his grandiloquence (G. Wilson Knight's "Othello music") in a manner that serves to distance him from conventional white notions of blacks as barbarians and beasts.[5] More than being simply articulate and sonorous, Othello is a consummate storyteller whose tales impress not only Desdemona but even the Duke, who observes that Othello's story "would win [his] daughter too" (I.iii.171). Othello's wondrous stories invariably draw attention to his stellar accomplishments—but in addition to presenting images of all sufficiency, they are infused with a pathos that gains him generous sympathy and tolerance from the Venetians.

There are times also when Othello goes to great lengths to efface himself, ingratiate himself, and evoke pity. Many critics have argued that Othello's excessive deference to the Venetians denotes a callow disavowal

---

5. The idea that Othello's way with words, his "music," is related to issues of race in the play would seem to be confirmed by *New York Times* editor Brent Staples, in his essay "Black Men in Public Space." In this essay, Staples discusses the problems of "image" encountered by people of color in U.S. cities today. He says: "Over the years, I learned to smother the rage I felt at so often being taken for a criminal. Not to do so would surely have led to madness. I now take precautions to make myself less threatening. [For example] I whistle melodies from Beethoven and Vivaldi and the more popular classical composers. Even steely New Yorkers hunching toward nighttime destinations seem to relax, and occasionally they even join in the tune. Virtually everybody seems to sense that a mugger wouldn't be warbling bright, sunny selections from Vivaldi's Four Seasons." Staples's frequently anthologized essay first appeared in *Ms.* magazine, September 1986.

of his identity as a black outsider, and that this naivete about his "place" as a black in Venice explains why he is so easily duped by the lies of a "true" Venetian like Iago. This view of Othello leads Anthony Barthelemy to conclude that Othello, as a Shakespearean black character, "never possesses the power or desire to subvert civic and natural order" (161).

To this charge of co-optation or "Uncle Tomism" in Othello, I would respond that Othello uses ingratiation, purposely, to smooth his way in a racist Venice. His intent is to achieve success and humanization for his blackness in moderate fashion. Othello's mode of achieving change differeniates him from Aaron, who would avoid racial conflict by leaving Rome to return "home"; from the "dark lady," who seemingly never appears in public with her white lover; and from Caliban, who attempts to raise violent revolt against his oppressors. Most simply, the choice between militancy or moderation in the need for change is endemic to all political contexts in which weaker forces struggle against those with more power. (In black–white race relations, the best example of this conflict is the militancy of Malcolm X and the moderation of Martin Luther King, Jr.) Hence, Othello has not forgotten that he is black, nor does he forget his cultural heritage or his history of enslavement. Rather he has taken a moderate course as he seeks to achieve personal success through the politic "humanization" of his blackness in Venice.

In a broader sense, Othello's deference to forces that have power over him is part of a larger issue of decorum and "place" in the play. That is, all the characters are very much concerned with their status in social hierarchies—whether in terms of public influence, like Brabantio; military rank, like Iago and Cassio; the proper place of fathers, daughters, wives, and "men"; or the proper "place" of a black in white Venice. Like Othello, the other characters are concerned with either maintaining their achieved "place" by any means they can or trying to improve their given status through some form of deference or ingratiation to those who have power to grant them what they seek. In one way or another, everyone has to be politic.

Thus, when Othello tells the Duke, "Rude am I in my speech . . . / And therefore little shall I grace my cause / In speaking for myself" (I.iii.81–89), we realize that this is far from true. And when Othello claims that "little of this great world can I speak / More than pertains to feats of broils and battles" (I.iii.86–87), we sense, likewise, that he exaggerates the extent to which his life has been "a flinty and steel couch of war" (I.iii.230). And after the bold fait accompli of his elopement with Desdemona, Othello is again politic—in deferring to the Duke's judgement, and by downplaying his sexual desires—thus refashioning the stereotype of blacks as lascivious beasts, which Iago and Roderigo have invoked to incite Brabantio (that is, the black ram tupping a white ewe). As Othello says:

> And heaven defend your good souls that you think
> I will your serious and great business scant,
> For she is with me; . . . no, when light-wing'd toys,
> And feather'd Cupid, foils with wanton dullness
> My speculative and active instruments,
> That my disports corrupt and taint my business,
> Let housewives make a skillet of my helm,
> And all indign and base adversities
> Make head against my estimation! (I.iii.266–74)

Although several critics have argued that these statements reveal the central patriarchal flaw in Othello's "love" for Desdemona, it seems to me that they are the finishing touches Othello gives to a muted image of black sexuality, an image that attempts to assuage conventional white fears of black lasciviousness.

This politic behavior determines, in part, Othello's unlikely marriage. Because Othello asks himself why he ever married (III.iii.246), we might presume that he had some reason for not marrying earlier. The most likely explanation for his extended bachelorhood is that the soldier's life has not allowed "skillets" to interfere with "service"; but it is interesting to speculate on the circumstances (beyond love) that lead him to marry this particular woman at this particular time, especially given the potential racial dangers of such a marriage.

After world travel, exploits, and wars, Othello has seemingly found a place for himself in Venice, even before his marriage to Desdemona. He is the Venetians' chief military officer; he speaks their language and is a Christian; he seems well connected socially and has loyal supporters; he has "fortunes" that revert to Venetian legal "relatives" on his death. Thus, despite his blackness, Othello is more integrated into the dominant community than are other Shakespearean black characters, and he is less socially isolated than Venice's own Shylock. Yet, although the cornerstone of black Othello's acceptance in Venice is his military indispensability, it is also true that this indispensability is subject to time. Being "no god" (III.iv.146), the strength of his mighty arm will decline as he ages—and Othello is already "getting older" at the start of the play. Thus, when we meet Othello, he is a man at the apex of his career and at a point in life where it would be plausible for him to be more open to the prospect of settling down. In this context, marriage to an admired and well-placed Venetian woman might bestow on him an ideal image of social (and human) sufficiency that would protect his blackness in Venice in his declining years.[6] This is not to suggest that Othello calculatingly directs his life toward this end, nor to doubt that he "loves the gentle Desdemona" (I.ii.25) as he says he does. Rather, the dramatic givens of the play—racism, Othello's age, and later, the correlation Othello sees between a successful marriage and a successful military "occupation"—simply emphasize the further advantages of his marriage to Desdemona at present.[7] As in "Beauty and the Beast," she will be the beautiful wife who will help to reveal the full humanity in Othello's blackness.

In the light of the discussion thus far, it is not surprising that Othello's concern for his image, especially in the context of his marriage, becomes the vulnerable spot that Iago attacks when he selects the marriage as the vehicle through which he will destroy the Moor.

III

The beginning of Act II presents an Othello who has defended himself in a judicious and politic manner against each racist charge leveled against him, an Othello at the high point of his powers. His facile victory over the Turks only further confirms the security of his place in Venice. At this point, Othello's romance seems "well-shipped" (II.i.47).

But Iago perseveres in his Vice-like effort to discredit the Moor and to transform this blithe romance into a dark morality drama. In seeking to turn Othello's unconventional virtue into conventional pitch, he applies jealousy, a potent morality drama temptation that might cause

---

6. Othello is not enfeebled; however, we may note that the play encourages us to accept the idea of aging as a motif of some consequence. We know that Othello contemplates his own "declin[e] / Into the vale of years" (III.iii.270) as a possible reason for Desdemona's ostensible unfaithfulness. More to the point is Iago's suggestion that no matter how faithful a man's service to the state, "when he's old" he is sure to be unceremoniously "cashier'd" (I.i.48).

7. Felperin sums up this line of argument succinctly: "As the living symbol of high Venetian culture, Desdemona is not simply a wife to Othello but the legitimating agent of his acculturation" (78). Peter Stallybrass states more simply: "Desdemona is the active agent of Othello's legitimization" (272).

anyone to miss a step. The jealousy that Iago grafts on Othello is, how-ever, simply the catalyst that brings to the fore a more prominent vul-nerability in Othello—a vulnerability of which not even Iago is fully aware and one that Othello can least defend himself against (as seems indicated by his swift, easy, and complete collapse): his fear of the loss of his image of "all in all" sufficiency in Venice. Thus, while the thought of Desdemona's unfaithfulness touches a raw nerve in Othello, it also raises the specter of a dashed opportunity (at a key point in his career) to preserve and even enhance the possibility of a safe and viable life in Venice—a city whose acceptance of blackness would seem to be contin-gent on his maintaining a flawless image of all-sufficiency.[8] Thus when Iago mounts his assault, the Moor loses rational control of a situation that, earlier in his life, he might have been able to control; or had Iago's evil not been quite so pernicious,[9] one he might have been able to ward off (as he does Brabantio's less potent challenge earlier on).

After what appear to have been years devoted to promoting an image of ideal blackness that allows him to claim his due and protect his place in Venice, Othello has, in fact, begun to reason and act on images of truth as if they were truth itself. His storytelling, for example, shows him using vivid and effective images of his past to win hearts and minds in Venice. These imagistic tales are essentially true but sound suspiciously similar to those titillatingly imagistic (but apocryphal) travel book stories so popular at the time. Even Othello's beautiful language is sprinkled with high-sounding neologisms (*provulgate, exsuffligate*) whose actual meaning and application are vague. Significantly, the things he cherishes most about his life as a soldier involve the outward trappings of war, the images of war rather than actual fighting:

> Farewell the plumed troop, and the big wars
> That makes ambition virtue; O farewell!
> Farewell the neighing steed, and the shrill trump,

---

8. It should be underscored again that, although Othello's preoccupation with im-age makes him more vulnerable to Iago's lies, this vulnerability should not be construed as an attribute of "blackness" that confirms him to be a stereotypical racial emblem. Like other somewhat less than ideal qualities in Othello, the Moor's anxious concern to be seen as all-sufficient derives largely from his desire to achieve his deserved place in Venice: to defend himself against a race-based antiblackness that would deny him his just rewards.

9. The play encourages us to equate Othello's vulnerability to Iago's lies with Cassio's susceptibility to wine. Hence, like Cassio, Othello is imbued with a poisonous force powerful enough to swiftly and completely bring about the destruction of his better self and give rein to his weaknesses and fallibilities.

The spirit-stirring drum, the ear-piercing fife;
The royal banner and all quality,
Pride, pomp, and circumstance of glorious war! (III.iii.355–60)

Ironically, there is a vast discrepancy between the image and the reality—between Othello's gestures and the fact that there is little or no concrete action to back them up. Othello helps to keep the peace in Venice ("Keep up your bright swords, for the dew will rust'em" [I.ii.58–59]), but no fighting actually occurs. In the ensuing sea battle with the Turks, strangely, a storm sinks the enemy ships, and Othello receives accolades wihout having fired a shot. Othello's scapegoating of Cassio on Cyprus saves him from having to "lift [his] arm" (II.iii.199) to quell further quarrels among his men.

The same dearth of substantive action prevails in situations occurring after Iago's lies about Desdemona have begun. For instance, the Moor's menacing threats against Iago in Act III and Emilia in Act V fall flat, as Iago slithers to safety and Emilia proclaims, "Thou hast not half the power to do me harm as I have to be hurt" (V.ii.163–64). Othello invokes black vengeance against Cassio but shuffles the job off onto Iago, and in the end, he sees the murder attempt fail. He is disarmed by Montano, and his final avenging lunge at Iago is ineffective. The only person he is physically violent with is Desdemona—and as Lodovico says, violence against a woman is not valorous. Othello does manage to take his own life—but this represents less an act of warlike power than the supreme gesture of powerlessness.[10]

The same empty gestures mark Othello's sexual power in the play. That is, despite all the talk about sexuality in *Othello*, there is little of it in the relationship between Othello and Desdemona. Although I disagree with those who suggest that Othello and Desdemona never consummate their marriage, the dramatic action of the play is orchestrated in a way that suggests that the couple's private time together suffers constant interruption. And after Iago's lies, sexual relations between the two seem simply unlikely. Also, although little reason exists to doubt that Othello loves Desdemona, many have noted how Othello often speaks of her in idealized Petrarchan terms—revealing his sense of her as a wonderful

---

10. The absence of concrete military power in Othello might be seen to further confirm his need to look ahead to a time when he would no longer be able to sustain his ideal soldier's image: a good marriage would be a hedge against any resulting loss of place in Venice.

"image" of womanhood rather than as a real woman to love. Thus, for Othello, Desdemona appears a "rose," a "perfect chrysolite," a "pearl" with skin as "white as snow" and as "smooth as alabaster"; his "soul's joy" to whom he would "deny nothing."

Given this tendency to objectify Desdemona as an "image" of beauty, and the way in which the play obscures real sexuality between them, Othello's reactions to Desdemona in the bedchamber scene just prior to her murder not only raise questions concerning his sexual power but also accentuate what lies at the heart of Othello's susceptibility to Iago's evil: his general propensity to treat abstract images as concrete realities. When Othello contemplates the sleeping Desdemona, with genuine ardor he murmurs words of Petrarchan praise and love. Then, when she wakens and invites him to bed, offering him, it seems, an opportunity to give his romance story a happy ending after all, the prospect of an enlivened and desirous Desdemona (as opposed to an alabaster figure) disorients Othello, and he draws back from the prospect of love made concrete and actual. Although it is easy enough to see Othello's withdrawal as the steeling of his resolve to carry out the execution, it also seems clear that it is not within the scope of his capabilities to move beyond an imagined view of love to its concrete reality. At the very end of the play, we do find Othello and Desdemona lying together on the bed; but the lifeless bodies only underscore the lost potential for real love—and even this final image of unity is disrupted by the presence of Emilia lying beside them.

IV

Othello's too-strong dependence on gestures and images—his taking them for truth—is the Achilles heel Iago exploits. Such gestures include the false images of Cassio's nonexistent dream, the misrepresenting dumb show of Cassio's cuckolding brag, and generally speaking, all circumstantial signs "which lead . . . to the door of truth" (III.iii.412–13). This dependence on image prevents Othello from seeing that the white antagonism he would defend himself against has undergone a change for the better—perhaps due to his own influence. That is, even with its dangers, Othello's Venice is not the antiblack and antilife "wilderness of tigers" that Aaron contends with in Titus's Rome; even the Venetians in *The Merchant of Venice* are more superciliously intolerant of cultural others, among them Moroccan princes and rich Jews, than is the case in *Othello*.

In fact, given Renaissance England's and Renaissance drama's image of Italian cities as hotbeds of intrigue and sin, all in all, Othello's Venice seems remarkably civilized. This is not to suggest that Venetian society is ideal; however, in key ways, it is more tolerant and accepting of Othello than he realizes. Othello's inability to perceive this, however, makes it impossible for him to read the signs of hope that exist for him in Venice— positive signs that would allow him to resist the fearful images of lost love, lost marriage and lost occupation, painted by Iago.

The leaders of the State indicate this change and hope. They ferret out the truth and have a clear sense of justice—traits that bode well for a black man wary of racist stereotypes, assumptions, and prejudgments by whites. The best examples of the State's pursuit of truth occur during the War Room scene in Act I. The Duke and several other leaders receive a flurry of confusing and conflicting reports about the strength and strategy of the enemy Turks. Obviously, these false reports foreshadow the seemingly true falsehoods that Iago will unleash on Othello during the course of the play. Through patience and good judgment, however, the Venetian leaders uncover the truth about the Turks, seeing through the false report of Angelo, one who, like Iago, should be "honest" but is not. Later, the State, through the Duke, challenges and dismisses Brabantio's accusations against Othello as "thin habits and poor likelihoods" (I.iii.108) and finally adjudges Othello a suitable husband for Desdemona. Further, no leader in the State denigrates Othello; and even when the truth of Othello's crime is known, Lodovico responds more in sorrow than in anger.

Corroborating and extending the idea that these Venetians are more unconventionally accepting of Othello's blackness than he realizes are the suggestions that Othello is not the only "outsider" in Venice, a remarkably healthy political and religious state whose power and success derive from cultural heterogeneity rather than from narrow ethnocentrism. This sense of Venice as an expansive, inclusive, and fluid society comes to us in part from the many references to people, places, and things that originate outside the city's ethnic and geographical boundaries but that, nevertheless, seem integral to Venetian life and perspective. The characters, for example, allude to crusadoes, carracks, guineas, coloquintidas, and Spanish swords; they have some knowledge of monkeys, baboons, aspics, crocodiles, locusts, and Barbary horses; they have been to or know about Aleppo, Rhodes, Cyprus, Egypt, Mauritania (and Moors). Cited also are the Pontic, the Propontic, and the Hellespont, as well as

England, Denmark, Germany, Holland, Rome, Sparta, and Verona. Venetian men are said to be partial to "foreign laps" (IV.iii.88), and the Venetian women would proverbially "walk barefoot to Palestine" (IV.iii.38–39) to find a good husband. All of these references connote a sense of cultural and geographic expansiveness. Then too, there is the well-known passage in which Emilia speaks to Desdemona at length about what she would do to gain "all the world": the "huge thing" of "great price" that she would risk "purgatory for" if she could have it for her labor (IV.iii.65–75). Even here, Emilia's reference serves as the culminating epiphany to over thirty allusions to the "world" in this play— from Brabantio who wants to be judged by "the world" (I.ii.72) if his accusation of Othello is false, to Iago's desire to bring his monstrous evil "to the world's light" (I.iii.402), to the Clown who would "catechize the world" (III.iv.13) to find Cassio.

Admittedly, other Shakespearean plays allude to places outside of the immediate dramatic setting. In *Othello*, however, the Venetians are construed to be the leaders of a group of Christian "others" who join together to oppose, not non-Venetians, but rather nonbelievers—in this case the infidel Turks: Florentines, like Cassio; Greeks, like Marcus Luccicios; Cypriots, who are old friends; black Moors "of here and everywhere" (I.i.137) like Othello. In fact, as Venice's field general, it is Othello's "occupation" to unite Florentines, Greeks, Cypriots, and Venetians alike under the Christian banner of the Venetian State and to serve the State in places like Aleppo, Rhodes, Cyprus, and Mauritania.

This general acceptance of heterogeneity and of the Other is particularized in Desdemona. She is the center of moral rightness and truth in the play,[11] and it follows that her views on blackness provide the best instruction regarding its meaning in the play. At the beginning of the drama, we are told that Desdemona's love for Othello derives from having seen "his visage

---

11. Despite Desdemona's Christian intention to mend evil with good, and her Christ-like sacrifice at the end, many critics have found fault with her as the voice of right reason in the play. Some have judged her to be a weak white foil who exists only for the purpose of dramatizing the black deeds of men; others have seen her as a beautiful, but naive and wayward romantic who wanders into dark and forbidden waters; still others have claimed that her Christ-like forgiveness of Othello is so ideal that it unfits her as a true sounding board for meaning in a mature Shakespearean tragedy. Notwithstanding these criticisms, Desdemona is the beacon of moral rightness in *Othello*, and her viability in this role is sustained in part by the fact that she is not the stock good angel of a morality drama or fairy-tale romance. That is, Desdemona is as prone to error and flaw as any character in the play; but, to a greater degree than all other characters, she has the ability to adapt and grow, and ultimately, through love and faith, to find out truth.

in his mind" (I.iii.252), thereby rendering Othello's racial blackness a moot issue in her affections for him. In Act III, after Desdemona discovers that she has misplaced the handkerchief, Emilia asks her if the Moor is jealous. Desdemona replies, "Who, he? I think the sun where he was born / Drew all such humours from him" (III.iv.26–27). Here, not only does Desdemona reject the conventional stereotype of black jealousy, but her speculation that Africa's hot climate is actually beneficial opposes the standard Renaissance view of Africa as the "foul furnace"[12] that turned Africans into hellish black devils. Futhermore, in a play that so earnestly questions whether the "best" women in a society ought not to marry their own kind, it is significant that, even after she has been called a "whore" and struck in public, Desdemona asserts that Othello's "[u]nkindness may do much, / And his unkindness may defeat my life, / But never taint my love" (IV.ii.161–63). When Desdemona affirms her love for Othello despite his behavior, the figurative sense of "unkind" as "unnatural" and thus "racially different" is heard as well, and Desdemona vows that—no matter what Othello has done, or why—she will not capitulate to the temptation to scapegoat his racial Otherness.

The idea of Othello's Venice as a heterogeneous state (and therefore more accepting of Othello than he realizes) is nevertheless confused by the racism and ethnocentrism that Iago advances in order to create a larger "place" or status for himself at the expense of an outsider. Moreover, although Roderigo, Brabantio, and (to a lesser degree) Emilia also foster racial divisiveness, these Venetians are as much under Iago's spell as Othello or Cassio.[13] It is Iago who sabotages the friendship, camaraderie, and love that has developed around, or in spite of, difference. He helps to poison the friendship between Brabantio and Othello and between Othello and Cassio; he tries to divide Cassio and Montano, the respective lieutenants of the newly combined Venetian and Cypriot forces. Most important, he poisons the love between Othello and Desdemona, in part by emphasizing their differences:

> Not to affect many proposed matches,
> Of her own clime, complexion and degree,

---

12. See Chapter 1 of E. Jones and pages 433–42 of Bartels for fuller treatments of sixteenth-century England's view of Africa.

13. In addition to hoodwinking both Othello and Cassio, Iago exploits Roderigo's desire for Desdemona and her "full fortune," Brabantio's paternal possessiveness, and Emilia's love for him.

Whereto we see in all things nature tends;
Fie, we may smell in such a will most rank,
Foul disproportion; thoughts unnatural.
. . . .
I may fear
Her will, recoiling to her better judgment,
May fall to match you with her country forms,
And happily repent. (III.iii.233–37; 239–42)

In general then, Iago seeks to turn fathers against daughters, husbands against wives, men against women, whites against blacks, and ultimately a heterogeneous Venetian society against itself.

Despite Iago's antiblackness, the play itself intentionally undercuts blackness as a signifier of evil by investing the white characters (even the more likable ones) with traits that are dark and sinister: Brabantio is exposed as a hypocrite and a racist; Roderigo is a fortune-hunter, a racist, and a would-be murderer; Emilia's loyalty and egalitarianism are diametrically counterposed by her slavishness, her deceit, and her bigotry; the suave Cassio has a nasty temper and a coarse side to his view of women. Even Desdemona seems to sway in the wrong direction when she attempts to redress Othello's demotion of Cassio. And Iago, of course, epitomizes the play's conversion of white to black as he plays the part of a Renaissance white devil. But the character who best exemplifies how the play transmutes the conventional meanings of black and white in *Othello* is Bianca.

Giving the name *Bianca* (that is, *white* in Italian) to a relatively substantial character in a play with a major black character is highly suggestive. As the character signifying whiteness, Bianca should, according to convention, be an ideal Petrarchan woman—which she is not. Yet, confusingly, a further reversal in Bianca's unconventionally "evil" whiteness occurs when she is said to be a whore in order to obtain the essentials of "bread and clothes" (IV.i.95). Also, in a play so obsessed with fidelity, Bianca loves but one man (although her profession gives her license to "love" many [IV.i.97]), and like Desdemona with Othello, she remains devoted to Cassio despite his ill-treatment of her.

But Bianca's most positive aspect is her implied rejection of Iago's hypocrisy and falsehood. At the end of Act IV, she rebels against Iago's and Emilia's efforts to bewhore her and to implicate her falsely in the wounding of Cassio. Even more significant is Bianca's earlier refusal to make a copy of Desdemona's stolen handkerchief: in refusing to fall in line with Iago's surreptitious effort to create a second (morality drama) story of infidelity with the handkerchief, she refuses to fabricate a false signifier of Othello's and Desdemona's romance. Moreover, in declining to "take out the work" (that is, destroy through replication) of the true love token (IV.i.153), Bianca is the first to reject outright Iago's evil designs. Her defiance signals a major turning point in the play, the point where other manipulated characters begin to throw off Iago's influence, thus bringing his plot to light.

The point here is that the conventional forms of antiblackness in this play occur almost exclusively in the context of Iago's fabrications about Othello and Desdemona. The racist sentiments in the play are uttered either by Iago or by characters over whom he has gained power through an exploitation of their frailties. As such, Iago spins an Archimago-like illusion of racial intolerance that distorts a truer (though certainly not perfect) reality of Venice that Othello does not discern.

V

Despite any sympathy we might have for Othello's need to foster an ideal black image in Venice, and despite our awareness of Iago's potent malignity, Othello remains culpable. Although his culpability ensues neither from his emblematic blackness nor (up to a point) from his "human" susceptibility to error and sin, Othello may be held accountable for his failure to read and understand the unconventional signs of hope in Venice that could have allowed him to see through Iago's false images.

In a sense, the question of Othello's culpability ought to be resolved when he realizes that he has foolishly killed a faithful wife, and seeing his error, embarks on what appears to be a reconciling course of tragic resolution. With good tragic form, Othello confesses his mistakes and then takes his own life in order to atone for his tragic folly. Thus, although Othello fails in his attempt to remake "Beauty and the Beast," he does manage to rework his part to fit that of the hero in a tragic romance ("I will kill thee, / And love thee after" [V.ii.18–19]). After all, to die by one's own hand while in the arms of one's slain lover is the stuff of tragic romance in *Romeo and Juliet* and *Antony and Cleopatra*. The point, however, is that although Othello realizes that he has mistakenly killed a faithful wife, and that a scheming ensign has gulled him, he never recognizes how his own too-strong dependence on images has contributed to the crime he has committed. This lack of recognition reveals his inability, even at the end, to see the whole truth. Thus, Othello's noble reconciliation at the end of the play is more ambiguous than it initially appears, and there is much in Othello's last words and deed to suggest that the image of blackness in this play is not redeemed.

For example, something seems awry in Othello's perception of reality when he describes Montano, the soldier who has disarmed him, as a "puny whipster" (V.ii.245). He understates the soldierly abilities of Montano and overstates his own capabilities. Some lines later, he seems to come to terms with his actual powerlessness when he admits that his threat against Gratiano is but a "vain boast" (V.ii.265). Yet it is disquieting that Othello should define his lost power as his inability to "control . . . fate" (V.ii.266), since he is at least partly to blame in the death of Desdemona. Othello cannot have fully come to terms with his own failings if he can refer to the Desdemona he has murdered as an "ill-starr'd wench" (V.ii.273). Just a few lines further, Othello asserts that Desdemona's faultless spirit "will hurl [his] soul from heaven, / And fiends will snatch at it" (V.ii.275–76); but despite his genuine anguish, he again misses the point when he fails to acknowledge not only Desdemona's commitment to their conjugal love but also the forgiveness and redemption she offers when she assumes responsibility for his crime.

The most telling instances of ambiguity concerning Othello's redeemed vision occur in his very last speech. Although the tone of Othello's once again noble words is lofty, the words themselves raise many questions about the clarity of Othello's vision and his motivations at the end. That is, although Othello claims to be heart-stricken over the senseless loss of the woman he loves, he begins his final speech with, "Soft you, a word or two . . . / I have done the state some service, and they know't" (V.ii.339–40). We have seen how Othello has used this ploy, understandably but manipulatively, to defend his ideal black image from racist attacks; but here, Othello's reinvocation of an earlier politic defensiveness seems uncontritely self-serving and unredeemingly out of place, not only in the light of his contrition but also in the light of his culpability in Desdemona's death.

Shortly thereafter Othello almost literally spells out how his part in recent events should be represented, in writing, to the Venetian State. As he has done in the past, Othello idealizes the image of himself that he would have Venice remember. When he tells Lodovico to "speak of my deeds as they are; nothing extenuate" (V.ii.343), he should mean, "Don't spare the awful truth"—but he probably does not. Further, in instructing Lodovico not to "set down aught in malice" (V.ii.344), Othello seems to say, "Don't tone down anything about me (for I am great of heart), but also, don't say anything that suggests that you don't approve of me." Othello thus asks us to keep our image of him not only grand but also uncritical—for his errors are but the consequence of "unlucky deeds" (V.ii.342). He goes on to fashion his future storied image of himself as "one that lov'd not wisely, but too well: / Of one not easily jealous" (V.ii.345–46). But is he completely truthful when he claims to have loved Desdemona "too well"? Did he love her so well that he judged her guilty on evidence that even Iago called circumstantial? Did he love her too well when he denied her the right to prove herself innocent? Can we ever accept his view that in killing Desdemona quickly he has somehow been "merciful" (V.ii.88)? And can we accept, without question or qualification, his assertion that he is not easily jealous in the absence of all resistance on his part against the lies of Iago? To raise such questions is to deny neither Othello's love for Desdemona nor the pernicious evil of Iago, but rather to gauge the degree to which Othello fully sees, understands, admits to, and mends the weaknesses within himself that have allowed Iago to bring forth the hideous scene that lies before him.

In short, the other characters in *Othello* come to terms with the truth, confess their disastrous errors, and go on to gain either real or symbolic salvation. Although Othello appears to undergo a similar process, his continued posturing prompts us to question whether he has recognized how his dependence on image has contributed to the tragic events—and in turn, to wonder if in fact he redeems himself with his dramatic self-sacrifice. In questioning the soundness of Othello's tragic resolution, we must also question whether he has seen the avenues of hope before him that might have saved his wife, his life, and his soul in Venice. That is, has Othello understood that Desdemona accepted him, loved him, and then saved him with her forgiveness? Does Othello (despite his error) see the possibility of redemptive vindication at the hands of a clear-sighted, just, and tolerant white Venetian state? And, in the context of the play as a morality drama, has Othello faith enough to believe that he will receive grace despite his earthy trials and sins?

VI

The last half of Othello's last speech is an imagistic travelogue of his sojourns culminating in his story of the slaughtered infidel. Othello then transposes the image of the slain infidel into a metaphorical image that represents his own faithlessness and penitent suicide. Putting a knife to his own throat is Othello's last grand gesture. Yet Gratiano startles us with his deflating observation that Othello's ostensibly noble and redeeming act mars "all that's spoke" (V.ii.358).

In the context of morality drama, Othello's suicide (especially with the signs of change and hope in Venice) denotes his capitulation to the last and most subtle deception of Vice—despair—the hopelessness that blinds one to the grace of God. Hence, at the end of the play, we find Othello to be in much the same predicament as Spenser's Redcrosse as he nears the end of his trials. Like Othello, the image-bound Redcrosse struggles with his fiend in an effort to come to terms with his lack of faith in a faithful woman. Having seen his errors, Redcrosse, like Othello, would redress his sins by doing away with himself at knifepoint:

> [The fiend] to [Redcrosse] raught a dagger sharpe and keene,
> And gave it him in hand: his hand did quake,
> And tremble like a leafe of Aspin greene,
> And troubled bloud through his pale face was seene
> To come, and goe with tydings from the hart,
> As it a running messenger had beene.
> At last resolved to worke his finall smart
> He lifted up his hand, that backe againe did start. (I.ix.51)

But unlike Othello, in the end, Redcrosse remains open to the truth of Una's love and forgiveness and God's grace—and pulls back from the pit to gain his salvation:

> "Come, come away, fraile, feeble, fleshly wight,
> Ne let vaine words bewitch thy manly hart,
> Ne divelish thoughts dismay thy constant spright.
> In heavenly mercies hast thou not a part?
> Why shouldst thou then despeire, that chosen art?
> Where justice growes, there grows eke greater grace,
> The which doth quench the brond of hellish smart,
> And accurst hand-writing doth deface.
> Arise, Sir knight arise, and leave this cursed place."

. . . .
So up he rose, and thence amounted streight. (I.ix.53; 54)

The trials of Redcrosse reflect the trials of morality drama protagonists generally; and to the degree that *Othello* is a play that incorporates the form and substance of morality drama, Othello's attempt to redeem himself through an otherwise noble suicide inadvertently leads him directly into the clutches of a hellish Vice. Thus, in the metadramatic struggle between genres, morality drama bests romance; for as Lodovico observes to Iago as the curtain is closed on the tragic bed, "[T]his is thy work" (V.ii.365).

My argument is that Othello's dependence on image at the expense of truth, reality, and hope (what the play calls "matter") is the "cause" of his downfall. More specifically, in the context of race, Othello continues to view his salvation in terms of his ability to build and live up to an ideal image—as valiant soldier, as fairy-tale husband, as the hero of a tragic romance—in order to redeem the integrity of his black humanity from denigration at the hands of conventionally hostile white "critics" (II.i.119) like Iago (or even those cited by Orkin). In this context of black survival, Othello's aims are fatal but not ignoble; consequently, his fall is more dramatically tragic than stereotypically evil—especially because the black image he strives to protect has found some measure of acceptance in Venice.

Devouring Discourses: Desire and Seduction in Othello

LUCILLE P. FULTZ

n her "Introduction" to *Othello: New Perspectives*, Virginia Mason Vaughan delineates the genealogy of *Othello* criticism, which according to her, "remained . . . a bastion of formalism and psychological analysis" well into the 1980s (13). Prior to this period, according to Vaughan, *Othello* critics were concerned with issues of textual history and authority, while debates swirled around issues of definitive editions and textual conflations. Vaughan maps the movement of criticism from controversies surrounding "which version was better" or "closer to Shakespeare's original text" to analyses of patterns of language and imagery, symbolism, and psychological motivations of characters. A major turning point in *Othello* criticism occurred in the 1980s with a shift toward feminist critique, deconstruction, and performance (14–18). Georgianna Ziegler, speaking of *Hamlet* criticism, contends that "in every age Shakespeare's text[s] [have] been subjected to the interests and the view of that generation" (1), and Jean E. Howard observes, "[W]e need more new readings of Shakespeare: readings which continue to bring to bear on these plays the human concerns which press on us now" (145). This is particularly applicable to *Othello* at present.

My own critique of *Othello* is situated in a postmodern moment that foregrounds discursivity as constitutive of the self and the worlds the self inhabits. Such a reading seeks to expose Iago's desire to locate power in discourse, a power that ultimately leads to Desdemona's murder and Othello's suicide. In other words, this study examines the ways in which Iago discursively problematizes Othello's marriage to Desdemona. To this end, Iago engages in what Michael Neill terms an "operation . . . principally aimed at converting the absent/present bed into a locus of imagined adultery by producing Othello's abduction of Desdemona as an act of racial adulteration" (391). Iago's campaign against the marriage begins in the opening scene and continues until he has ensnared Othello into his trap of "racial adulteration" by convincing him that Desdemona is unfaithful to him mainly because of his race. By opening the play with Iago's base commentary on Othello's marriage, Shakespeare foregrounds marriage as the thematic and discursive issue in the play. Commenting on Iago's influence and Othello's vulnerability as an alien in Venice, G. M. Matthews contends that despite his physical and cultural difference, Othello is "a great human being who . . . recognizes (within the limits of his social role) only universal humane values of love and loyalty," which he loses once he allows himself to become "vulnerable to irrational, unhuman forces, embodied in Iago" (123).

Othello offers an expansive view of the ways in which language works against certain speakers and is twisted and perverted in the mouth of a dishonest practitioner. By playing on the ambiguities and ironies inherent in language, Iago is able to use the seductive dimensons of discourse to achieve diabolical ends. Through a consciously selective use of language, Iago distorts reality and manipulates others so that they unwittingly play into his hands. In short, Iago listens for the spaces and slippages in discourse in order to play upon latent and manifest fears. As Kenneth Burke observes, "Iago, to arouse Othello, must talk a language that Othello knows as well as he, a language implicit in the nature of Othello's love as the idealization of his private property in Desdemona." Although Iago's language is the "dialectical opposite of Othello's," Burke continues, "it so thoroughly shares a common ground with Othello's language that its insinuations are never for one moment irrelevant to Othello's thinking" (414). Ultimately, Iago's double discourse destroys Othello and Desdemona by distorting their love and their most intimate relationship. I wish to argue that by analyzing Iago's control and manipulation of discourse, we can better understand Othello's downfall.

Othello is at one level a dramatization of the mechanism and failure of language, a dialectic between reality and "invention." Iago's diabolical, insatiable desire, bounded only by Desdemona's death, moves within a socially established discourse that feeds on itself and devours other discourses in its wake. Language in *Othello* is, then, not merely a dramatic vehicle or tool; language is the element of thematic concern. Language confirms, indicts, and convicts.

The marriage of Othello and Desdemona, with which the play opens, seems to suggest that deeply entrenched prejudices—suspiciousness of other races and cultures, of those who are "alien" and do not seem to belong—are about to be overcome and there is a possibility of social transformation. But such a possibility is challenged at the very moment of its inception, even before the marriage is consummated, because Iago insists—even in the face of Brabantio's acquiescence ("Gone she is, / And what's to come of my despised time / Is nought but bitterness" [I.i.159–61]) and the Duke's sanction of the marriage on the grounds of Othello's character ("If virtue no delighted beauty lack, / Your son-in-law is far more fair than black" [I.iii.285–86)])—that marriage to a black man is not proper for a Venetian woman. Consequently, Iago jealously guards what is putatively now his exclusive sphere of influence in order to avenge himself on the Moor by challenging his humanity and coextensively his right to be wedded to Desdemona.

Through a shrewd insight into the desires and fears of others, and through a radical inversion of their discourses, Iago fulfills his own desire for revenge and control. Anthony Kubiak argues that Iago's "terrorist discourse" is far "more potent" than Othello's physical violence because it "operates through the *effect of discourse on seeing.*" Such a *seeing*, Kubiak further states, "engenders the perjury and its vengeance" (63). Thus, in order to manipulate and/or forestall truth/proof, Iago constantly resorts to this terrorist discourse by substituting a "manifest discourse" (Baudrillard, 53) for ocularity and by positing a discourse that contradicts or delays verification. In short, Iago manipulates discourse as a medium of power.

Iago's desire constitutes and controls the dramatic movement of *Othello*. His conviction that Brabantio will object to his daughter's marriage on racial grounds provides Iago with the terms for a disruptive discourse, the first in a series of rhetorical gestures that jeopardize rather than undermine and dissolve Desdemona's marriage to the Moor. Iago intends not merely to call attention to "a sexual union represented as a form of pollution" (Tennenhouse, 89) but to destroy the partners in this union as well. As Michael Neill observes, Iago keeps the "real imaginative focus of the action always the hidden marriage-bed . . . within which [he] can operate as a uniquely deceitful version of the *nuntius*, whose vivid imaginary descriptions taint the vision of the audience, even as they colonize the minds of Brabantio and Othello" (396).

The structure of any play resides, in large measure, in the words of characters. The structure of *Othello* resides in the words of the character who simultaneously has control of her or his own discourse and the discourse of others. Both Desdemona and Iago evince their ability to expropriate other characters' discourses. But in the final analysis, Iago subverts Desdemona's linguistic power, not so much by dominating her discourse directly as by controlling the discourse of those in close communication with her.

It is interesting to note that near the opening of the play, Iago tells Roderigo to call up Brabantio, rouse and incense him with "timorous accent and dire yell" (I.i.74). Iago's directive is metalinguistic, one that announces Iago's awareness of language and its power to persuade, to excite and incite. He says as much in a soliloquy:

> When devils will the blackest sins put on,
> They do suggest at first with heavenly shows
> As I do now. For whiles this honest fool
> Plies Desdemona to repair his fortunes,
> And she for him pleads strongly to the Moor,
> I'll pour this pestilence into his ear. (II.iii.318–23)

The lines to Roderigo, then, indicate Iago's modus operandi. In order to "poison" Brabantio's "delight," Iago bombards him with gross images of Othello:

> Even now, now, very now, an old black ram
> Is tupping your white ewe. . . .
> . . . the devil will make a grandsire of you. (I.i.89–92)

Iago posits physicality and sexuality as the essential markers of the Moor's humanity and continues this line of discourse in the face of Brabantio's disbelief. But Iago's language and intent are so egregiously offensive that poetic discourse cannot accommodate them and gives way to debased prose:

[Y]ou'll have your daughter cover'd with a Barbary horse, you'll have your nephews neigh to you, you'll have coursers for cousins, and jennets for germans. (I.i.111–13)

In notable contrast to Roderigo's discourse which invokes Othello's race ("thick lips," "lascivious," and "extravagant and wheeling stranger"), Iago's "diseased preoccupation" (Neill, 397) with Othello's sexuality results in a bestialization of the Moor and a devaluation of his marriage by making it *sound* obscene. His vision, as Kubiak points out, is "transformative and perjured" (24), a vision he imposes through language. Principally, Iago's aim is to control the discursive field. Such control resides in the hybrid nature of his discourse. Thus, *Othello* is as much about the ways in which one discourse is able to devour other discourses as it is about Iago's diabolical revenge on the Moor. In short, *Othello* is about the failure or fulfillment of desire through the loss or adroit use of discursive power.

Iago, as Margaret Ranald observes, is a "skillful opportunist who turns situations to his own account." His discursive power is cumulative; it relies on repetition and insinuation. He is aware of Desdemona's naivete about the "wickedness of the world outside" and knows "inexperience and decency blind her to the possibility that her motives might appear questionable and her actions capable of misconstruction" (136, 137). As Ranald further observes, Iago uses this naivete to undermine Desdemona's virtue and invert the "warm[th] and vital[ity]" she evinces in her spontaneous espousal of Cassio's cause (144). She is, thus, caught in a web of words spun by Iago from the matrix of male domination, "the pernicious effects of chastity . . . a doctrine men impose upon women" (Snow, 387). To achieve his purpose of undermining Desdemona's chastity, Iago concludes that his most effective method would be "to abuse Othello's ear / That [Cassio] is too familiar with his wife," since Cassio has "a smooth dispose / To be suspected, framed to make women false" (I.iii.378–81). Although Othello is to be the dupe of Iago's performative gestures, it is clearly Desdemona who must suffer character assassination via the male order.

At this point, a review of Jean Baudrillard's theory of seduction might help us better articulate the theater of discourse in *Othello*, since his theory accommodates my reading. Baudrillard observes that "in seduction . . . it is manifest discourse—discourse at its most superficial— that turns back on the deeper order (whether conscious or unconscious) in order to invalidate it, substituting the charm and illusion of appearances" in contrast to *"all meaningful discourse [which] seeks to end appearance."* But, Baudrillard continues, "inexorably, discourse is left to its appearances, and thus to the stakes of seduction, thus to its own failure as discourse" (53–54). It is in this light that we might examine the use of discourse in *Othello*, especially discourse as manipulated and enjoyed by Iago, who, as Roy Roussel observes, shows the "seducer's fascination with the spectacle of his own manipulation and control" (725). In other words, Iago is seduced by his own ability to seduce. Baudrillard describes this autoseduction as the moment when "perhaps discourse is secretly tempted . . . by the bracketing of its objectives, of its truth effects which become absorbed within a surface that swallows meaning. . . . [I]t is the original form by which discourse becomes absorbed within itself and emptied of its truth in order to better fascinate others: the primitive seduction of language" (54).

Reading *Othello* in the context of Baudrillard's seduction theory permits us to examine discourse motivated by desire. To begin with, it is worth remarking that marriage between Desdemona and Othello stems from Desdemona's desire for knowledge about Othello and the seductive power of that desired knowledge. For example, when asked about his use of charms to win Desdemona's affection, Othello argues that his narrative discourse was the charm, the power, he employed. Observing Desdemona's eagerness to hear him recount his exploits, Othello states that he:

> Took once a pliant hour and found good means
> To draw from her a prayer of earnest heart
> That would all my pilgrimage dilate
> Whereof by parcels she had something heard,
> But not intentively. I did consent. (I.iii.150–54)

Desdemona confirms the force of Othello's narrative discourse, its seductive power, by hinting that he propose marriage, by preferring him to men of her own race and class:

> I saw Othello's visage in his mind
> And to his honors and his valiant parts
> Did I my soul and fortunes consecrate. (I.iii.248–50)

"I saw Othello's visage in his mind" is the critical line because it simultaneously discloses Desdemona's awareness of Othello's race and her ready acceptance of his mind (his intellectual and narrative powers) above any thoughts of race. She insists that she has looked beyond the physical—which on the surface seems of no consequence to her—into the soul of the Moor and likes what she discovers. But her dismissal of his face underscores her recognition of the fact that Othello's race does matter. At the same time, she readily submits to his maleness as evinced by her unquestioned "duty" to him—a duty dictated by tradition and gender.

Desdemona's statement cannot be contradicted by Brabantio, but it is too much for him to accept. And he is prepared to lose his daughter rather than accept the Moor as an affine:

> I here do give thee [Othello] that with all my heart
> Which, but thou has already, with all my heart
> I would keep from thee. (I.iii.191–93)

Brabantio's pronouncement on his daughter's behavior in marrying Othello without permission is precisely the utterance that opens a space for Iago to work his will on the Moor and undermine the union that Iago himself finds most repugnant: "Look to her Moor, if thou hast eyes to see: / She has deceived her father and may thee" (I.iii.288–89), words Iago will later reiterate to Othello.

Othello and Desdemona use language to "deliver" what Baudrillard terms "real meaning," "truth," or honest discourse, in contradistinction to Iago's manifestly perjured discourse. If, as Baudrillard observes, seduction sports "triumphantly with weakness, making a game of it with its own rules," then we cannot rightly call Othello's narrative of his personal history, recited at Brabantio's and Desdemona's requests, a seductive act. Seduction robs discourse of its "sense and turns it from truth" by causing "manifest discourse"—the surface meaning—to "say what it does not want to say; it causes determinations and profound indeterminations to show through in manifest discourse." It is, then, the responsibility of interpretation to "break the appearance and play of the manifest discourse" (53). Interpretation is vital to a deeper understanding of the ways by which discourse operates in *Othello*, where, as Kubiak convincingly argues, "we can begin to see how the language of the theatre *within the theatre* is . . . always eminently terrorist because of language's failure to adequately state its intentions" (63). Yet early in *Othello*, language does achieve what Roland Barthes terms its "adequation of enunciation" (208) through Othello's and Desdemona's performative gestures.

For example, when Othello is accused of bewitching Desdemona, and thus marrying her without her "knowing" what was happening to her, he defends himself on discursive grounds: he argues from the force of his narrative, categorically stating that it was language's power to re-create the images of his exploits that merited Desdemona's affection. [Though he declares at one point that he is "rude" of speech "[a]nd little blessed with the soft phrase of peace" (I.iii.81–82), we are perhaps not meant to take the declaration seriously.] Othello won her father, too, initially:

> Her father loved me, oft invited me,
> Still questioned me the story of my life
> From year to year—the battles, sieges, fortunes,
> That I have passed. (I.iii.127–30)

Othello—like any "author" recognizing that his words have not merely conveyed their intentions but have moved to another level of meaning beyond their author's expectation—realizes that the more he reiterates his deeds of valor and his triumphs over adversities, the closer Desdemona is drawn to him:

> This to hear
> Would Desdemona seriously incline;
> . . . .
> She would come again, and with a greedy ear
> Devour up my discourse. (I.iii.144–49)

In other words, Othello tells the Venetians, Desdemona was moved by his deeds and seduced by his discourse:

> She thanked me,
> And bade me, if I had a friend that loved her,
> I should but teach him how to tell my story,
> And that would woo her. (I.iii.162–65)

In fact, Othello's rehearsal of the scene clearly reveals that Desdemona, not he, was the seducer:

> Upon this hint I spake:
> She [first] loved me for the dangers I had passed,

And I [in return] loved her that she did pity them.
This only is the witchcraft I have used. (I.iii.165–68)

Asked to corroborate Othello's testimony, Desdemona, like Othello, preempts her father's argument by taking the discursive initiative: she expropriates her father's discourse of "obedience" and, like Othello, demonstrates language's ability to state the bald truth as she understands it, a truth by which she lives. She brilliantly turns her father's discourse on duty back on him without hint of conscious irony, but rather by a conscious rhetorical gesture. Because she wants desperately to have his approval, she reaches for the best way to articulate that duty—by placing her duty on par with her mother's, a claim her father cannot gainsay:

My noble father,
I do perceive here a divided duty:
To you I am bound for life and education;
My life and education both do learn me
How to respect you. You are lord of all my duty;
I am hiterto your daughter. But here's my husband;
And so much duty as my mother showed
To you, preferring you before her father,
So much I challenge that I may profess
Due to the Moor my lord. (I.iii.178–87)

Both Desdemona and Othello demonstrate that "real meaning" and "manifest discourse" are not necessarily mutually exclusive, that they can operate simultaneously toward a mutual telos at this juncture. The tragedy occurs when the two pull in opposite directions and when Othello and Desdemona, especially Desdemona, lose the discursive advantage.

Iago's observation of Desdemona's "seduction" of Othello and her discursive power over her father, no doubt, warns Iago against a direct attempt to seduce her to leave Othello. Having seen her turn male discourse back on her father and the Senate in her resolve to remain with Othello by arguing that it was she, not Othello, who did the seducing and by requesting and obtaining from that august body permission to join Othello in Cyprus, despite the fact that it is a site of battle, Iago surely realizes that Desdemona can discursively match him. Witness, for example, her astute comparison of her decision to marry Othello to a battle and her boldness in trumpeting the implications of that decision to the world:

That I did love the Moor to live with him,
My downright violence and storm of fortunes
May trumpet to the world. (I.iii.244–46)

Iago most surely observes that Desdemona belies what Teresa De Lauretis terms "the web of the male Oedipal logic" in which "the little girl has no other prospect but to consent and be seduced into femininity" (52). Desdemona preempts her father's traditional right to make a "proper" choice for her.

Iago's power to manipulate discourse, however, gives him the dramatic edge over Desdemona. The motivation for linguistic manipulation, and thereby manipulation of human beings, stems from Iago's perception—whether real or imagined—that he has been superseded by an inferior military man, namely Cassio, and that he has been cuckolded by Othello. Furthermore, he "smarts under neglect" by a general he deems racially inferior to himself. This conviction that he has been slighted, Harley Granville-Barker contends, is the "immediate spring" of Iago's desire to denigrate the Moor (125).

Lacking a sphere of influence within the civil and military hierarchy, Iago locates his power in the manipulation of discourse. And, ironically, in the final analysis, Othello is seduced by his own discourse because the language Iago employs to defame Desdemona and challenge Othello's manhood is Othello's, albeit perverted and polluted.

Iago plays upon what Philip McGuire terms the "deliberate disjunction of action and feeling" to accomplish his goal of turning Othello into an animal. In other words, Iago employs "rhetoric to undercut reason" (205). The play is, then, to borrow from McGuire again, "an imitation of an action of knowing and judging"; an "assay on the limits of intelligence and natural passion, deception deftly and most intelligently practiced" (209) through terrorist discourse. Kubiak adds to this when he states that Iago "terrorizes Othello with the most subtle shift of seeing refracted through an almost imperceptible misdirection of the eye—a misdirection effected through Iago's words" (63–64).

Roderigo and Othello challenge or try to circumvent such terrorist discourse when they ask Iago to substantiate his verbal claims with objective proof. They, especially Roderigo, recognize the tension between Iago's discourse and objective reality; yet ironically, they must rely on Iago, whose discourse they question, to resolve that tension. Although Othello is satisfied to have Iago supply the evidence, Roderigo threatens to see for himself—to confront Desdemona directly now that he has begun to "find [him]self fopped" (IV.ii.190). When threatened by Roderigo's decision to confront Desdemona, however, Iago proves that he still controls the discourse, which he quickly interposes between Roderigo's demand for proof and his own will to power. Moreover, according to Kubiak, Iago knows that "ocularity in which [Roderigo] seeks his truth is as much a failure as the language that directs it." Kubiak describes the failure of ocular proof in *Othello* as the "violence of failed seeing—the desire to see, seeing desire, seeing what one has been told (not) to" and adds that "both seeing and speaking" in Othello are ensnared by a "falsely assumed empiricism" that relies not on proof but on Iago's capacity "to reproduce or rehearse 'the Same,' that impossibility" (66). If sight is not to be trusted, then discourse must bear the greater responsibility for proof, which should, therefore, be an incontrovertible proof that does not rely on but rather opposes and exposes seduction. Baudrillard formulates this opposition between ocularity and discourse: "All appearances conspire to combat and root out meaning (whether intentional or otherwise), and turn it into a game . . . one that is more adventurous and seductive than the directive line of meaning" (54).

Roderigo first challenges Iago's discourse in Act IV when he realizes that he has been duped: "I *heard* too much; for your words and performances are no kin together" (my emphasis). He protests Iago's failure to deliver on his promises and decides to "make [him]self known to Desdemona":

> If she will return my jewels, I will give over my suit and repent my unlawful solicitation; if not, assure yourself I will seek satisfaction of you. (IV.ii.193–96)

There will be no further deliberation on this issue, and Iago knows it. Now he must retreat from dilatory,[1] verbal strategy to direct action. Hence the fabrication about Cassio's delivering a message that will send Othello and Desdemona to Mauritania and the proposal to murder Cassio: "I will show you such a necessity in his death that you shall think yourself bound to put it on him" (IV.ii.231–32). Iago's "show" will, of course, be verbal.

---

1. Patricia Parker notes that Iago gains power over Othello "at the threshold of the great temptation scene . . . through those pauses, single words and pregnant phrases which seem to suggest something secret or withheld, a withholding which fills the Moor with the desire to hear more" (54).

Roderigo's recognition that Iago's words are at odds with his actions—promises without proof, discourse without substance—begins the ineluctable drive toward the failure of Iago's disruptive discourse. Roderigo's threat to confront Desdemona engenders a quick and strategic discursive move on Iago's part. Roderigo's suspicions coupled with Othello's desire for "ocular proof" sorely undermine Iago's discourse. Thus, discourse cannot serve Iago in this crisis of credibility and therefore must be "redeployed as action" (Baudrillard, 54). He must stage another scenario while he recovers the discursive ground, first, by praising Roderigo's decision and then by forestalling that decision. It is noteworthy that at this juncture, Iago shifts from poetic discourse to prose, a clear indication of his failure to control his best weapon, language, and of his diminishing power to manipulate Roderigo:

> Why, now I see there's mettle in thee, and even from this instant do build on thee a better opinion than ever before. Give me thy hand, Roderigo. Thou has taken against me a most just exception; but yet I protest I have dealt most directly in thy affair.

Roderigo counters that he has seen no evidence to support Iago's claims: "It hath not appeared." Iago concedes as much but does not stop at mere concession: he inverts Roderigo's argument:

> I grant indeed it hath not appeared; and your suspicion is not without wit and judgement. But, Roderigo, if thou hast that in thee indeed, which I have greater reason to believe now than ever—I mean purpose, courage, and valour—this night show it. If thou the next night following enjoy not Desdemona, take me from this world with treachery, and devise engines for my life. (IV.ii.200–11)

Clearly, Iago is weakened by Roderigo's threat of intervention, a threat that not only will expose his machinations vis-à-vis Roderigo but also will expose Iago's entire charade. Iago skillfully diverts Roderigo from his failure to deliver on his promises. This scene brillfully illustrates Baudrillard's observation that sedution stems from weakness, not power: "To seduce is to appear weak. To seduce is to render weak" (83). Iago is unquestionably the "seduced" in this scene because Roderigo has weakened Iago's ability to control him by words alone.

Othello is marked by a series of seductive gestures that lead to the untimely and unwarranted death of Desdemona. In *Othello*, the contours of desire are shaped by individual discourse and gestures of seduction.

Iago's desire to bend Othello to his will is contingent upon his power of seduction. Iago's desire constitutes and controls the dramatic center, while Desdemona's position as object of male desire—her marriage to the Moor and Roderigo's desire for a sexual union with her—constitutes the thematic center of the drama. Iago's actions circulate around this marriage plot. Desdemona's elopement with a black man provides the basis for Iago's seduction of Roderigo, Brabantio, and Othello, while her position as Othello's wife provides the ground on which Iago's vengeance operates.

Iago recognizes power when he meets it. He recognizes the strength of Desdemona's resolve, which makes the Senate agree to her remaining with him even in Cyprus. Thus, Iago elects to work toward denying Desdemona her desires by manipulating those around her and by subterfuge, or what Baudrillard calls seduction or a turning "from one's own truth" or leading another "from his/her truth." It is precisely Iago's desire to lead Desdemona from the Moor's bed that results in her tragic death. Very early on, Iago insists to Roderigo that Desdemona will turn from Othello once his narrative becomes tiresome and she is forced to see him in racial terms, that is, see him as black. He insists that Desdemona's violent love for the Moor, engendered by his "bragging and telling her fantastical lies" (II.i.213), will eventually be destroyed by ocularity: "Her eye must be fed. And what delight will she have to look on the devil?" (II.i.215–16). Being sated, Iago contends, Desdemona will see the physical reality of Othello:

> When the blood is made dull with the act of sport, there should be, again to inflame it and to give satiety a fresh appetite, loveliness in favour, sympathy in years, manners and beauties: all which the Moor is defective in. Now for want of these required conveniences, her delicate tenderness will find itself abused, begin to heave the gorge, disrelish and abhor the Moor. (II.i.216–22)

Iago articulates this thesis of Desdemona's "momentary" infatuation with the Moor and true attachment to the younger, handsome Cassio not only to Roderigo but to Othello as well. Only instead of stating it openly, he makes insidious suggestions—"Did Michael Cassio, / When you wooed my lady, know of your love?" (III.iii.93–94)—that force Othello to voice doubts about Desdemona's fidelity. The conversation proceeds with Iago's saying little by way of direct accusation but suggesting a great deal, insinuating his thoughts into Othello's psyche:

By heaven, he echoes me,
As if there were some monster in his thought
Too hideous to be shown. (III.iii.109–11)

Finally, Othello, seduced into believing his wife has been unfaithful, becomes totally confused about his own thoughts. So muddled, in fact, is Othello at this juncture that he fails to note and pick up Iago's overt admission of treachery, "[O]ft my jealousy / Shapes faults that are not" (III.iii.148–49), or heed his warning, "O beware, my lord, of jealousy" (III.iii.167).

Othello, at first, defends Desdemona's virtue, her playful spirit and easy show of affection for others: "Where virtue is, these are more virtuous" (III.iii.188). He defends her honesty on the grounds that she chose him despite his race. But Iago returns to his discursive strategy by echoing Brabantio's warning:

She did deceive her father, marrying you;
And when she seemed to shake and fear your looks
She loved them most. (III.iii.207–9)

Edward Snow brilliantly observes that the "decisive moment in Iago's seduction" occurs when Iago gets Othello to see Desdemona "in terms of Brabantio's warning" (399). Snow further argues that Othello's reference to Desdemona's reputation being as "black as [his] own face" suggests that he is being manipulated by a language "calculated to *make* him despise himself because he is black" (401).

Subtly goaded by Iago, Othello admits, "I think my wife be honest, and think she is not, / I think thou art just, and think thou art not" (III.iii.385–86). But, Othello continues, Desdemona has made an unnatural match by marrying him, her "nature erring from itself" (III.iii.229), a point Iago seizes on to undermine Othello's faith in Desdemona's love and acceptance of him. He reminds Othello that Desdemona refused numerous "proposed matches / Of her own clime, complexion and degree" (III.iii.231–32), implying that Othello is not on the same human level as the Venetian suitors.

Doubting/trusting both his wife and Iago, Othello asks Iago for a "living reason," actual proof of Desdemona's infidelity. Iago obliges with a performance calculated to remove all doubt: Cassio's discourse of love ostensibly spoken during sleep. Iago cleverly reminds Othello that what he has reported is only a dream; Othello counters that it is "a foregone conclusion" (III.iii.429). At this juncture, Iago sets the discursive stage for the tragic conclusion. All that remains is ocular proof misdirected and interpreted by Iago. Finally, what Othello sees is infected by his desire, a desire informed through Iago's words. Othello's murder of Desdemona results from his own victimization by Iago. Iago is partially correct when he tells Emilia, "I told [Othello] what I thought, and told no more / Than what he found himself was apt and true" (V.ii.175–76).

The circulation of desire in *Othello* and the concomitant acts that affect desire provide an insight into Iago's decision to manipulate others discursively. Iago's narrative is directed toward a conclusion that satisfies his desire for power through discursive control, whereas Desdemona's narrative moves along an axis of desire for happiness through a shared experience. Iago's and Desdemona's interlocking desires collide through Iago's attempts to break Othello's hold on Desdemona and through Desdemona's efforts to influence Othello on Cassio's behalf. Out of this matrix of interlocking and conflicting desires comes Iago's seduction of Othello.

Iago's seductive power is situated in his ability to manipulate the sociolect,[2] a hybridization of a desire to manipulate and destroy Othello, who is for Iago the locus of misplaced power and the object of illegitimate desire. Iago's enterprise is, then, to desempower Othello, not by making Othello undesirable to Desdemona (which he realizes he cannot do) but by turning Othello against Desdemona.

To achieve this end, Iago employs another of his dramatic skills— acting. Granville-Barker observes that Iago assumes a dual acting role— he his both the persona Iago of the play *Othello* and the character who exploits the role of actor to accomplish his desired goal:

> The medium in which Iago works is the actor's; and the crude sense of pretending to be what he is not, and in his chameleonlike ability to adapt himself to change of company and circumstance, we find him an accomplished actor. (162)

---

2. Michael Riffaterre notes that the socioelect is the site of "myths, traditions, ideological and esthetic stereotypes . . . harbored by a society," as well as the site of "ready-made narrative and descriptive models that reflect a group's idea of or consensus about reality." Iago refers to Othello in animalistic terms to play to the Venetian socioelect. His references to Othello as "an old black ram," "the devil," and "a Barbary horse" reveal Renaissance stereotypes and, more important, play upon the racial fears of the Western male (130).

Both the pleasure and the success of Iago's enterprise are contingent upon what Roussel terms the "seducer's fascination with the spectacle of his own manipulation and control" (725), while Baudrillard argues that seduction derives its "passion" and "intensity" not from an "energy of desire" but rather "from gaming as pure form and from purely formal bluffing" (82). "Gaming" and "purely formal bluffing" describe Iago's method precisely and completely.

The so-called "brothel scene" represents the triumph of Iago's gaming and bluffing. Iago's strategy proposes to expose Othello's gullibility and confirm his contention that Othello is not quite on the same human level with Desdemona and is therefore not a suitable mate for her. This strategic move by Iago clearly indicates that Othello is the object of Iago's seduction, not Desdemona. It is as though Iago seeks Othello's moral and mental downfall, in part, because he cannot match Othello's physical prowess and narrative skill. What he seeks, and what he succeeds in effecting, is the undermining of the Moor's intelligence and coextensively his humanity. The outcome of the play turns, then, on Iago's seduction of Othello and Othello's collusion in his own downfall, and that collusion becomes the ultimate sign of Iago's mastery of multiple discourses.

Bibliography

Adams, Abigail. *Letters of Mrs. Adams, the Wife of John Adams*, 2 vols., ed. C. F. Adams, Boston, Charles Little & James Brown, 1840.

Adams, John. *Diary and Autobiography of John Adams*, 4 vols., ed. Lyman H. Butterfield, Cambridge, Mass., Harvard UP, 1961.

Adams, John Quincy. "Misconceptions of Shakespeare, Upon the Stage" and "The Character of Desdemona" in James Hackett, *Notes and Comments upon Certain Plays and Actors of Shakespeare with Criticism and Correspondence*, New York, Carleton, 1863.

Africanus, John Leo. *The History and Description of Africa*, 3 vols., tr. John Pory. Ed. with an Introd. and Notes, Robert Brown, London, Lincoln's Inn Fields, 1896.

Althusser, Louis. "Ideology and Ideological State Apparatuses," *Lenin and Philosophy and Other Essays*, New York, Monthly Review Press, 1971.

Bartels, Emily C. "Making More of the Moor: Aaron, Othello, and Renaissance Refashionings of Race," *Shakespeare Quarterly, 41* (1990), 433–54.

Barthelemy, Anthony Gerard. *Black Face, Maligned Race: The Representation of Blacks in English Drama from Shakespeare to Southerne*, Baton Rouge & London, Louisiana State UP, 1987.

Barthes, Roland. *Image, Music, Text*, New York, Hill & Wang, 1977.

Baudrillard, Jean. *Seduction*, tr. Brian Singer, New York, St. Martin's Press, 1990.

Berger, Arthur Asa. *Signs in Contemporary Culture: An Introduction to Semiotics*, New York & London, Longman, 1984.

Bernal, Martin. *Black Athena: The Afroasiatic Roots of Classical Civilization: Volume 1, the Fabrication of Ancient Greece, 1785–1985*, New Brunswick, Rutgers UP, 1987.

Berry, Edward. "Othello's Alienation," *Studies in English Literature, 30* (1990), 315–33.

Boaden, James. *Memoirs of the Life of John Philip Kemble, Esq.*, 2 vols., London, Longman, 1825.

Bradbrook, M. C. *Shakespeare: The Poet in His World*. London, Methuen, 1978.

Bradley, A. C. *Shakespearean Tragedy*, London, Macmillan, 1904.

Braxton, Phyllis, "The Moor and the Metaphor," *South Atlantic Review*, 55 (1990), 1–17.

Brown, William Wells. *The Rising Sun; or The Antecedents and Advancement of the Colored Race*, Boston, A. G. Brown, 1874.

Bulman, J. C., and Coursen, H. R. eds. *Shakespeare on Television: An Anthology of Essays and Reviews*, Hanover & London, UP of New England, 1988.

Burke, Kenneth. *A Grammar of Motives*, Berkeley, U of California P, 1969.

————. "Othello: An Essay to Illustrate a Method," *Othello: Critical Essays*, ed. Susan Snyder, New York, Garland, 1988.

Burton, Robert. *The Anatomy of Melancholy, What It Is, With All the Kinds, Causes, Symtomes, Prognostics, and Several Cures of It*, London, J. & E. Hodson, 1804.

Butcher, Philip. "Othello's Racial Identity," *Shakespeare Quarterly*, 3 (1952), 243–47.

Calderwood, James L. *The Properties of Othello*, Amherst, U of Massachusetts P, 1989.

Cantor, Paul A. "Othello: The Erring Barbarian among the Supersubtle Venetians," *Southwest Review*, 75 (1990), 296–319.

Carlisle, Carol Jones. *Shakespeare from the Greenroom: Actors' Criticism of Four Major Tragedies*, Chapel Hill, U of North Carolina P, 1969.

Carpentier, Alejo. *Explosion in a Cathedral*. New York, 1989.

Chupa: Maria Anna. *Anne, the White Woman in Contemporary African-American Fiction: Archetypes, Stereotypes, and Characterizations*, Westport, Greenwood Press, 1990.

Coleridge, S. T. *Coleridge's Shakespearean Criticism*, 2 vols., ed. T. M. Raysor, Cambridge, Harvard UP, 1930.

Collier, Jeremy Payne. *Memoirs of the Principal Actors in the Plays of Shakespeare*, London, Shakespeare Society, 1846.

Cooper, Anthony Ashley. 3rd Earl of Shaftesbury, *Characteristics*, ed. J. M. Robertson, London, Jonas, 1964.

Cowhig, Ruth. "Blacks in English Renaissance Drama and the Role of Shakespeare's Othello," *The Black Presence in English Literature*, ed. David Dabydeen, Manchester, Manchester UP, 1985.

Davis, Angela Y. *Women, Race and Class*, New York, Vintage Books, 1983.

DeLauretis, Teresa. *Alice Doesn't: Feminism, Semiotics, Cinema*, Bloomington, Indiana UP, 1984.

DeMendonca, Barbara Heliodora C. "Othello: A Tragedy Built on a Comic Structure," *Aspects of Othello*, ed. Kenneth Muir & Philip Edwards, Cambridge, Cambridge UP, 1977.

Dollimore, Jonathan. "The Cultural Politics of Perversion: Augustine, Shakespeare, Freud, Foucault," *Genders*, 8 (1990), 1–16.

Dorman, James H. *Theater in the Ante-Bellum South 1815–1861*, Chapel Hill, U of North Carolina P, 1967.

Dunn, Esther C. *Shakespeare in America*, New York, Macmillan, 1939.

Edelstein, Tilden G. "*Othello* in America: The Drama of Racial Intermarriage," *Region, Race, and Reconstruction: Essays in Honor of C. Vann Woodward*, ed. J. Morgan Kousser & James McPherson, New York, Oxford UP, 1982.

Eden, Richard. *The First Three English Books on America [1511]–1555 AD*, ed. Edward Arber, Birmingham, 1885.

Eliot, T. S. *Selected Essays*, London, Faber & Faber, 1956.

Fanon, Frantz. *Black Skin, White Masks*, tr. Charles Lam Markham, New York, Grove Press, 1967.

Farjeon, Herbert. *The Shakespearean Scene: Dramatic Criticisms*, London, Hutchinson, n.d.

Felperin, Howard. *Shakespearean Representation*, Princeton, Princeton UP, 1977.

Fiedler, Leslie A. *The Stranger in Shakespeare*, St. Albans, Paladin, 1974.

Findlater, Richard. *The Player Kings*, New York, Stein & Day, 1971.

Fitzgerald, Percy. *The Life of David Garrick*, 2 vols., London, Tinsley Bros., 1868.

Frederickson, George. *The Black Image in the White Mind: The Debate on Afro-American Character and Destiny, 1817–1914*, New York, Harper & Row, 1971.

Gardner, Helen. "The Noble Moor," *Interpretations of Shakespeare; British Academy Shakespeare Lectures*, selected by Kenneth Muir, Oxford, Clarendon Press, 1985.

Gerard, Albert. " 'Egregiously an Ass': The Dark Side of the Moor. A View of Othello's Mind," *Aspects of Othello*, ed. Kenneth Muir & Philip Edwards, Cambridge, Cambridge UP, 1977.

Gildon, Charles. "Remarks on the Plays of Shakespeare." *The Works of William Shakespeare*, ed. Nicholas Rowe, Vol. 7, New York, AMS Press, 1967.

Giraldi, Giovanni Battista (Cinthio). *A Hundred Tales*. Ferrara, Italy, 1565.

Gohlke, Madelon. " 'All That Is Spoke Is Marred': Language and Consciousness in *Othello*," *Women's Studies*, 9 (1981–82), 157–76.

Granville-Barker, Harley. *Prefaces to Shakespeare*, London, Sidgwick & Jackson, 1945.

Grebanier, Bernard. *Then Came Each Actor*, New York, David McKay, 1975.

Grimsted, David. *Melodrama Unveiled: American Theater and Culture, 1800–1850*, Chicago UP, 1968.

Harlow, Barbara. "Sentimental Orientalism: *Season of Migration to the North* and *Othello*," *Tayeb Salih's "Season of Migration to the North": A Casebook*, ed. Mona Takieddine Amyuni, Beirut, American University of Beirut, 1985.

Hawkes, Terence. *Shakespeare's Talking Animals: Language and Drama in Society*, Totowa, Rowman & Littlefield, 1973.

Hawkins, F. W. *The Life of Edmund Kean*, 2 vols., London, Tinsley Bros., 1869.

Hazlitt, William. *Complete Works*, ed. P. P. Howe, 21 vols., London, J. M. Dent, 1930.

Hedgecock, Frank A. *David Garrick and His French Friends*, London, Stanley Paul, n.d.

Heilman, Robert. *Magic in the Web: Action and Language in Othello*, Lexington, U of Kentucky P, 1956.

Hill, Erol. *Shakespeare in Sable: A History of Black Shakespearean Actors*, Amherst, U of Massachusetts P, 1984.

Himes, Chester. "Dilemma of the Negro Novelist in the U.S.A.," *New Black Voices: An Anthology of Contemporary Afro-American Literature*, ed. Abraham Chapman, New York, New American Library, 1972.

————. *The Primitive*, New York, New American Library, 1955.

Hodge, Robert, and Kress, Gunther. *Social Semiotics*, Ithaca, Cornell UP, 1988.

Holbein, Woodrow L. "Shakespeare in Charleston, 1800–1860," *Shakespeare in the South: Essays on Performance*, ed. Philip C. Kolin, Jackson, UP of Mississippi, 1983.

Holderness, Graham. *Shakespeare's Histories*, New York, St. Martin's Press, 1985.

Hooks, Bell. *Yearning: Race, gender, and cultural politics*, Boston, South End Press, 1990.

Howard, Jean. "Scholarship, Theory, and More New Readings: Shakespeare for the 1990s," *Shakespeare Study Today*, ed. Georgianna Ziegler, New York, AMS Press, 1986.

Howard, Jean, & O'Connor, Marion. eds. *Shakespeare Reproduced*, New York, Methuen, 1987.

Hoyt, Edwin P., *Paul Robeson: The American Othello*, New York, World Publishing, 1967.

Hudson, Theodore R. *From LeRoi Jones to Amiri Baraka: The Literary Works*, Durham, Duke UP, 1973.

Hunter, G. K. "Othello and Colour Prejudice," *Interpretations of Shakespeare: British Academy Shakespeare Lectures*, selected by Kenneth Muir, Oxford, Clarendon Press, 1985.

Hutton, Laurence. *Curiosities of the American Stage*, New York, Harper & Bros., 1891.

Johnson, Lemuel. *The Devil, the Gargoyle, and the Buffoon*, New York, Kennikat Press, 1971.

Johnson, Samuel. *Samuel Johnson on Shakespeare*, ed. William K. Wimsatt, Jr., New York, Hill & Wang, 1960.

Jones, Eldred. *Othello's Countrymen: The African in English Renaissance Drama*, London, Oxford UP, 1965.

Jones, LeRoi. *Dutchman and The Slave: Two Plays by LeRoi Jones*, New York, William Morrow, 1964.

————. *Home: Social Essays*, New York, William Morrow, 1966.

————. "An Interview with LeRoi Jones by Sidney Bernard," *Literary Times*, May–June 1967.

Jordan, Winthrop D. *White Over Black: American Attitudes Towards the Negro, 1550–1812*, Chapel Hill, U of North Carolina P, 1968.

Kubiak, Anthony. *Stages of Terror: Terror, Ideology, and Coercion as Theatre History*, Bloomington, Indiana UP, 1991.

Lamb, Charles. *The Complete Works and Letters of Charles Lamb*, ed. Bennett A. Cerf & Donald S. Klopfer, New York, Random House, 1935.

Lawlor, John. *The Tragic Sense in Shakespeare*, London, Chatto & Windus, 1960.

Leavis, F. R. *The Common Pursuit*, London, Chatto & Windus, 1953.

Levi-Strauss, Claude. *Race and History*, Paris, UNESCO, 1952.

Lewes, George Henry. *On Actors and the Art of Acting*, Leipzig, Bernhard Tauchnitz, 1875.

Loomba, Ania. *Gender, Race and Renaissance Drama*, Manchester, Manchester UP, 1989.

Lower, Charles B. "Othello as Black on Southern Stages, Then and Now," *Shakespeare in the South: Essays on Performance*, ed. Philip C. Kolin, Jackson, U of Mississippi P, 1983.

Mannoni, O. *Prospero and Caliban: The Psychology of Colonization*, New York, Vintage, 1983.

Marcus, Leah. *Puzzling Shakespeare*, Berkeley, U of California P, 1988.

Marowitz, Charles. "An *Othello*," *Open Space Plays*, selected by Charles Marowitz, London, Penguin, 1974.

Marshall, Herbert, & Stock, Mildred. *Ira Aldridge: The Negro Tragedian*, London, Camelot Press, 1958.

Marx, Karl, & Engels, Frederick. *The German Ideology*, ed. C. J. Arthur, New York, International Publishers, 1970.

Mason, Philip. *Prospero's Magic: Some Thoughts on Race and Class*, London, Oxford UP, 1962.

Matthews, G. M., "*Othello* and the Dignity of Man," *Shakespeare in a Changing World*, ed. Arnold Kettle, London, Lawrence & Wishart, 1964.

McGuire, Philip C. "*Othello* as an 'Assay on Reason,'" *Shakespeare Quarterly* 24 (1973), 198–209.

Morozov, Mikhail M. *Shakespeare on the Soviet Stage*, tr. David Magarshack, London, Soviet News, 1947.

Morris, Charles. *Signs, Language and Behavior*, New York, Prentice-Hall, 1946.

———. *Signification and Significance: A Study of the Relations of Signs and Values*, Cambridge, M.I.T. Press, 1964.

Nazareth, Peter. "Othello—Exploited Black or Posturing Leader of the Afro-Asian Delegation?" *An African View of Literature*, Evanston, Northwestern UP, 1974.

Neill, Michael. "Unproper Beds: Race, Adultery, and the Hideous in *Othello*," *Shakespeare Quarterly*, 40 (1989), 383–412.

Newman, Karen. "Femininity and the Monstrous in *Othello*," *Shakespeare Reproduced*, ed. Jean Howard & Marion O'Connor, New York, Methuen, 1987.

Orkin, Martin. *Shakespeare Against Apartheid*, Craighall, A. D. Donker, 1987.

Parker, Patricia. "Shakespeare and Rhetoric: 'Dilation' and 'Delation' in *Othello*," *Shakespeare and the Question of Theory*, ed. Patricia Parker & Geoffrey Hartman, New York, Methuen, 1985.

Perceval, John. *Report on the Manuscripts of the Earl of Egmont*, 2 vols., Dublin, John Falconer, 1909.

Phillips, Caryl. *The European Tribe*, New York, Farrar Straus Giroux, 1987.

Ranald, Margaret Loftus. *Shakespeare and His Social Context*, New York, AMS Press, 1977.

Richardson, Sandra Lee. "Sweet Meat from Le Roi: The Dramatic World of Amiri Baraka," DAI, Stanford University, 1979.

Riffaterre, Michael. *Fictional Truth*, Baltimore, Johns Hopkins UP, 1990.

Robeson, Eslanda Goode. *Paul Robeson, Negro*, New York, Harper, 1930.

Robeson, Paul. *Here I Stand*, Boston, Beacon, 1958.

Rose, Mark. "Othello's Occupation: Shakespeare and the Romance of Chivalry," *English Literary Renaissance*, 15 (1985), 293–311.

Rosenberg, Marvin. *The Masks of Othello*, Berkeley & Los Angeles, U of California P, 1961.

Roussel, Roy. "The Project of Seduction and the Equality of the Sexes in *Les Liaison Dangereuses*," *Modern Language Notes*, 96 (1981), 725–45.

Rymer, Thomas. *Critical Works*, ed. Curt A. Zimansky, New Haven, Yale UP, 1956.

Said, Edward W. *Orientalism*, New York, Random House, 1979.

Salgado, Gamini. *Eyewitnesses of Shakespeare: First Hand Accounts of Performances, 1590–1890*, New York, Barnes & Noble, 1975.

———. Introduction, *Othello*, ed. Gamini Salgado, New Swan Shakespeare, Advanced Series, London, Longman, 1976.

Segal, Lynne. *Slow Motion: Changing Masculinities, Changing Men*, New Brunswick, New Jersey, Rutgers UP, 1990.

Shattuck, Charles H. *Shakespeare on the American Stage*, 2 vols., Washington, Folger Shakespeare Library, 1976.

Snow, Edward A. "Sexual Anxiety and the Male Order of Things," *English Literary Renaissance*, 10 (1980), 384–412.

Snyder, Louis. *The Idea of Racialism: Its Meaning and History*, Princeton, D. Van Nostrand, 1962.

Sollors, Werner. *Amiri Baraka/LeRoi Jones: The Quest for a "Popular Modernism,"* New York, Columbia UP, 1978.

Spivack, Bernard. *Shakespeare and the Allegory of Evil*, New York, Columbia UP, 1958.

Stallybrass, Peter. "Patriarchal Territories: The Body Enclosed," *Othello: Critical Essays*, ed. Susan Snyder, New York, Garland, 1988.

Stanislavsky, Konotatin. *Stanislavsky Produces Othello*, tr. Helen Nowak, London, Geoffrey Bles, 1948.

Styron, William. *The Confessions of Nat Turner*, New York, Signet, 1966.

Taylor, Gary. *Reinventing Shakespeare*, New York, Weidenfeld & Nicholson, 1989.

Tennenhouse, Leonard. "Violence Done to Women on the Renaissance Stage," *The Violence of Representation*, ed. Nancy Armstrong & Leonard Tennenhouse, New York, Routledge, 1989.

Tokson, Elliot H. *The Popular Image of the Black Man in English Drama, 1550–1688*, Boston, G. K. Hall, 1982.

Topsell, Edward. *The Historie of Foure-Footed Beastes*, London, William Jaggard, 1607, Amsterdam, Theatrum Orbis Terrarum, 1973.

Variorum: Othello, vol. VI (1886) of *A New Variorum Edition of Shakespeare*, ed. H. H. Furness and others, Philadelphia, Lippincott, 1873–1955.

Vaughan, Virginia Mason & Cartwright, Kent. eds. *Othello: New Perspectives*, Rutherford, Fairleigh Dickinson UP, 1991.

Velikovsky, Immanuel. *Oedipus and Akhnaton*, New York, Pocket Books, 1980.

White, Richard Grant, *Shakespeare's Scholar*, New York, D. Appleton, 1854.

Williams, Gwyn. *Person and Persona: Studies in Shakespeare*, Cardiff, U of Wales P, 1981.

Winstanley, Lilian. *A History of Shakespearean Criticism*, 2 vols., ed. Augustus Ralli, London, Oxford UP, 1932.

Ziegler, Georgianna. ed. *Shakespeare Study Today*, New York, AMS Press, 1986.

Contributors

MYTHILI KAUL is at present Professor of English at the University of Delhi (India). She has published articles on Shakespeare in *Notes and Queries*, *Forum for Modern Language Studies*, *Hamlet Studies*, *The Upstart Crow*, and *Shakespeare Yearbook*.

PLAYTHELL BENJAMIN, an award-winning journalist, is a contributing editor with *Emerge* and a regular contributor to *Village Voice*. He is currently completing a novel.

SHELIA ROSE BLAND has acted with theater groups in New Orleans and is a member of the Society of Stage Directors and Choreographers. A former resident director, Guthrie Theatre, she lives in Minneapolis where she works as a freelance director and occasionally teaches at the University of Minnesota, Metropolitan State University, and the Minneapolis College of Art and Design.

ELLIOTT BUTLER-EVANS, Associate Professor of English and former director of the Black Studies Center at the University of California at Santa Barbara, is the author of *Race, Gender, and Desire: Narrative Strategies in the Fiction of Toni Cade Bambara, Toni Morrison, and Alice Walker*.

MARYSE CONDÉ, well-known novelist, playwright, and critic, is Professor in the Department of French and Romance Philology at Columbia University. Her novels include *Segou-les Murailles de terre* and the prize-winning *Moi Tituba, sorciere noire de Salem*, and *La Vie scelerate*.

LUCILLE P. FULTZ is Assistant Professor of English at Rice University, associate editor of *Sage*, and co-editor of *Double Stitch: Black Women Write about Mothers and Daughters*.

EARLE HYMAN has been acclaimed as one of the finest Othellos of the century. His other highly successful roles include that of Rudolf in *Anna Lucasta*, Mister Johnson in *Mister Johnson*, and James Tyrone in *A Long Day's Journey into Night*. He is the recipient of the Theatre World, CRY statuette (Norway), and Actors Studio awards.

JACQUELYN Y. McLENDON is Associate Professor of English at the College of William and Mary. She is the author of *The Politics of Color in the Fiction of Jessie Fauset and Nella Larsen* and articles on African American women's writings.

JAMES A. McPHERSON, Pulitzer prize-winning novelist and short story writer, is the author of *Hue and Cry*, *Elbow Room*, *A World Un-suspected*, and *The Prevailing South*. A former MacArthur Prize Fellow, he is at present Professor of English, Writers Workshop, University of Iowa.

S. E. OGUDE is Professor in the Department of English and Literature at the University of Benin, Nigeria.

ISHMAEL REED, distinguished novelist, poet, and essayist, is co-founder and editor (with Al Young) of *Quilt* magazine. He is best known as the author of *The Free-Lance Pallbearers*, *Yellow Back Radio Broke Down*, and *The Terrible Threes*.

EDWARD WASHINGTON, Assistant Professor of English at Mansfield University, has published articles on Shakespeare's *Lucrece* and *Titus Andronicus* and is currently working on a book-length study of Shakespeare's black characters.

JOHN A. WILLIAMS, author of twelve novels and nine nonfiction books, is Paul Robeson Professor of English and Journalism at Rutgers University.

AL YOUNG, co-founder and editor (with Ishmael Reed) of *Quilt* magazine, is a novelist, poet, writer of screenplays, and a professional musician. He is the winner of the CCLM Award for Poetry and the Joseph Henry Jackson Award. Currently he teaches literature and creative writing at the University of California, Santa Cruz.

Index

actors portraying Desdemona: (Peggy)
Ashcroft, 101, 103, 107; (Uta)
Hagen, 16, 23, 102, 103–4; (Dame
Madge) Kendall, 101
actors portraying Iago: (Charles)
Kean, 115; (Ian) McKellen, 115
actors portraying Othello: (Ira)
Aldridge, 12–14, 99–101, 103,
114, 139; (Thomas) Betterton, 3, 5;
(Edwin) Booth, 10–11; (Avery)
Brooks, 104; Burbage ("Dicke
Burbidge"), 3; (Richard) Burton,
115; (Laurence) Fishburne, 19;
(Edwin) Forrest, 10; (David)
Garrick, 3; (Moses) Gunn, 18;
(Anthony) Hopkins, 19; (Earle)
Hyman, 18; (Henry) Irving, 11, 14;
(Samuel L.) Jackson, 104; (James
Earl) Jones, 18, 19, 104; (Edmund)
Kean, 7, 115, 163; (John Philip)
Kemble, 3, 6; (William) Marshall,
18–19, 104, 139; (John) Neville,
115; (Laurence) Olivier, 3n, 19, 27,
115, 163; (Anthony) Quayle, 115;
(James) Quin, 3; (Ralph)
Richardson, 27; (Paul) Robeson,
15–18, 23, 100–103, 106,
108, 114–15, 139, 163; (Wayland)

Rudd, 15; (Tomasso) Salvini, 11;
(Godfrey) Tearle, 115; (Henry)
Watkins, 11; (Orson) Welles, 115;
(Willard) White, 115; (Paul)
Winfield, 18; (Donald) Wolfit, 19
Adams, Abigail, 6
Adams, John, 6n
Adams, John Quincy, 6–7, 9–10, 153
Addison, Gayle, 111
Africanus, John Leo, 2, 149
afterlife, 74
Aldridge, Ira, 12–14, 99–100, 101,
103, 114, 139
Aldridge's Othello, 12–14
Al-Ghazzali, 70
all-male cast: accentuates humor, 39;
in Elizabethan times, 37;
melodrama, 38; *Othello* production
using, 29
Antony and Cleopatra, 69, 74, 183
arrogance, Othello's, 54–55
Ashcroft, Peggy, 101, 103, 107: and
(Paul) Robeson, 103
assumptions, about motivation, 48

Bandman, Daniel, 8
Baraka, Amiri, 121n, 122, 122n, 134,
135n